WHO MAKES WAR

ALSO BY JACOB K. JAVITS

Order of Battle: A Republican's Call to Reason
Discrimination, U.S.A.

WHO MAKES WAR

The President Versus Congress

JACOB K. JAVITS

with DON KELLERMANN

WILLIAM MORROW & COMPANY, INC. New York 1973

For Marion, Joy, Joshua, and Carla in the hope that I may communicate to them something of my devotion to the American idea.

PRINTED IN THE UNITED STATES OF AMERICA.

LIBRARY OF CONGRESS CATALOG CARD NUMBER 73-9354

ISBN 0-688-00189-0

1 2 3 4 5 77 76 75 74 73

FOREWORD
by Barbara W. Tuchman

Two processes in human affairs that may be taken for granted are the nature of power to increase itself until it meets limits and the nature of mankind to make war. Both processes have been more than normally active over the past generation of American experience, to the point that they now confront us in this decade with two issues demanding immediate control. The first is the constitutional issue caused by the expanded power of the presidency which has dangerously upset the careful tripartite balance and separation of powers upon which this state was founded. The second is the war-making issue which is included in the first.

These are not huge inhuman forces before which we are helpless. They have been recognized and challenged by the War Powers Act introduced by Senator Javits and co-sponsored by fifty-eight other Senators, which was passed by the upper house in April 1972 and is now again before Congress. While it does not solve the constitutional issue all at once, it does put a primary and necessary measure within our reach.

War is old but Executive gigantism for this country is new. Man has been making war on his own kind ever since he separated himself from the ape by acquiring tools and, along with tools, weapons. From the earliest Sumerian sculpture of helmeted soldiers with spears and shields to the B-52s over Vietnam—a matter of some six thousand years—the record can hardly tell of a generation from which the clash of arms was absent. Historians have calculated that up until the Industrial Revolution war occupied more man-hours than any other activity except agriculture. The experience of our own century, the Terrible Twentieth as Churchill named it, does not suggest any diminution of the habit. William James concluded that men fight out of the "rooted bellicosity of human nature," a proposition that would be hotly disputed by Marxists and other optimists on the theory that war is not genetic but societal. I cannot say why men fight but only, as a historian, that they do; and not any less today than when the body-count was calculated by the number of foreskins of Philistines or the height of a pile of skulls, but rather more. Since the habit invariably inflicts harm and misery, our purpose must be to put it under as strict controls as possible.

One control that I believe the American people now owe to the world is to limit the capacity of their own Executive to wage presidential war. The intended check on this possibility formulated by the framers of the Constitution was to invest Declaration of War, and therefore consent, in Congress. The check was adequate until recent presidents took to circumventing its clear intent by going to war without Declaration. Our longest, most disputed war has been waged under emergency powers left over from Korea.

Declaration is not a mere matter of semantics or obsolete protocol. It is of the essence in so far as we wish to retain a system in which the people, through their representatives in Congress, have a rein upon policy. For a war that is not sufficiently and clearly in the national interest to sustain a Declaration by Congress cannot be warranted. The very absence of Declaration indicates deficiency in the *casus belli* and uncertainty of the national interest.

In the course of Senator Javits' narrative we can see the intent and the functioning of the war-making power emerge and, in our own time, as Executive gigantism takes effect, assume a strange new shape. One reason for this development is that the American Chief Executive is not anchored in a cabinet and advisers who stand upon an independent constitutional footing. Meanwhile, as the country has moved into a dominant world

position and the domestic areas of federal function have multiplied and grown more complex, the presidency has steadily extended its reach, while the Congress has abdicated in proportion
—until this session. Now the need for constitutional reform has
become apparent, not to restore the eighteenth-century model,
but to confirm its classic balance of powers and validate its
restraints upon the Executive for late-twentieth-century conditions. The War Powers Act is the first step.

March, 1973

FOREWORD
by Alexander M. Bickel

FOR a good many years, the issue of the President's independent war powers has been like the weather; nearly everybody has discussed it but nobody has done anything about it. Jacob K. Javits, however, has tried mightily, and there is now a fair prospect that he may succeed.

He has, of course, not been alone. Other efforts, directed specifically at the Vietnam war, have been made, and in drafting his own War Powers Bill Senator Javits has had the collaboration of colleagues, notably Messrs. Eagleton of Missouri and Stennis of Mississippi and former Senator Spong of Virginia. But as long ago as 1970, Senator Javits was among the first to see that general legislation was needed. He perceived that if Congress was ever to resume exercise of its share of the war power through specific actions, it would have to begin by reallocating a share of the responsibility to itself in a general, declarative statute.

Owing to an extended practice of independent Presidential initiatives, Congress no longer knew its place, Senator Javits realized; it had lost its bearings in the field of foreign and war policy. And so a quasi-constitutive act of standing forth before the people as a sharer of responsibility was needed on the part of Congress. That is what Senator Javits and his collaborators drafted, shepherded through the Senate in 1972, and introduced and are leading toward passage again in 1973.

In this fluent and instructive volume, Senator Javits and Mr. Kellermann make the case for the Javits bill chiefly on the historical principle. They rehearse the episodes, few of them to be counted among the glories of American history, which have denuded the Congress of its portion of the war power and have ended by establishing the imperial Presidency. To be sure, some of the things Presidents have done on their own independent authority in the past have been great and good things, and Lincoln's actions in the singular circumstances of the outbreak of civil war were not only great and good but different in legal contemplation from the international use of force. Yet the result of the entire course of events recounted in this book, the good actions as well as the doubtful and the deplorable ones, is now such an imbalance of power in favor of the President as a democratic government of separated and checked powers cannot safely tolerate. It is time to restore, with due regard to modern conditions, a nearer approach to the original scheme of the American Constitution.

In accordance with the intent of the Framers of the Constitution, the Javits bill sanctions independent Presidential action, of an essentially defensive nature, in true emergencies. Otherwise, and aside from full-scale declarations of war, the bill makes provision for specific authorizations by Congress of Presidential use of force in international relations. The emphasis is on the word "specific." There are to be no more Tonkin Gulf resolutions, authorizing everything and nothing, and no implicit ratifications of on-going Presidential wars, without the assumption of responsibility, as by appropriating money.

The internationalist credentials of Senator Javits are solid. No one can plausibly suspect a measure that bears his name— or for the matter of that, the names of his collaborators—of being neo-isolationist in spirit. The United States remains a world power and the world remains nuclear and peace uncertain. Our security and the peace of the world continue to depend in substantial measure on credible commitments undertaken by the United States and on a credible American capability to act in a crisis. That capability now rests uneasily and in the view of many people unconstitutionally with the President. Far from eroding it, the Javits bill would substantially enhance it. Under the bill, the United States will be able to make credible international commitments through specific legislation implementing treaties and other agreements. There will be no doubts, such as are now widely entertained, about the power of the President to act in a crisis when that power has been explicitly conferred upon him by specific legislation dealing with specific American commitments.

The long story of Presidential war-making detailed in this book is often unedifying. Nor would a full history of Congressional attitudes in matters of war and peace always please us. There is no assurance of perfect wisdom in Congress any more than in the Presidency, on domestic problems or foreign. But Congress and the President, acting together, are all we have got institutionally. The only assurance, which Senator Javits to his great credit has labored to provide us, lies in constitutional legality of process, in discharge by Congress and the President together of the duty to explain, justify and persuade, and thus to define the national interest by evoking it.

May, 1973

ACKNOWLEDGMENTS

THIS book, in which a historic constitutional issue has been followed through the course of two hundred years of the American story, is the end product of an effort to which many have contributed their time and talents. First, I wish to express my debt to members of my Washington staff who developed the idea for the War Powers Act, which is at the heart of this book. They are Frank Cummings, who was my Administrative Assistant, Charles Warren, my principal legislative aide, and Peter Lakeland, my foreign policy aide.

Also, I wish to express appreciation to my colleague John Stennis of Mississippi, the Chairman of the Senate Armed Services Committee and my earliest and staunchest partner in the proposed legislation, and to Senator Thomas Eagleton of Missouri, who made such important and original contributions to the War Powers Bill. Senator Lloyd Bentsen and Senator Robert Taft, Jr., contributed, through their own versions, to the final result. Former Senator Hiram Spong, who floor-managed the 1970 legislative effort, was also of enormous assistance in bringing this issue to the forefront of public attention.

My particular gratitude is due to Professor Vincent Carosso, Director of Graduate Studies in History at New York University, for his careful reading of the manuscript and the thoughtful comments he offered as the book took shape. I am greatly indebted to Ilana Stern for her perseverance and dedication throughout long months of research on American political history as it relates to the history of the conflict over War Powers. My thanks also to Winslow Wheeler of my Washington staff for examining the record of my own twenty-seven years in Congress in connection with my responses to the successive crises that have beset the United States during my years of public service. I wish also to thank Dean Robert McKay of New York University School of Law for his unfailing support and help in response to the War Powers Bill.

Hillel Black, who edited *Who Makes War*, was a source of great encouragement and gave unstintingly of his intellectual resources during the months of the book's development. His judgment and observations were enormously helpful in maintaining the integrity of the theme and assuring that the story of the conflict over War Powers was told with clarity and precision.

I wish to take particular note of the generosity of two distinguished Americans, Barbara W. Tuchman and Professor Alexander M. Bickel, in authoring forewords to this book. Their observations on the crisis over War Powers in these pages lend added significance to the theme and the issue. Indeed, Professor Bickel has been a most skilled and ardent advocate of the War Powers Bill and will have had a vital role in its enactment into law.

Finally, I would like to thank Don Kellermann, who helped in the research and organization of this book and who collaborated with me in its preparation, for his unfailing graciousness and understanding of my time and space problems in getting the book completed.

CONTENTS

[xiii]

NOTE: Italicized phrasing throughout text indicates author's emphasis unless otherwise noted.

No one will question that [the war] power is the most dangerous one to free government in the whole catalogue of powers. It usually is invoked in haste and excitement when calm legislative consideration of constitutional limitation is difficult. It is executed in a time of patriotic fervor that makes moderation unpopular. And, worst of all, it is interpreted by judges under the influence of the same passions and pressures.

Supreme Court Justice Robert Jackson
Woods v. Miller Company (1948)

The Congress shall have power . . .

To define and punish piracies and felonies committed on the high seas, and offenses against the law of nations.

To declare war, grant letters of marque and reprisal, and make rules concerning captures on land and water.

To raise and support armies, but no appropriation of money to that use shall be for a longer term than two years.

To provide and maintain a navy.

To make rules for the government and regulation of the land and naval forces.

To provide for calling forth the militia to execute the laws of the Union, suppress insurrections, and repel invasions.

To provide for organizing, arming, and disciplining the militia, and for governing such part of them as may be employed in the service of the United States, reserving to the States respectively, the appointment of the officers, and the authority of training the militia according to the discipline prescribed by Congress. . . .

ARTICLE 1, SECTION 8
The Constitution of the United States

AUTHOR TO READER

Who Makes War has turned into one of the great political questions of our time. The men who shaped our fundamental law would have found this a surprising development. For the group gathered in Philadelphia to write an American Constitution shared a heritage of antipathy to vesting the war-making power in one hand. They equated such concentration with monarchy at its worst. They regarded it as an opening to tyranny and they thought they were there to prevent its recurrence.

Two centuries later we find ourselves debating the question of war powers in the context of historical developments that have eroded the constitutional protections formulated in 1787. That erosion has been slow but steady. The process has accelerated over the past twenty years and it eventually involved us in a Vietnam War that divided the American people as only once before. Not since the Civil War had this country experienced such intense and widespread dissent from official policy. Never before in our history had we engaged in a national adventure so bitterly divided among ourselves. That division was a reflection, in part, of the complete frustration of the popular will by those with the powers to govern. The bitterness that has recently poisoned so much of our public dialogue will hopefully disappear. But we must prevent its recurrence if we are not to jeopardize our survival as a free people.

No individual and no particular set of political circumstances have triggered the process whereby presidential authority has come to dominate the decisions that determine whether or not the United States makes war. It is the cumulative effect of historic precedent that has produced a situation totally antithetical to the principles which animated the framers of the Constitution.

From the administration of George Washington to the administration of Richard Nixon, the pressures of international crises and war have generally encouraged the expansion of executive authority. President after President has been enabled by the sheer force of events to swallow up much of the power constitutionally assigned to the Senate and the House of Representatives. The question we face is whether to permit that executive aggrandizement to continue unabated or whether to restore the constitutional balance envisioned by the founders of the Republic.

The issue has to be settled and I believe that it must be settled by the recapture of some of the congressional authority surrendered in the past. My judgment is that the time to act is now. For there inheres in the Presidency of the United States today entirely too much power over war for the security of our freedom.

One of the pet illusions of the American people is that "it can't happen here." But it can. We are as vulnerable as any other people to threats to the constitutional structure of our government and to our fundamental liberties.

As we look to the future we must realize that a renewed sharing of power between President and Congress is necessary to our political and social health, to our freedom. We must reduce the number of things done in secret. Many of the thousands of executive agreements between the President and Chiefs of State throughout the world must be subjected to the "advise and consent" authority entrusted to the Senate by the Constitution or be enacted into law by both houses.

While there is no need for the legislative branch to become involved in housekeeping arrangements whereby small Marine detachments are stationed abroad as embassy guards, there is every reason to require the Senate's consent to major national commitments. A situation in which the United States becomes involved in Brazilian security arrangements or the air defense of Spain is no small matter. But arrangements like these have been cloaked in the greatest secrecy. The congressional efforts now under way to alter this pattern of executive decision-making are similar to the legislative effort to restore the power to make war to its proper constitutional equilibrium. War is just too dangerous, too costly, too awful, to be entrusted to a small group of men making decisions in secret without the full participation of the elected representatives of the American people.

At the beginning of our involvement in World War II, U.S. Attorney General Robert Jackson acknowledged presidential obligation to conform to constitutional requirements in activities relating to war and treaty-making. He did so, it is true, in the context of stretching executive power at the expense of Congress. But he exercised care to acknowledge the constitutional frame. A quarter of a century later we heard Undersecretary of State Nicholas De B. Katzenbach declare at a congressional hearing that to all intents and purposes a President has the right to engage the country in war on the basis of his "inherent powers" as Commander in Chief. These differences in attitude are expressive of great changes in a short period of time. Yet they illustrate only a fractional portion of the enormous expansion of executive power since World War II.

In the firm belief that an examination of the events that have led us to the current impasse over the power to make war can be helpful in its resolution, I have attempted in the following pages to recapitulate the relatively little-known history of the struggle over this issue until it has burgeoned into a full-blown constitutional crisis. Although I have introduced legislation designed to restore the constitutional balance, and although I am convinced of its efficacy, the important thing is that we find a way to solve the problem that is satisfactory to Congress, the President and the people.

This book was conceived and written before the Watergate scandal had come to light. Watergate is now seen to hinge on the power of the Presidency and to challenge the American structure of government at its very foundation.

I cannot, therefore, address myself to the aggrandizement of the presidential and the erosion of the congressional war power without taking into account the lessons of Watergate. That shock to the nation's sensibilities can be seen as an almost logical outgrowth of the continuous extension of presidential authority without regard to the constitutional precept of separation or balance of power.

Watergate came about, at least in part, because the Presidency had become an office of such awesome authority that those close to an incumbent Chief Executive seemingly could be led to believe that they were above the law, especially when they felt able to cite "higher" grounds of loyalty to the President and "National Security" as justification for their actions.

In this sense, Watergate lends added importance and emphasis to the narrative that follows in this book. It demonstrates what can happen even in the Presidency when inordinate power is vested or thought to be vested in a single hand. The lessons to be drawn from this history of the abandonment of constitutional constraints seem to be applicable to every phase of our national life. Watergate amplifies the need to act on the story told and the solutions proposed in these pages. It demonstrates also that while the nation's governmental structure is strong and resilient and able to absorb great shocks, it needs also to take the measures dictated by historical necessity in order to safeguard democratic institutions.

My purpose in writing this book is to broaden the discussion of a fundamental constitutional question and to stimulate among the American people an even greater awareness of how important it is to find a responsible answer to the question of Who Makes War.

I

The General,
the Delegates and
the Constitution

PHILADELPHIA was a suitable place to make a new beginning. In the summer of 1787 the Quaker City was the center of much of the nation's intellectual and political life. It was appropriate for the American Philosophical Society, the country's first association of scholars, to make its home there. The city's long tradition of freedom of inquiry and religion stretched back a century to the days of founder William Penn, and it was in the steeple of Philadelphia's State House that the Liberty Bell had tolled in 1776 to proclaim the Declaration of Independence.

Now, eleven years later, the Constitutional Convention would bring to the nation's largest city some of the most distinguished men in the land. To the residents of a provincial city, even a great one, it was an unusual sight. Through May and into early June, the delegates rode into town. The parade was to continue in and out of Philadelphia during the summer months and turn into an exodus of exhausted and successful lawmakers in mid-September.

For eight weeks the Convention performed its labors in the discomfort of heat and humidity hardly suitable to intense intellectual effort. Yet that Convention's deliberations produced an instrument of government that has served the United States for nearly two hundred years.

The delegates bore names we have come to identify with

the musty odor of ancient elementary-school history books and mythical cherry trees. But George Washington and Benjamin Franklin, James Madison and Alexander Hamilton were not figures in an Independence Day pageant. They were vital and incisive men determined to find a way to stable and effective government for the recently confederated thirteen American States.

Washington, a vigorous man of fifty-three, brought to Philadelphia a reputation as America's first citizen. The principal hero of the War for Independence was physically powerful, the possessor of a notoriously ferocious temper that had been mastered and chained beneath the gravity of an impassive exterior. Contemporary descriptions reflect a general recognition that intense passions and vigorous appetites moved within the General, even as he controlled them with an iron will. He commanded respect and deference from men who found it difficult to bow to the notion of natural superiority. The quality to which they deferred had nothing to do with the Sunday School piety proclaimed to generations of American schoolboys. George Washington was ill-served by his idolators, whether they were portrait painters like Peale or hagiographers like Parson Weems.

Among the delegates was Gouverneur Morris. A transplanted New Yorker, Morris was destined to play a key role in the Convention's deliberations as a member of the Pennsylvania delegation. His wit and intellect were matched by a charm that beguiled women and brought him the friendship and admiration of many of the country's most important men. General Washington's cool demeanor was a challenge to a man of Morris' character. During a dinner at which several of the delegates were discussing the Virginian's reticence, Morris wagered that he would throw his arm about the General and engage him in an intimate "man to man" conversation. A few days later he met the General at a social gathering given at the home where Washington lodged. Morris, seeing the Convention's president standing near a fireplace, strode to his side and laid his hand on Washington's shoulder. "Well General—" he began. That was the end of the conversation. Morris, recalling the episode, remarked that Washington gazed at the offending hand and then looked away. The younger delegate said that his hand fell to his side and that he wished he had been able to "sink through the floor." The incident underlines the awe in which Washington was held not only in Philadelphia but in the country at large.

For eight years he had served as Commander in Chief of the Army of the Revolution. He represented, as did no other figure, the values and the triumph of the War for Independence. His presence at the Convention endowed the proceedings with the advantage of association with "the greatest character in America." And the men who deliberated at Philadelphia intended him to play a central role in whatever government evolved out of their consultation. The fact that George Washington would wield the executive powers meant that they would be executed by the one citizen to whom universal admiration was accorded.

We may live under the rule of law, but the men who wrote the Constitution had good reason to be aware that law, like most other human institutions, is shaped and given its texture by those who have the power to interpret its dicta and execute its mandate. The Constitution-makers had been war-makers first. They had been active participants in events that gave them every reason to be wary of concentrated power and suspicious of office with a potential for tyranny. They were in Philadelphia to hammer out an instrument for effective government. But they were also there to protect the people from abuse of its powers.

The fifty-five Convention delegates represented constituencies with interests that conflicted almost as much as they were conjoined. Large states were held suspect by small. Commercial and manufacturing interests were at odds with the planters and the farmers. The slaveholding states sent their best men to a Convention in which they were obliged to defend an institution about which many of them felt guilty and all felt ill at ease. Prospects for success were not bright. But in the summer and fall of 1787 the drive to survive overcame the centrifugal forces of disparate interest and a Constitution of "checks and balances," an instrument of "divided powers," emerged from the heat-ridden chamber in the Pennsylvania State House where the delegates deliberated.

Every single clause of the proposed Constitution had been examined and questioned, revised and re-revised. There were occasions on which the delegates appeared uncertain as to which branch of government was the natural executor of what power. In some cases powers were taken from one authority and given to another. Wherever possible they were divided so as to create a balance that best assured the interests of all. The Constitution-makers had written a document that would develop into a symbol of the virtues of intelligent compromise.

The compromises they arranged, and the expressed views of some of the Convention delegates, have resulted in one of the great American sports—Constitution wrestling. For two hundred years politicians, lawyers and parties at interest have been able to find sustenance for their views on government simply by pushing and hauling at a document that of necessity was at times ambiguous. A situation requiring a system of checks and balances was bound to produce a people with a sharp collective eye on the weights and measures.

No article, no clause in the document taking shape in Philadelphia would be of more significance than those elements dealing with the power to make war. The England from which the delegates had torn their liberty made war at the word of its king. To the Americans this was an eight-year reality rather than a constitutional abstraction. British troops and ships of war had concentrated their destructive power over the length and breadth of the thirteen Colonies. Some of the most moving language in the Declaration of Independence describes the experience with fierce and intense indignation:

> The history of the present King of Great Britain is a history of repeated injuries and usurpations . . .
>
> He has kept among us in times of peace, standing Armies without the consent of our legislatures . . . He has abdicated government here, by declaring us out of his protection and waging war against us . . .
>
> He has plundered our seas, ravaged our coasts, burnt our towns and destroyed the lives of our people . . .

In the wrong hands, the power to make war could have consequences that the men gathered in Philadelphia would not choose to see again. It was a power that could not only wreak havoc; it had countless times changed the very nature of the relationship between the citizen and his government. Washington himself had been delegated dictatorial powers when he served as Commander in Chief. On December 27, 1776, a bill was passed in the Continental Congress that said in part:

> Resolve, that General Washington . . . is vested with full, ample and complete powers to raise and collect together, in the most speedy and effectual manner [troops] . . . to establish their pay . . . to displace and appoint all officers . . . to take wherever he may be whatever he may want for the use of the army . . . to arrest and confine persons . . . disaffected from the American cause.

A six-month time limit was placed on the General's wide-ranging authority, but Congress voted him similar powers twice more. On each occasion he surrendered his prerogatives without protest on the date designated by Congress. These episodes were recalled during the debate over ratification of the Constitution, when Governor Edmund Randolph of Virginia catalogued the evils that would follow dissolution of the Union, and compared the situation to the Revolutionary era. He said, "Such was the situation of our affairs then that the power of Dictator was given to the Commander in Chief to save us from destruction." Patrick Henry, speaking to the same issue, appeared to regard temporary dictatorship during periods of emergency as preferable to the evils of the new Constitution:

> In making a dictator we followed the example of the most glorious, magnanimous and skillful nations. In great dangers the power has been given. America found a person for that trust. She looked to Virginia for him. We gave a dictatorial power to hands that used it gloriously; and which were rendered more glorious by surrendering it up. Where is there a breed of such dictators? Shall we find a set of American Presidents of such a breed? *Will the American President come and lay prostrate at the feet of Congress his laurels?* I fear there are few men who can be trusted on that head.

Henry's contemporaries (he refused to serve in Philadelphia because of his opposition to a stronger central government) preferred a constitutional system to the chance that new George Washingtons would appear at every moment of national need. They were justified in the judgment that Washington's capacity to resist blandishment was likely to be unique. Only four years prior to the Convention he had again underscored his devotion to Republican institutions by his behavior during what has come to be called the Newburgh Conspiracy.

Newburgh, a small community in New York State, was headquarters for the Continental Army's northern encampment in 1783. General Washington's troops waited that winter for an agreement that would bring peace to America for the first time in eight years. Negotiations with the British were well under way and only the terms of the victory were to be settled. But the winning American Army was riddled with discontent. It had been offered no laurels, no loot and all too little gratitude. Congress either refused to abide by its agreement to provide half-pay pensions after demobilization, or so diluted the arrangement as to render them worthless.

The new Confederation's Congress had little or no authority to fund its activities as a government, let alone settle a debt of honor with troops who were no longer necessary to survival. Petition after petition by Army representatives had been considered, ignored or postponed and the bitterness at the Newburgh encampment grew in intensity. Some of the younger officers considered their situations to be desperate. Many of them had been soldiers through adolescence and early manhood. They felt now that they were to be cut adrift and sent into civilian life without compensation or prospect. Despite the difficulties of military life, service under a Commander almost all of them revered had provided a life style they feared to change. The indifference of the Government to their needs stoked the fires of rebellion throughout late 1782 and early 1783. At this juncture the interests of discontented officers and of civilians wishing to establish a strong national government, appeared to merge.

The unhappiness of some of Washington's soldiers was matched by the feelings of a number of the Confederation's leading politicians who despaired of the new Government's fiscal integrity. The national power to levy taxes was inhibited by state veto. The ability to borrow at reasonable rates had vanished. The Army's disaffection appeared to Robert Morris (the Government's financial agent) to be a tool with which to persuade the Congress to vote the Government adequate taxing power. It was a dangerous game which Morris and several associates, including Alexander Hamilton and Gouverneur Morris, were about to play. Although the events that unfolded in Newburgh and Philadelphia are shrouded by time and the disingenuous attitudes of most of the participants, they appear to have incorporated all of the elements of a threat to the civil power. For the first time in American history the military was used to lobby on behalf of public measures beyond its competence.

It began in the last week of December, 1782, when Major General Alexander McDougall and two fellow officers appeared before the Congress in Philadelphia with a petition from the Army at Newburgh. For six months the Army had negotiated unsuccessfully with the state governments. Now, on the eve of demobilization, its representatives appeared at the nation's new capital to urge their cause. "We have borne all that men can bear . . . our private resources are at an end." They asked only "for an honorable and just recompense for several years' hard service" during which they had become "worn down and exhausted." The officers offered to accept a cash settlement in lieu of the pension commitment. Many of them had gone without pay for months and their requests were reasonable. But, then as now, some Congressmen balked at outside pressure. The Newburgh representatives concluded their reasonable protestations with a thinly veiled threat. They said "any further experiments on their patience may have fatal effects."

Hamilton and Madison both saw that the Army's petition provided new leverage on behalf of a national taxing power. Secret letters to General Knox, Washington's principal aide, were sent by the petitioners and their political mentors, urging him to announce support of a funding system so that the troops could be paid. Correspondence strongly implying the threat of mutiny—a refusal to demobilize at war's end—involved General Gates, the hero of Saratoga as well as an embittered enemy of the Commander in Chief. Groups of dissident officers appear to have been organized to threaten the Congress if the funding measure was not accepted and acted upon. But it was early in the history of the United States and Congress refused to bow to lobbying from the armed forces. When the bitterly disappointed military delegates returned without firm commitments from Philadelphia, word of their failure circulated instantly.

At that point, a document couched in the most inflammatory terms was circulated by one of General Gates's senior aides. It recalled the humiliation of past treatment by Congress, demanded an end to "meek language and entreating memorials," and suggested that in its extremity the Army, "inviting the direction of your illustrious Commander," retreat to the wilderness and dissolve its bonds with a government that had treated it with "rudeness and dishonour." This "Newburgh Address" made the rounds of the encampment so quickly that General Washington immediately accepted the implied challenge to congressional authority.

When he learned that a group of officers had called for a meeting to hear the report of the returning delegates, Washington responded at once. Fully aware of the emotional pitch to which his officers had been raised, he issued a general order that opened with the following disdainful observation:

> The commander in chief, having heard that a general meeting of the officers was proposed to be held this day at the new building, in an anonymous paper which was circulated yesterday by some unknown person, conceives, although he is fully persuaded that the good sense of the officers would induce them to pay very little attention to such an irregular invitation, his duty, as well as the reputation and true interest of the Army, requires his disapprobation of such disorderly proceedings.

The General went on to call his own meeting for the following Saturday morning. He indulged an ironic touch by requesting General Gates to preside "and report the result of the deliberations to the Commander in Chief." The Commander in Chief, however, was not satisfied to permit the "deliberations" to take place without his own views being taken into account. When Gates opened the proceedings before officers packed into a new building designed for social events, he was confronted by George Washington asking "permission" to address the officers.

It would be inaccurate to describe Washington's remarks as "impassioned." He was not that kind of man. Indeed, he referred in passing to the "passions" roused by the pamphlet urging the Army to defy Congress. Rather, Washington's speech was a recollection of his own faith in his officers, the trials they had shared, and an affirmation of the cause for which they had suffered.

> . . . in the attainment of complete justice for all your toils and dangers, and in the gratification of every wish, *so far as may be done consistently with the great duty I owe my country and those powers we are bound to respect,* you may freely command my services to the utmost extent of my ability.

He heaped scorn on those who suggested "this dreadful alternative of deserting our country in the extremest hour of her distress, or turning our arms against it." Washington said that the idea of forcing Congress into "instant compliance" had "something so shocking in it that humanity revolts at the idea." He expressed "horror and detestation" of "the man who wished under any specious pretenses to overturn the liberties of our country and who wickedly attempts to open the floodgates of civil discord, and deluge our rising empire in blood."

When George Washington left that meeting, the Newburgh Conspiracy was over. The officers passed a series of resolutions reaffirming their loyalty to the country and the civil power. They promised that "no circumstances of distress or danger shall induce a conduct that may tend to sully the reputation and glory which they have acquired at the price of their blood and eight years faithful service." After thanking the Commander in Chief for his address the officers told the world that they "view with abhorrence and reject with disdain" the propositions made in the call to mutiny. Washington's role in preventing the seeds of civil discord from taking hold in the military reflected a conservatism of the highest order. His principal interest was the preservation of liberty. There was in him, and his contemporaries knew it, no shadow of Caesar.

[9]

When the Convention sat four years later, not one of the delegates would dispute the assertion of Thomas Jefferson, who had remarked of the Newburgh Conspiracy that "the moderation and virtue of a single character has probably prevented this revolution from being closed as most others have been, by a subversion of that liberty it was intended to establish."

Although Jefferson's observations were in full accord with their own, the delegates realized that the office of the Presidency offers great temptation to those who would exercise its authority. Despite the enormous respect in which Washington was held, the delegates in Philadelphia were concerned with those who would come after. The Convention debate over the war powers offers evidence of that concern, and of a firm resolve to combine effective use of the power to make war with restraints insuring that one man alone would be unable to change the state of the nation from peace to war.

We have a diary account of the Convention mood as recalled by Georgia delegate Abraham Baldwin, who wrote that the Convention had limited the "ultimate tendency" to monarchical power when it made the Executive "dependent on the states at large and impeachable." He emphasized that the Constitution also vested Congress with power over the Army and Navy and the right to make war and peace. "These were delicate things, on which all felt solicitous and yet all were unanimously convinced that they were necessary."

The question of who was to make war and restore peace was only one aspect of the problem. The degree and range of the power itself caused considerable debate. Standing armies were altogether unpopular in the United States during the early days of the Republic. Americans had good reason to associate a professional soldiery with tyranny and oppression. Their experience with George III's Hessians had done nothing to diminish such fears. Madison himself observed that "armies in time of peace are allowed on all hands to be an evil." Although he thought it unwise to prohibit a standing army in case of need, he voted for a proposal to limit such a force to a specific number to be determined by the Convention. Others put the case even more strongly. George Mason of Virginia wished to insert a clause in the Constitution that would specifically assert the dangers of a standing force. He suggested that the clause in which Congress is empowered to call out the militia (Article 1, Section 8) be prefaced with the words *"and that the liberties of the people may be better secured against the dangers of standing armies in time of peace."*

Despite the still fresh memory of the Newburgh Conspiracy, Gouverneur Morris opposed the measure because of what today would be called its "public relations impact." He said such a motion would give a "dishonourable mark" to the military. Roger Sherman of Connecticut, however, told the Convention that he favored reasonable restrictions on the number and continuance of an army in time of peace.

Sherman's remark, even as he voted to empower the new Congress to raise armies and to support them, reflected a general discomfort with the entire question of the war powers. These men were realists. One of them had observed that the principal reason for making a new Constitution was to provide for the common defense. But it was no easy thing for any of them to decide in whom or in what body to entrust the power of the sword.

Perhaps Woodrow Wilson best described the dilemma confronting the Constitution-makers. A century after the great Convention had completed its work, the President-to-be published a treatise on constitutional government. In it he wrote, "It is difficult to describe any single part of a great governmental system without describing the whole of it. Governments are living things and operate as organic wholes."

The fullness of Wilson's perception was denied to all but the most brilliant of the delegates in Philadelphia. They didn't have ten decades of constitutional practice to look back on. Their concern was to put together a working structure and they attempted to compartmentalize that structure in order to achieve the just balance that was one of their principal objects. While there was complete and sensitive recognition of the immense significance of the power to make war and maintain the peace, there was less than full awareness that a good many of the other powers they were to deal with impinged sharply on the power to make war. Hamilton and Madison, neither of whom had the faintest glimmering of the nature of modern conflict, came closer than any of the others to articulating the constitutional potential for aggrandizing the power of the executive office, no matter how it was described on paper.

Writing as Publius in the *Federalist Papers*, Hamilton discussed the war powers as they were framed in the newly written and still unratified Constitution:

> These powers ought to exist without limitation, because it is impossible to foresee or define the extent and variety of national exigencies . . . it must be admitted as a necessary consequence that there can be no limitation of that authority . . . that is, in any matter essential to the formation, direction, or support of the *national forces*.

Clinton Rossiter has observed that "Hamilton had a healthy bias in favor of the Presidency because he was obsessed with energy." In our own day we have seen the savage consequences of executive energy applied in the wrong place on behalf of the wrong purpose at the wrong time.

In the early Federalist era, writing a few short years after the Constitution had taken effect, Hamilton, in pursuit of that "executive energy," was already engaged in the work of broadening the constitutional base for the President's war powers. He contended that inasmuch as the President was the sole organ of foreign policy he exercised authority that could "determine the condition of the nation, though it may in its consequences, *affect the exercise of the power of the legislature to declare war*."

Madison, on the opposite side of the question, replied to Hamilton at the urging of his mentor and emerging party leader, Thomas Jefferson. Madison charged that his fellow founder used the Constitution's "executive power" clause as a convenient cloak for the assumption of "policy forming powers constitutionally independent of direction by Congress, though capable of being checked by it." Both of these men had fought with vigor and valor to shape the very document they now disputed. The debate on the war powers clause at the time it was hammered out provided no inkling that they would later see it from such different angles of vision. Certainly enough time had been given to arguing the question.

On August 17, 1787, the Convention's Committee on Detail recommended to the Convention that the legislature be given the power "to make war." Charles Pinckney, averse as he was to giving the President the power of a "Monarch," was troubled at the delays in deliberations he foresaw if the power was given to the *entire* Congress. He thought the members of the House of Representatives were "too numerous" to make decisions of such consequence. The South Carolinian asked that the Senate be endowed with the war power because it would be "more acquainted with foreign affairs and more capable of proper resolutions" than the other house. Pierce Butler of South Carolina agreed with his compatriot that the House was not a suitable instrument of such power. He asked that the Convention empower the President to make the great decision because he "would have all the requisite qualities and *will not make war but when the nation will support it.*"

Other delegates did not share Butler's confidence. Elbridge Gerry rose to say that he "never expected to hear in a republic a motion to empower the Executive alone to declare war." His view was given added support by a thoughtful comment that Virginia's Colonel George Mason threw into the debate. He remarked that he too was convinced that it was unsafe to hand such power to the Executive and he told the delegates that he was for "clogging rather than facilitating war; but for facilitating peace."

It was at this point that the Convention took an ironic turn. Gerry of Massachusetts, always on guard against potential executive encroachment, drew attention to another problem confronting the new Government. If Congress was not in session and an enemy attacked the United States there would be no constitutional method by which to defend the country. Gerry and James Madison moved that the word "make" be changed to "declare." In that way, it was asserted, the power to change from a state of war to peace would be retained by the legislature, but the means "to repel attack" would be at hand. George Mason, yet another believer in the legislative authority, also endorsed the change. The vote in favor of "declare" rather than "make" was unanimous in the wake of the admonition from Rufus King of Massachusetts that the phrase "make war" might be understood to "conduct" it, which was an executive function. The retroactive ambiguity bestowed on the Convention's decision by lobbyists on behalf of executive branch prerogative is particularly bemusing, when one considers that those most articulate in behalf of the change were also those most determined to keep the essential power to determine war or peace in congressional hands.

Only Connecticut's Roger Sherman foresaw the consequences of a semantic switch. He remarked that the original phrasing "stood very well" and that "the Executive should be able to repel and not to commence war." Sherman's warning words went unheeded simply because most if not all of the delegates believed that the problem had been solved, when the Convention endowed Congress with the authority to raise and support armies and navies, make rules and regulations for the military forces, call out the militia and to exercise all of the *policy* functions associated with the war power. The executive role, in the Convention's view, was to be limited to the function of Commander in Chief.

Washington's previous military service and his presence on the scene in Philadelphia account in large degree for the simple three-word description of the presidential role in relation to questions of war and peace. "Commander in Chief"—that is all the Constitution says and the record indicates debate on only one aspect of the question. Colonel Mason questioned the advisability of the President taking personal command of troops in the field. Hamilton, as a matter of fact, wrote a plan of government that expressly forbade such command unless authorized by the United States Senate. The New Jersey plan, representing the aspirations and the fears of the small states, specifically provided that no member of the Federal Executive would assume personal command of any troops "as General or in other capacity." The absence of debate on the question at the Convention itself adds dimension to the significance of the Washington presence. For the presidential office was partially tailored to the expectation that he would be its first occupant and he had long ago proven what a proper commander in chief does and how he behaves.

Only later, during the period when state conventions were called on to ratify the Constitution, was the question raised with any force. Several states accepted the new document as the law of the land; but they proposed amendments requiring the Commander in Chief to refrain from assuming personal command of troops in the field. One Carolinian was bitterly dissatisfied. "General Washington is all very well," he is reported to have said. "But what of General Shlushington?"

Americans of this generation have good reason to understand the ease with which a President may breach the constitutional wall that separates his powers from those of the Congress. The surprising fact is that at least a few of the Constitution-makers were fully aware of what some of them saw as possibility and others as peril. James Madison breathed life into the Constitution. He was devoted to the principles woven into its fabric. But Madison understood that no document of itself could resist the twin forces of fear and violence. In the midst of the debate on standing armies he told his fellows:

In time of actual war, great discretionary powers are constantly given to the executive magistrate. Constant apprehension of war has the same tendency to render the head too large for the body. A standing military force with an overgrown executive will not long be safe companions to liberty. The means of defense against foreign danger have always been the instruments of tyranny at home. . . . Among the Romans it was a standing maxim to excite war . . . and throughout Europe, the armies kept under pretext of defensive need are really kept to enslave the people and alarms of foreign danger help tame the people.

II

Who Makes Neutrality?

WHEN George Washington took office as President of the United States, he began a process that has continued with little interruption for almost two hundred years. The presidential situation exemplifies challenge. Its horizons sometimes appear limitless to its occupant. In Washington's case there was considerable truth to the appearance. He assumed executive power over a thin strip of land stretching from Maine through Georgia and west to the Mississippi River. What lay below the Georgia border was known to hold future potential as American territory and the land beyond the Mississippi provided food for the dreams of adventurers and spoils for the pockets of speculators in national futures. What was later called manifest destiny already beckoned the fringe of Americans huddled along the Atlantic coast. As a matter of fact, in 1789 Americans were no longer huddling, but uncoiling themselves slowly across the continent.

In every great people there is an arrogance closely linked to joy. It is, in the early stages of development, awareness of possibility that can only be analogous to youthful men and women sensing that the world is open to them. Later, perhaps, that quality can turn into what Senator Fulbright has described as the "Arrogance of Power." But when Washington and his Cabinet took office, when the first Congress sat in New York, they had before them only a barely touched canvas on which to paint the beginning of the history we examine today.

Washington's Cabinet and that first Congress began immediately to establish, and almost as rapidly to break, a stream of precedents for future politicians to weigh in their own calculations as to the possibility of political action. In a sense, the statutes enacted by Congress during that first session were an extension of the Constitution itself. Indeed the first decade of congressional legislation could be called, without too much license, an extension of the Philadelphia Convention. The same could be said of the evolution of the Cabinet.

Washington may have been a military man, but as President of the United States he served metaphorically as the captain of a ship on a shakedown cruise. We are accustomed to a Cabinet structure in which the Secretaries function as supervisors of the great bureaucracies. Many of them, in our own time, find it almost as difficult as an ordinary citizen to make an appointment with the President of the United States. Not so in the early days. Policies that cut across departmental lines were thrashed out in Cabinet meeting. Written recommendations on military and foreign policy, on Indians and presidential relations with the Congress were sought from Cabinet members and given considerable weight by the President himself.

The Chief Executive had not yet achieved the level of power that immersed all other personalities in the dignity of his office. Alexander Hamilton, the first Secretary of the Treasury, and Thomas Jefferson, Washington's first Secretary of State, were imposing figures in their own right. More important, they represented two entirely opposed views as to the powers and duties of the central government and they fought out these differences within the first administration. Hamilton's burning desire to establish the national credit and to establish a thriving commercial and manufacturing community under the umbrella of federal power was countered by Jefferson's concern for the preservation of "agrarian virtue" and of the rights of the states to govern themselves. These political differences between two men of genius and character resulted almost immediately in the formation of political parties and in a change in the way in which the executive branch conducted its business.

Washington's first impulse had been to incorporate into the

Administration all sections of the country and all views of government. The perpetual conflict between Hamilton and Jefferson and their followers convinced him that he had been in error. When Jefferson resigned his post in 1793, the President realigned the Cabinet so as to reflect the federalism of the Hamiltonian views that more closely approximated his own.

No dilemma confronting the President reflected the "faction" in his Cabinet with more clarity than the battle over the Neutrality Proclamation of 1793. It was the first significant assertion of presidential war power outside the explicit constitutional frame and it occurred in the midst of a struggle between the two great maritime powers of England and France. That war, as fortune had it, also closely reflected the divisions between the Federalists and the Republicans, as Jefferson's followers were coming to call themselves. (It should be noted that while many among the Republicans had been opposed to the Constitution some of their most influential leaders in the new Government had been active participants in shaping the new law. James Madison, the "Father of the Constitution," was the leader of the Republicans in the House. Some had switched sides. Patrick Henry, who had bitterly opposed what he considered to be the Constitution's potential for tyranny, was now a Federalist. The Constitution ended one ideological drama and created another with a revised cast of characters.)

It was a Frenchman who triggered the first constitutional crisis over the war power. Citizen Edmond Charles Genêt was the selection of the new French Revolutionary Government to serve as minister to its American ally. That "ally" was most uneasy in its relationship to the only power which had recognized its existence and given it military aid in the struggle for independence. Now, a few short years later, France had undergone its own revolutionary paroxysm, emerging with its king overthrown and a government dominated by "democrats." To the Republicans the change was a matter of joy and an opportunity to express the brotherhood of the two movements for freedom. But many of the Federalists found themselves questioning the exact meaning of the "defensive" alliance with France and its status as a result of the overthrow of the monarchy. There was, in truth, little resemblance between the bourgeois Revolution in the United States, fought in large degree over property rights, and the bitter war between a starving, illiterate and impassioned French peasantry against the despotic monarchy that had sucked the marrow of its substance over hundreds of years. That didn't prevent the American people, at a distance of three thousand miles, from choosing up sides with a vengeance. The large majority, hating the old enemy, grateful to the French who had stood by them, was enthusiastically in favor of the French cause. The Hamiltonians, on the other hand, were strongly opposed to war with England.

Jefferson, whose enthusiasm for the cause of French liberty cannot be questioned, did not share his followers' appetite for American involvement in the European conflict. He was as much a realist as Hamilton and he knew that war with England could bring nothing but disaster. America's standing army had been disbanded after the Treaty of Paris except for a small force stationed on the northwest frontier to fight the Indians. There was literally no navy at all. By 1785 Congress had sold the three vessels remaining from the Revolutionary flotilla. The purpose of statesmanship is survival and war with England was no way to survive.

France, in addition to the enormous popular support it enjoyed, could point to two treaties with the new nation that gave her ground for special consideration. If the United States could not afford war with England it could equally ill afford war with the adventurous French who were in the process of throwing the great powers of Europe into paroxysms of fear. In a letter to Madison, Jefferson remarked that the United States found itself in the position of walking a diplomatic "tight rope." Citizen Genêt, arriving at Charleston, South Carolina, to take up his American ministry couldn't have cared less about the United States Constitution, but his presence and his actions created the first great constitutional conflict over presidential war power.

Genêt was an attractive figure. He was twenty-eight years old and bore himself with the exuberance of a revolutionary riding the crest of a wave of success. Revolutionaries do not find themselves in that situation with too much frequency and Genêt's enthusiasm is understandable. The hindsight of history nevertheless obliges us to question the judgment of the French "directory" in its choice of this particular minister. Genêt had been at the Russian court in St. Petersburg, where he had so offended the Czar by his revolutionary pronouncements that it was thought the better part of discretion to bring him home. The government, which at first had intended to send him to Holland, decided that the fervor of his sentiments deserved the reward of assignment to the libertarian atmosphere of the United States. There were passions to be stirred in the friendly American air. But, as it turned out, Genêt would have done his country less damage if they had given him to the Dutch.

He appeared on the scene as a conquering hero, rather than the ambassador of a foreign power. When his ship anchored at Charleston, a stronghold of French sentiment, he made a triumphant progress all the way up the coast on the way to present his credentials to the President of the United States. Pro-French dinners, toasts and parades marked the procession and Washington expressed intense annoyance at the undiplomatic journey. But Genêt's behavior mirrored considerably more than insensitivity and vanity. He was out to enlist material American support and later claimed that Governor Moultrie of South Carolina encouraged him in his plans. Genêt immediately began commissioning American ships and men to take arms against England as privateers preying on British commerce on the high seas and along the American coast.

The way Genêt read France's treaties with the United States he had every right to take such action. Washington and his Cabinet, despite the differences among them, did not believe the treaties should be so interpreted. If France was entitled to the privileges of an ally, there was considerable question as to whether the United States should permit such provisions to take effect under circumstances in which this country could not protect herself against British depredation. In any case, Genêt's failure to come directly to Philadelphia to call on the President and the Secretary of State set exactly the wrong tone for a mission of extreme delicacy. Jefferson's natural sympathy for the French cause was offset by Genêt's arrogant display, and Hamilton, friendly to British power and the possibility of future trade relationships, was enabled to bring the neutrality issue to a head within the Cabinet. That issue goes to the heart of Who Makes War, because it raises the question of who is empowered to keep the nation at peace.

The first move in the direction of the Neutrality Proclamation of 1793 came in a series of questions Washington addressed to his Cabinet officers. He asked them to comment on the obligation of the United States to receive Genêt as France's minister and to consider the advisability of a new look at the Treaty of Alliance of 1778. Jefferson, on receiving the President's questions, remarked to a friend that he saw Hamilton's hand in their formulation.

Then as now, party politics and questions of high policy were often inextricably tied together. The precept that the Constitution is a "living document" really means that it pulses with the life of partisan strife and the conflict of opposing views as to what it says and what it implies. Nowhere is this more evident than in the controversy over neutrality. The real question, as Jefferson and Hamilton both saw it, was "Neutrality for whom?" Neither wished to become involved in the conflict but they were intensely partisan in their views of how they wished the struggle to end. Jefferson, as Secretary of State, often disparaged the Federalists in conversation with Genêt. Some writers feel the French minister was given undue encouragement by the warmth of their early interchanges. Hamilton, on the other hand, gave George Hammond, the British minister, what amounted to blow-by-blow accounts of the meetings of the Cabinet. In a later age, both men would have been considered guilty of the grossest indiscretion. They held office at a time when codes of public conduct were in the process of formation and there were few if any guidelines as to what was improper in the political arena.

Washington himself, ostensibly above the battle, lent added fuel to the quarrel by the tone of his questions on neutrality. He received in reply a unanimous expression that the United States should stay out of the war. Beyond that, there were differences among the ministers both in nuance and posture. Hamilton questioned the advisability of receiving Genêt. He also thought that the provisions of the treaty with France ought to be put into suspension. Hamilton noted that the United States had made its arrangements with the French king and that if his heirs should recover their power they might well take exception to this country's engagement with the revolutionaries. Jefferson's response that treaties are made with nations and not individuals was acknowledged to be correct; but he lost on the essential point. For Washington, with a majority of the Cabinet behind him, decided to issue a declaration of neutrality in the war between England and France. Jefferson's principal concern was that the declaration be couched in gentle terms that would enable France to continue to regard the United States as a friend and supporter.

His rival, on the other hand, wanted to underline the presidential decision to assert American neutrality. (If Hamilton could anger the French in the process, then all the better.) The Treasury Secretary proposed that the declaration include language that would emphasize American intent to engage in "conduct friendly and impartial towards the belligerent powers." That was the language Washington used and he further forbade individual American citizens to engage in unneutral acts under the penalty of law. As the dispute engaged the Cabinet's attention, it raged within party circles and the national press.

When Jefferson contended that the President's right to issue such a proclamation was an encroachment on the congressional war power, he opened for the first time the great question with which we are plagued two hundred years later. Jefferson's first concern was to maintain good relations with France and he didn't hesitate to use the Constitution to that end. He had a good case, even though he lost. The Virginian contended that only Congress could change the nation from peace to war and that a declaration of peace implied a future intent that only Congress constitutionally could determine. Hamilton took the argument to the press. In a series of articles he developed his own attitudes toward "the executive power" as it is described in the Constitution. Hamilton's key argument was that the President had a right to issue such a proclamation both as the man charged with the responsibility for foreign affairs *and as Commander in Chief, when Congress was not in session.*

Although James Madison took up the journalist's cudgels at Jefferson's behest, it was too late. Washington signed the proclamation while Congress was in recess and the passage of time made the issue of legislative control *irrelevant to the action.* It was not to be the last occasion on which presidential initiative presented a scattered and divided legislature with what appeared to be a *fait accompli.* Even in those early days it was all too easy to let the past go unchallenged and concentrate on the future.

Looking back to the first time the war powers question was raised we can't help but note that the constitutional issue has been repeatedly ignored or obscured. The attention of the policymakers invariably focuses on the achievement of their objectives. Nowhere is this better illustrated than by what occurred in the aftermath of the Neutrality Proclamation.

Citizen Genêt was quite willing to accept the Neutrality Proclamation as valid so long as it didn't interfere with his own activity. He went merrily along disregarding its provisions, commissioning American ships to raid British shipping and bringing in British prizes to American ports where he calmly auctioned them off to the highest bidder. Repeated protests from his former friend, Jefferson, went unheeded. Finally, one of Genêt's prizes, *The Little Democrat (The Little Sarah* before her capture as a British merchantman), was outfitted as a warship while in port in Philadelphia. Under the provisions of the proclamation, the ship was forbidden to leave port. The United States had little or no means to enforce such a prohibition and Genêt refused to obey the request. *The Little Democrat* sailed off to raid British shipping from Maine to Georgia. Genêt's action infuriated and humiliated Jefferson. But Genêt had done even worse. During an interview with a Pennsylvania official, the French minister asserted that he would "appeal [over Washington's head] to the people." That remark put a period to a chapter in American history. His words were widely circulated and stirred such resentment that the ardent French sympathizers of the past found themselves turning away from the cockade in a display of loyalty to their own officials and, most importantly, to their new institutions.

Genêt himself had stretched official tolerance beyond its limits. Jefferson transmitted to Paris a collection of the "diplomat's" insolent communications to the State Department and asked that the French recall the passionate minister to his own shores. They complied, and sent such a strong reprimand to Genêt that he had every reason to expect the guillotine if he returned home. The emotional Frenchman therefore created another precedent for us to consider. He asked for political asylum and was allowed to remain in the United States. He later married into a distinguished New York family, became a United States citizen and disappeared into comfortable obscurity.

The name of Edmond Charles Genêt is considerably more than a footnote to history. His personality offered the first administration not only a blatant challenge to its prestige from abroad, but an opportunity to assert its authority at home. In the struggle to maintain American neutrality, to assure American survival, a very small but significant step had been taken in asserting executive power at the expense of congressional prerogative. Although the Hamiltonians took pains to tie the Neutrality Proclamation to the absence of Congress and though they insisted that it reflected no intent to extend executive prerogative, the strength of its assertions and prohibitions belies the caveat. The issue of who has the power to *declare* peace is the obverse side of the issue of Who Makes War. The Constitution had been given its first new reading.

III

President Adams Wages "Quasi-War"

ALTHOUGH we live in an era in which emphasis must be laid on restraint of the executive power, it was not always so. Nor, if history continues to weave new strands into old patterns, will it hold true through all our tomorrows. The early years of the Republic offer solid evidence that the Constitution as written provides protection against abuses of power by *any* of the three branches of government. The period also provides ample illustration of the amazing facility with which even the greatest of men can deceive themselves, when such deception is necessary to achieve a political ambition or a policy aim. The "Quasi-War" with France is a case in point.

John Adams became President in 1797, after eight years in the Vice Presidency, a place he described as "irksome and wholly insignificant." Such a position was completely out of keeping with the self-appraisal of one of America's leading statesmen.

Adams' career stretched back to the days when he had the courage to defend British soldiers in the case of the Boston Massacre. He had been the prime mover behind the choice of Washington as the Continental Army's Commander in Chief. It was fortunate that he had a good opinion of himself, for he was to be the victim of intense dislike and caricature throughout his public career. Only the unquestioned quality of his past services to the country had brought him its highest office. He made little attempt to hide a high temper and his love of pomp offered his enemies an inviting target. During the first administration it was learned that Adams wished to be called His Excellency and, because of his substantial appearance, he was given the title "his rotundity." But beneath the scapegoat surface was a keen mind and a commitment to a republic of variable interests in viable equilibrium.

Adams assumed the Presidency at a time in which partisan wrangling between the Federalists, his own party, and Jefferson's Republicans was reaching new intensity. Washington's disappearance from the scene had removed whatever restraint had existed in the feuding about the nation's direction. To compound the problem, Adams was not the undisputed leader of his political associates. Hamilton, who had been Washington's leading adviser, was, in fact, the head of the Federalist party. The Cabinet members (retained in office by the new Chief Executive) offered their loyalty to Hamilton rather than to the President. Only Adams' vanity could have blinded him to the fact that most of the business of the government was in actuality directed by the handsome New York attorney, who now held no public office. Adams' political life was further complicated by Thomas Jefferson's election to the Vice Presidency. The new President thus found himself with the leader of the opposition party as his potential successor. Although Adams and Jefferson had once been close friends, political differences had long separated them and the President was isolated in his own national house. He shared with Hamilton an aversion to Jefferson's belief that serving the interests of the small farmer would assure a successful American future. The Federalist leaders were also wary of the democratic base of Jefferson's support and they were convinced that the new nation's strength could best be fostered by dedicating a strong central government to the expansion of business and industry. But Hamilton's dynamism and the natural inclination of his fellow Federalists to turn to him for leadership made a split with Adams inevitable.

Adams was also the first of a long and unbroken line of Presidents to inherit the problems left behind by their predecessors. Indeed, he remarked to his wife Abigail that Washington, at the Adams inauguration, had looked as though he wished to say, "I am fairly out and you are fairly in. See which of us will be the happiest."

One of the legacies with which Adams had to contend was a war with France, undeclared and, to the degree possible, unfought by the United States. That war and its domestic consequences unseated John Adams at the end of his first term and destroyed the Federalist party in the bargain. The similarity to certain recent events is striking, but there were also differences marked by the relatively close observance of constitutional principles in those early days and by the President's seeming vacillation on the question of war or peace.

The hostilities with the French resulted directly from the unfriendliness of Washington to the revolutionary government, and, particularly, from a treaty signed by this country with Britain that explicitly recognized England's interpretation of the rules of war at sea. Despite the warmth for the French cause felt by many or most of the American people, relations between the governments deteriorated dramatically. French privateers and warships drew a noose around American shipping in the Atlantic and in the West Indies. A dramatic rise of 600 percent in insurance rates for American shipowners reflected the nation's impotence. The contempt which a powerful France felt for American might was justified by the paucity of the new Republic's military resources. It also underlined the fact that most Americans weren't sure just who the enemy was. The American Navy's inadequate equipment exemplified the national unwillingness to spend its citizens' money on a military establishment. The ironic fact that both Britain and France, and their colonies in the Indies, needed goods supplied by American ships further complicated matters. For the very merchants most affected by the depredations of French and British privateers were most reluctant to strengthen the naval forces. It was estimated that for every ship intercepted and hauled off, three got through. Profits were high and payment of the "freight costs" appeared to some to be not only the better part of valor but good Yankee business sense.

The Jeffersonians, for totally different reasons, wished to

avoid war with France at almost any cost. They felt that the treaty John Jay had signed on behalf of the United States with the hated British king justified the French in their attacks on American shipping. The French cannon fire amplified the rage felt by many Americans at Jay's "surrender" to British interests.

Any Republican doubt on the matter was resolved by the presence in Congress of a strong "High Federalist" faction that demanded a declaration of war with France. These Hamiltonians represented the acute political view that the Federalist party was in deep political trouble. Increasing numbers of Republican candidates were taking power in the states and seats in Congress. Head-counters looked to the election of 1800 with considerable misgiving. But a war with France, a crusade in which the Republicans would be tarred with the enemy brush, seemed to offer a way out. Personal factors too, played a role. Military glory had thus far evaded Alexander Hamilton. He saw a conflict with the French as an opportunity to lead American forces in the conquest of New Orleans and the Floridas. An American Empire was already shaping in the forge of Hamilton's imagination.

The situation was hardly comfortable for President Adams. His office required him to protect American interests but he knew that he led a divided country and he feared a declaration of war against France without a unified public behind him. Adams determined, early on, to resist the war spirit while asserting American rights on the high seas. His position was paradoxical; the more so because his Cabinet members in their written recommendations to him sometimes offered word-for-word repetitions of the instructions of Alexander Hamilton.

The President was determined to go before Congress in a special session on May 15, 1797. He wished to "consult and determine on such measures as in their wisdom shall be deemed meet for the safety and welfare of the said United States." Adams wrote that he wished to settle "all disputes with France," but, as historian Alexander De Conde wrote, "he dreaded war less than disgrace." It is interesting to note that whatever actions the Executive deemed fit to take on his own, he was always aware of the obligation to consult with Congress. There was never a question in Adams' mind of taking a national position without regard to the views of the body empowered to declare war. But Adams was pilloried by all parties for all of the wrong reasons.

While the President prepared to ask congressional approval for a peace mission to France, Jefferson, "the Peacemaker," wanted no part of a special session. Because Adams intended to couple his suggestion for a new approach to the French with requests for a stiffening of our military posture that might appear to the French to be belligerent, Jefferson wrote that the Federalists were "taking the high ground of war." Hamilton, agreeing with his enemy's assessment, was so confident that France would refuse to treat that he endorsed the mission wholeheartedly. When war came, he told his party comrades, he wanted it to be apparent that the conflict had been forced on the United States. There were to be no fingers of accusation pointed at the Federalists as the "war party." That too has a contemporary ring.

Adams' attempt to increase our armed power threatened at first to give him the worst of all worlds. Congressional response to his requests for increased military strength was mixed. His proposal for a mission to France was threatened with delay because of dissatisfaction with its composition. But finally a commission composed of Elbridge Gerry, John Marshall and Charles Cotesworth Pinckney was empowered to negotiate with the ever-changing French Republic. That quality of change in France was one of the factors that made dealing with her so difficult. Governments rose and fell and the only motif that ran through them was a common corruption that finally erupted in what has come to be called the XYZ Affair; an effort to force a bribe of $250,000 from the American peace commissioners as the price for talking at all. This extortion by Messrs. X, Y and Z on behalf of the French Foreign Minister Talleyrand completely turned American public opinion about, and resulted in a fervor for war with the French that embraced many of the embarrassed Republicans.

But before that piece of comic opera was put on public display, a stream of bitter invective flowed between Congress and the Executive. The special session had exacerbated the passions of both sides. Adams failed to achieve unity behind his foreign policy and found himself increasingly marked by the "French Party," as he called the Republicans, as a President who wished to lead his country into war. Although he was later to see no way out of the conflict with France, the President at that stage wished to make every effort to come to an accommodation. He was rewarded by Jefferson's observation that in both France and the United States the executive branches wished to make war and that only legislative restraint had prevented that result.

As French depredations continued on the high seas, the American negotiators persisted in their attempts to break through the impasse of requests for money bribes. When Adams' Secretary of State, Timothy Pickering, learned what had happened in Paris he ordered the mission home immediately. Adams himself was angered to an extraordinary degree. His first inclination was to ask Congress for a declaration of war, but he diluted the message because of *his fear that he would be refused*. The balance of constitutional forces was at work. No matter the merits of the cause (the Republicans did not yet know about the XYZ Affair) the Executive could not commit the United States to a course of military action without congressional endorsement. It should be further observed that Adams, throughout his term of *office, felt differently at different times about the need for war with France*. Constitutional restraint operated at this point as a form of imposed wisdom. The President limited himself to a request for arms manufacture, coastal protection and for the revenue to pay for increased military outlay. It was the latter request that came back to haunt the war-makers in a later revulsion of public opinion.

The President's relatively mild message was received with hostility by the pro-French Republicans. The newspaper *Aurora* rejected his account of French activity and charged him with delivering a "war message." The Republican organ said that *Adams had declared war without going to the Congress* and that the Constitution was endangered. The facts, in this case, were quite different. Adams, patiently for a man of his character, was waiting for a rise on the scale of French belligerency to rally behind him the public opinion necessary to fight a national war. Other Presidents have exercised considerably less discretion with even more at stake in terms of the life and death of innocent people.

Congressional resolutions opposing even limited armament for defense forced Adams to disclose the events that had occurred in Paris. He sent to the House of Representatives all of the dispatches from his peace commissioners. The entire story of the indignities to which they had been subjected and a detailed account of the bribery attempt were included. The XYZ Affair was made to order for presidential need. The people and the Congress turned from their close emotional ties to the French. The tricolor was no longer worn as decoration in public. French revolutionary songs were no longer sung with fervor in public places. The end of an era of strong affection for foreign causes and a shift to concern with national self-interest was about to begin. But the long delays in communication, the straining between the President and Congress over their rights with regard to the war power, also produced an unlooked-for result. In the hour of Federalist triumph, events took shape that were to keep the *quasi* in quasi-war.

The President at first gloried in the new tide of public enthusiasm for his position and glowed at the sweep of national anger with the French. He succumbed to the political temptation to tie his opposition at home with the enemy abroad. "Foreign hostility" and "domestic treachery" were often linked in his public language. The resentment and the fear stirred by release of the XYZ papers manifested themselves in willing congressional endorsement of Adams' call for a large Army under the command of Washington. (Adams was humiliated when the retired Cincinnatus demanded that Hamilton be called as second in command; but he acceded.) The Alien and Sedition Acts, designed to silence the voices of dissent, were also promulgated by a Congress with increased Federalist representation. Taxes on land and houses were voted to finance a new Navy that would attack the French on the high seas at any time in any place. Since the war, momentarily at least, was being fought at sea, a Department of the Navy was created for the first time in American history. Everything was marshaled for war —everything, that is, except the House of Representatives. Despite the pressure from the executive branch and from the Federalist majority in the Senate, there was still enough sentiment against going to war to make a declaration doubtful. That doubt was enough to limit American-French hostilities to naval engagements while the representatives of both countries, official and unofficial, tried to come to an accommodation.

The first hint of the possibility of peace arrived in the United States with the return of John Marshall, one of the commissioners involved in the XYZ Affair. When he reported to the President that the French gave signs that they were ready to negotiate, it afforded Adams an opportunity to seek an alternative to a formal declaration of war. There just might be the chance for profitable talk—meaningful negotiation.

There were other signs pointing to a slim possibility for peace. An American Quaker doctor named Logan who visited France with introductions to high French officials from prominent Americans, including Vice President Jefferson, returned home with Foreign Minister Talleyrand's disavowal of the XYZ bribery attempt. The French official had indicated to Logan that a new delegation would be more than welcome to discuss the possibility of reestablishing Franco-American relations. Adams, suspicious at first, was reassured by reports from his own son John Quincy, then serving as minister to Berlin. For internal reasons having to do with France's concerns in Europe, a conflict with the United States had become increasingly unappealing.

But even as the prospects for negotiation took a turn for the better, war fever intensified at home. Newspaper editors opposed to the Federalists were prosecuted and jailed. National security was used as a shield for repression. Hamilton, himself no soft-hearted lover of Republicans, asked his partisans, "Why establish a tyranny? Energy is a very different thing from violence." In another moment, more representative of his attitudes at the time, Hamilton suggested that war with France might afford the opportunity for land armies to conquer the Floridas and Louisiana, and, he said, we ought "to squint at South America."

But it was the new American Navy, off the ways at last, that swept into the Caribbean and engaged French men-of-war with notable success. Commodore Thomas Truxton, commanding the *Constellation*, captured the French thirty-four-gun frigate *L'Insurgente*. He remarked that the French captain told him that their countries were at peace and that this engagement would put them at war. "If so I am glad of it," said Truxton, "for I detest things being done by halves."

President Adams had good reason to be satisfied that things were being paced by halves rather than wholes. For as a grudging Congress gave acquiescence to his "half-war," as the Hamiltonians in his party pressed for more action, word came from Europe that it was time to reenter negotiations with the French. John Adams' statesmanlike response to the new situation cost him reelection to the Presidency but it prevented the United States from becoming deeply involved in a major war with the most powerful military force in Europe. Napoleon had arrived on the scene and conflict with the United States was irrelevant to his particular vision of the future of the French Empire.

American agents at The Hague were approached by French representatives. Assurances were given that the French would be receptive to a mission from the United States and Adams prepared to commission the American minister at The Hague as his representative. A bitter quarrel with the Hamiltonians in his own Cabinet and with pro-war Federalist Senators ensued and a compromise was worked out. Oliver Ellsworth, the Chief Justice of the United States, was named as chief of a three-man mission to conduct the negotiations.

The timing was propitious, for the American war fever that had been raised after the XYZ papers were released was quickly broken by the medicine of taxation. The landowners and slaveholders who were hit by revenue collectors in order to fund the Quasi-War became less than militant in their advocacy of war. State and local elections indicated a resurgence of Republican strength and the Federalists fought more bitterly among themselves than against the French or the Republicans.

Adams learned that he had been steadily deceived by his Cabinet over a period of three years and he split his party irreparably when he relieved the Secretaries of State and War. National discord was intensified by the passage of the Alien and Sedition Acts. They symbolized to a divided country the despotism thought to have been escaped with the War for Independence. Thomas Jefferson (the chief beneficiary of the backlash) was elected President of the United States in a contest in which the principal Federalist leaders were opposed to their own Chief Executive.

One of Jefferson's first acts was to sign a treaty with France that had been negotiated by his predecessor's peace commissioners. The agreement's provisions are of little consequence today. The United States was assured of relief from further French sea assault and her earlier alliance with France was nullified. That had been a key Federalist objective. Napoleon for his part was now free to pursue his ambitions for empire without the American thorn in his side. But the importance of the episode lies not in who got what out of a quasi-war, but in who did what; and in the complexity of motive that moved each of the parties into positions strikingly different from those with which they had begun. The key factor in preventing large-scale war was widespread public opposition and the expression of that opposition in Congress. It should be remarked that this view is not consistent with those held by some of the Hamilton Federalists. Their contention was that Congress lagged behind the people in acceptance of the conflict. If election returns mean anything at all, they proved the Federalists were wrong.

Whatever the truth, the constitutional factor was at work. Vacillation as to a proper course of action was apparent in the behavior of most of the key participants in the executive branch. Hamilton spoke of war on one day and the advantages of peace on the next. Washington, in retirement at Mount Vernon, saw no possibility of an accommodation on one occasion and later remarked on the necessity for further attempts to reach agreement.

But it was Adams who was President and it was his behavior that invites comparison with the course of later Chief Executives. Two hundred years after the fact we have had more than sufficient time to contemplate the Ellsberg Papers of that day; they came from a multitude of sources and they reveal that nothing in the craft of statesmanship is immutable. Most things can be revised and altered and set into new directions, and if necessary, withdrawn from consideration. Only war itself, once begun, takes on an inevitable dimension of tragedy.

John Adams was a veteran of public life by the time he entered the Presidency and he knew that to be true. His own intelligence, his Cabinet advices (often intentionally misleading) led him down the road to war more than once. His anger at French intransigence brought him to the point of drafting a belligerent request for a declaration of war. But he never made it. Time and new information and shifting public attitudes changed his mind several times during the period of the Quasi-War. In the end, he and the country muddled through without slipping into the chasm.

Those shifting perspectives would have been to no avail without the constitutional restraints to which Adams felt forced to bow. His "vacillation" was simply a response to his new information, and his willingness to do what was right no matter what the personal cost testifies to the need for institutional barriers against impulsive action. The division of the war powers between the President and Congress is such a barrier. Without that division of power, the time-consuming and involved negotiations of American diplomats, the change in the presidential attitude toward the question of peace and war and the public opposition as expressed in Congress would have been to no avail. Without that one small clause in the Constitution that "Congress shall have power to declare war," John Adams would have been unable in his later years to remark that his decision to send a final peace mission to France was "the most disinterested, the most determined and the most successful of my life."

IV

Jefferson's
Private War

DEBATE and legislative enactment are the tools of the trade for
members of the Senate. We usually concentrate on the immediate problem at hand. Only when we confront the great issues that
strain and divide us are we obliged to take the long retrospective
view. Vietnam, in our time, is that issue. That miserable war
has given us pause. The issues it raises about the way we conduct
our national affairs have driven me to the pages of history
where I find strange analogies that sound the themes of the
present.

I have always held the conviction that history is at least partially the character of the men and women who make it. Study of
the relations between Congress and the President has reaffirmed
that conviction. A new element of awareness has, at the same
time, entered my assessment of the historic frame in which we
help to make our own futures. Obscure events, apparently marginal to the fortunes of nations, have often set us on a course we
had no intention of taking. Just as we sometimes misjudge each
other, misread the characters of those closest to us, so we sometimes fail to see the full characters of those who have dominated
the pages of our history.

Thomas Jefferson wrote more public documents and private
papers than any other great figure of the past. One of his biographers has observed that the very quantity of the record hides

the man. He can be made to say and to represent anything. Despite the variety of materials a dominant theme has emerged. One imagines Jefferson would have found it to his liking, and in it there are large truths. But while the third President is most often perceived as a philosopher of egalitarianism, as the great "small *d*" democrat, as the apotheosis of the American experiment, there are other facets to that portrait. One of them is particularly relevant to the exercise of presidential power. Thomas Jefferson's use of that power in the war with the Barbary pirates appears in many ways to be filled with a presidential will to make war out of personal conviction unmatched until the days of the struggle in Vietnam.

Jefferson took office in a revulsion against centralized authority. His own political leadership as well as his incisive writing had played a large role in stimulating that revulsion. He saw the central government as a potential enemy of liberty and looked to the states as guardian of the rights of the people. Jefferson was particularly critical of the tendency of the President to take on too much responsibility for the establishment of policy. It will be recalled that he bitterly opposed the Neutrality Proclamation as an invasion of congressional prerogative. During the Quasi-War with France, he regarded much of the Administration's activity as a cover for the aggrandizement of its own power. But Jefferson was a complicated person and the high mountain of the Presidency offers a panorama beyond the range of a Vice President's vision. We must remember also that Thomas Jefferson had been in public life for thirty-two years when he took the oath of office. During that period he had developed strong attitudes toward the requirements of American policy. While he often shifted course, with some of his closest companions completely unaware of the change in tactical direction, he remained remarkably consistent in the nature of his ultimate goals. His personality prevented him from publicly assuming an authoritarian stance. He appears to have been mildness itself and exerted a great charm on those he chose to admit to his intimate circle. Politicians are frequently accused of using people. Jefferson was a politician and he used people magnificently. More often than not he used them to great ends.

But the Virginian's shyness and his libertarian attitudes tended to obscure on occasion a unique vigor of purpose. Hamilton, when Jefferson's election became apparent, remarked consolingly to a fellow Federalist that the office would not wither from lack of use.

Jefferson's great enemy was correct in his conclusion. The tools of Jefferson's choice were quite different from those of his predecessors, but they were enormously effective in assisting him to achieve his goals. And they stretched markedly the fabric of the Constitution he was sworn to uphold and had promised to construe within the narrowest of limits. Nowhere is that more evident than in the way he dealt with the menace of the Barbary pirates.

The American conflict with the Barbary Powers is a fascinating illustration of the enormous change that has taken place in war. It gave full scope to the quixotic impulses of seamen and adventurers, and it offers a splendid case study of a President who got Congress to give him a good deal of what he wanted, but who took the rest on his own. Jefferson's Presidency was filled with echoes of his public past. He knew as well as any man in America what the Barbary problem was and he had his own ideas of how to solve it. But at no time did he press as hard publicly on behalf of those ideas as he had fifteen years earlier when he served as minister to France. Those were the days when he and John Adams, then minister to Great Britain, were still close friends. Their correspondence about the Barbary pirates illustrates passionate conviction on Jefferson's part that the only way to deal with the Barbary Powers was *to build a navy and to drive them from the seas.*

The Barbary Coast stretches along North Africa's Mediterranean shores from Egypt to the Atlantic. Four principal powers, Algiers, Morocco, Tripoli and Tunis, terrorized the sea-lanes during the centuries between the fall of Spain to the Christians and the advent of American commerce under an American flag. The history of these depredations is rooted in the conquest of much of Europe and Africa by the followers of Islam and the almost unending waves of war and migration that produced a North African population dependent in large degree on piracy for its sustenance. The major European powers regarded the

Barbary incursions on their coasts and the looting of their commerce as nuisances worthy of an occasional forceful reply, but more easily assuaged by the form of treaty and the substance of tribute. The moral implications of so dealing with a group of pirates may be questionable. North African war vessels were manned by flag-flying thieves who took prisoners from European ships, used them as galley slaves, sent the women off to harems, put others in chains and held them for ransom. But the European powers were concerned principally with their own rivalries, and the highest bidder was often able to enlist one or more of the Barbary Powers as an ally in commercial war against a less lavish Christian power. The question of humanity was raised only as a tactic for negotiation. In any case, during the early days, the Christian powers took their own slaves from Moorish ships, so it was *quid pro quo*.

Pride did not enter the game in the case of Great Britain. England paid lavishly despite Barbary's awe of her naval power. The treaties she signed now and again with the Dey of Algiers, or the Pasha of Tripoli or the Bey of Tunis, gave her commerce and her people a relatively high degree of freedom of the seas. So long as American shipping sailed under the British flag, the Colonies too were protected by British might and by British arrangements. But in 1783 that happy state of affairs came to an end. United States shipping was on its own. Thomas Jefferson, as minister to France, had been close to the Mediterranean scene at that time, and as President of the United States he dominated it when American interests were asserted some quarter century later.

The Stars and Stripes were not greeted with hurrahs when the newly independent Yankee shipping entered the coastal waters. The Barbary Powers sensed easy prey and began to take ships and crews into custody. In 1785 the brig *Maria*, out of Boston, was hauled into port. In rapid order ships bearing the names *Dauphin* and *Betsy* were also boarded and captured. An early account by John Foss, an American seaman enslaved and held for ransom, described the situation.

Foss recalled that his ship, the *Polly*, was boarded by a fierce horde of bearded Moslems after the ship had been tricked into close proximity to a pirate vessel. The American prisoners were stripped of their clothes and given "vermin infested" rags to replace them. Taken to Algiers, they were marched through the streets to the loud applause of "thousands of malicious barbarians," and brought before the Dey himself. That personage comforted his new slaves with the words, "Now I have got you, you Christian dogs. You shall eat stones!"

The slaves were hurled into dungeons and fettered with chains and shackles weighing up to forty pounds. Their fate was to be used as labor in mountain quarries outside of Algiers, where they blasted and dragged tons of rock for miles at a time, under the threat of the whip.

Foss's account was repeated in substance by others who followed him into captivity and it echoes the pathetic tales told by those who had been ransomed in the earlier days when American shipping had been under British "protection." Some victims served the rest of their lives in slavery, while others were held for as long as ten years before adequate funds secured their release. But the increasing savagery of the Barbary attacks, and the apparent helplessness of the Confederation government to stop it, brought the issue into the forefront of the public business.

Jefferson and Adams were commissioned by the new government to attempt to sign peace treaties with the Barbary rulers. Their efforts were futile inasmuch as the bribes authorized by the Confederation Congress were pitifully small compared to the demands made by the pirates.

Our interest in the developing conflict with the Barbary States relates to Jefferson's attitude. Jefferson and Adams met in London and discussed every aspect of the problem. When Jefferson returned to his post in Paris, they continued their discussion in correspondence. His letters to John Adams embodied a conviction that Jefferson, though he later hid it well, took with him into the White House.

I acknowledge, I very early thought it would be best to effect a peace through the medium of war . . . 1. Justice is in favor of this opinion. 2. Honor favors it. 3. It will procure us respect in Europe and respect is a safeguard to interest.

4. It will arm the federal head with the safest of all the instruments of coercion over its delinquent members.

Jefferson's views are even more sharply and interestingly expressed in a letter to James Monroe. Writing in August of 1786, fifteen years before he became President, he said:

> . . . the necessity that the United States should have some marine force, *and the happiness of this*, as the ostensible cause of beginning it, would decide on its propriety. . . . every rational citizen must wish to see an effective instrument of coercion, and should fear to see it on any other element than the water. A naval force can never endanger our liberties, nor occasion bloodshed; a land force would do both.

Jefferson, then, obviously regarded the Barbary actions as a rationale for the Navy he regarded as a necessity. Adams, who endorsed the continued payment of tribute as sanctioned by precedent and the practice of older and larger powers, did reply nevertheless to the key point in the Jefferson letter. "I agree in opinion of the wisdom and necessity of a Navy for other uses . . . I will go all lengths with you in promoting a Navy, whether to be applied to the Algerines or not."

These two men, so different in their political philosophies, and leaders of parties tied strongly to opposing foreign interests, nevertheless followed remarkably similar impulses with regard to the war power, when they assumed the Presidency under the new Constitution. The record indicates however that Adams, the Federalist, the endorser of vigorous central power, deferred far more to congressional prerogative than did his successor. For all his temper, for all his occasional sword-rattling, Adams kept it in the scabbard because the Constitution obliged him to do so.

Jefferson, the "Republican," had an extraordinary ability to ally himself with constitutional principles while at the same time he directed presidential hostilities four thousand miles from home; the country's first "democratic" Chief Executive also arranged for a secret alliance with a puppet ruler who would serve the interests of the United States as seen by an American President. Manner is in some cases the very heart of matter.

In 1795, in order to palliate the increasing arrogance of the Barbary corsairs, Adams had signed a treaty with Algiers that called for payment of $642,000 in cash and an annual shipment of naval stores. Congress was appalled by the fact that twenty-three American vessels and one hundred nineteen prisoners had been captured by the Barbary pirates during a two-month period. Finally, the legislators authorized the creation of the United States Navy. But anger was salted by parsimony and the popular fear of a military monster. The bill passed by only eleven votes and was restricted by conditions that made it difficult for Jefferson to use the new fleet to full effect.

Shortly after the new President took office in 1801, the Pasha of Tripoli sent a company of soldiers to the American consulate, where they cut down the flagpole. This quaint custom signified that the Pasha was angry enough to consider himself at war with the United States. The issue, as usual, was money, and how to extort more of it from distant and pitiful America.

One reason the Pasha felt able to intimidate the Americans was the fact that months earlier the United States had been humiliated when one of its principal warships succumbed to the threats of the Dey of Algiers. The *George Washington*, with twenty-four guns and a crew of one hundred and thirty, had been in port in order to deliver the annual American treaty booty. The Dey commanded the ship's captain, William Bainbridge, to proceed to Constantinople with a shipment of goods for the Sultan. When Bainbridge refused, the weakness of his position was pointed out. His ship would never leave the harbor without being blasted from the water by Algerine shore batteries. Bainbridge decided that in a Navy with only fourteen frigates on the water, it would be foolhardy to lose the *George Washington*. The insult was compounded by the Dey's order that the American flag be struck and that the Algerine flag be flown during the voyage.

Yussuf Karamanlis, the Tripolitan Pasha, was a man who sensed weakness. He had seized his throne by intrigue and murder. The principal victim had been his oldest brother. In the aftermath of the American humiliation at Algiers, Yussuf refused to discuss his demands for Yankee tribute with James

Cathcart, the American consul. Cathcart, a former seaman, had been captured and enslaved for ten years before his release. His dispatches home and those of his fellow consuls, William Eaton in Tunis and Richard O'Brien in Algiers, were long cries of frustration at American impotence in Barbary. Each of them had repeatedly called for the use of force in dealing with the threats of the Barbary rulers. The long distances between Africa and the United States, combined with bitter political infighting at home, resulted in almost total lack of response to their pleas. But the episode of the *George Washington* spoke louder than the words of the new country's diplomats. Although mighty England could afford to tolerate a few Mediterranean pirates the new Republic at last felt called upon to assert its rights. The assertion was couched in ambiguous terms that reveal something of the new President's intentions and the artifice in which he cloaked them.

Word from Africa indicated to the State Department that war with Tripoli was likely. But Jefferson had received no communication that the event had occurred at the time he sent a so-called "squadron of observation" to the Mediterranean. In a letter to be delivered to the Pasha of Tripoli, the President remarked that the squadron's purpose was to "superintend the safety of our commerce and to exercise our seamen in nautical duties." He then said, *"We mean to rest the safety of our commerce on the resources of our own strength and bravery in every sea."*

The Secretary of the Navy ordered Commodore Richard Dale to sail for Gibraltar. There he was to take soundings as to the state of international affairs. If the Pasha of Tripoli had declared war the Americans were to blockade the Tripolitan coast. If not, a letter from Jefferson was to be delivered and American amity was to be assured. Dale, of course, learned of the flagpole episode and conducted himself as an officer in a Navy at war.

The next months and years saw the small United States Navy engaged in actions against the corsairs that reflected the validity of the President's twenty-year faith that American force would restrain the corsairs from interference with our Mediterranean commerce. Names like Dale, Preble, Sterett and Decatur were recorded as heroic figures in the annals of United States valor. The Tripolitan brigands were revealed as "Paper Tigers." A nineteenth-century biographer of Jefferson summed up the President's military accomplishment when he wrote that there was "something really exquisite in Jefferson's turning the infant Navy of the infant government to a use so legitimate."

Our concern is with a different aspect of the question. Did Jefferson's actions accord with constitutional precept? Glenn Tucker, a writer on the Barbary Wars and on naval affairs, has observed that a naval officer at that time was "the United States on the firing line." Did a President of the United States have a right to put Commodore Dale and his several successors on the firing line? There were those who thought not.

Jefferson took office on March 4, 1801. Two months later a Federalist newspaper, the *New England Palladium*, was able to say in its columns that "it is extraordinary that our government has not yet caused official publication to be made of the state of our affairs with the Dey of Tripoli." The truth, of course, was that the executive branch had ample written evidence of that state of affairs and that the Administration was even then looking for a commodore to lead its squadron to the Mediterranean.

Jefferson, although he was beginning a new policy without reference to the Congress, was careful to move slowly. Initial instructions were phrased with such reticence that Commodore Truxton, his first choice, refused the assignment. He felt that his orders were not sufficiently flexible to enable him to take effective measures against the potential enemy. During the years of Jefferson's first administration those initial instructions were stretched to a point reminiscent of orders and interpretations of orders given in our own day. It took even the new President's own party some time to catch up with him.

The *Aurora* was a Jeffersonian newspaper. In December of 1800 it suggested that a Navy was not necessary to protect American commerce and that there would be no danger to our ships, "if they never take long voyages to sea." By June of 1801, after Jefferson had assumed the Presidency, *Aurora* changed its position. The paper now declared that "Dale has orders to defend the honor of his country and to protect its commerce by affording convoys, when required, to American vessels trading in the Mediterranean." Almost at the same time, the Philadelphia *Gazette*, once an advocate of strong federal action, demanded that the executive branch inform the people as to the situation in Barbary. In every case in which the Federalists attacked Jefferson on the Barbary issue and on the Navy there was implied or specific reference to congressional prerogative. The case, on this level, had considerable substance. For at the same time as our naval forces were engaged in hostilities with the Barbary pirates, the Jefferson Administration attempted to overthrow the Pasha of Tripoli and replace him with still another brother. The job was very nearly done with the aid of the United States Marines.

V

To the Shores
of Tripoli

WILLIAM EATON, the United States consul in Tunis, was a former
Army officer. He had served with distinction as a young Vermont
volunteer during the Revolution and when the war was over he
went on to conduct a series of derring-do missions for government
officials. In Africa he found himself in a situation that went
against the New England grain. Eaton was an acute observer and
he sensed immediately that Barbary would crumble under the
impact of relatively little force. His letters are filled with expressions of anger at the way the United States submitted to North
African humiliations. He began to plan an expedition that would
first topple the Bey of Tunis from his throne, and then, in an
early version of the domino theory, result in the fall of the other
North African tyrannies.

Eaton's project was stymied at first by the fact that his Washington superiors paid him very little attention. He received few
if any instructions, and as a rule, they related to ways to pacify
the Bey. Directions as to the purchase of "gifts" of diamond-
encrusted rifle barrels and similar trifles are still in the national
archives. Eaton followed orders, but, thousands of miles from
home, he had also engaged in private business on his own behalf. He made and then lost a fortune in the Mediterranean trade.
His attitude toward the piracy problem was best expressed in the
view that "there is no access to permanent friendship without pav-

ing the way with gold or cannon balls." He made it plain to the Secretary of State that his own preference was for the cannon balls. Eaton's chance came when he visited with his fellow consul James Cathcart. They devised a plan whereby Hamet Karamanlis would become the new Pasha of Tripoli. In point of fact, Hamet had been in line for the throne. He fled the country when his younger brother, Yussuf, killed the former Pasha, assumed the power himself and began to look for Hamet.

Eaton located the royal refugee in Malta and made a vague proposal of alliance with the United States. When Hamet, a man with a great desire for survival and very little of Eaton's zest for adventure, gave tentative agreement, Eaton increased the tempo of his communications with Washington.

His unrelenting efforts eventually bore the fruit of official approval when James Madison, Jefferson's Secretary of State, authorized the expenditure of $20,000 to subsidize a Hamet land force. He instructed Commodore Samuel Barron, the latest in a series of Mediterranean naval commanders, that Eaton was to be assisted in implementing the scheme. "With respect to the Ex-Bashaw of Tripoli [Hamet] we have no objection to you availing yourself of his cooperation against Tripoli . . . in such an event you will, it is believed, find Mr. Eaton useful to you . . ." In such ways do envoys become generals. For Eaton now located the hapless Hamet hiding with a few other royal refugees in the desert outside Alexandria. After securing Hamet's commission as commanding general, he asked Barron for the assistance of one thousand United States Marines to make the long march through the desert to the city of Derna. It was there that Eaton planned to fight the first battle against the Pasha. Derna was Tripoli's second largest city and Eaton was convinced that if it fell, Tripoli itself, like a cluster of rotten dates, would fall to the ground. Barron, however, although obliged to cooperate, was still the man in charge, and he saw little merit in giving a civilian command of his Marine contingent. The two men compromised. Eaton was given *ten* Marines under the command of Lieutenant Presley N. O'Bannon. Those ten Marines almost did the job.

Doling out his subsidy, and a good deal of his own money, Eaton recruited hundreds of Arabs, including their women and children, as Hamet's crusade made its way to Derna. There were repeated episodes in which the putative Pasha evidenced a lack of taste for the risks and attempted to scurry back to Alexandria. On one occasion the Arab troops threatened to kill Eaton, the Marines and a few Greek mercenaries for good measure. But the march continued through the desert. Eaton's contingent made its way through Tobruk, Sidi Barani, Sollom and Bombe. It was as though the nineteenth-century adventurer was tracking out Montgomery's line of pursuit of Rommel through the African desert.

At long last the "force" arrived before Derna and Eaton was proven right. He and O'Bannon led an attack that resulted in the fall of the city. The Marines had arrived at the shores of Tripoli.

To this day historians will argue the question whether William Eaton and O'Bannon's Marines could have taken Tripoli itself. They were not given the chance. The Pasha, frightened by Eaton's success, evidenced a new willingness to settle his differences with the United States, and an American envoy who had been empowered by Jefferson to make a treaty achieved a better agreement than any that had been completed in prior history. Tripoli agreed to give up all American prisoners for a payment of $60,000 and agreed further, *to cease demanding tribute of American shipping or the United States Government.*

The Eaton march to Tripoli had other side effects. Shock waves of fear of the American fighting men had spread throughout the Barbary Powers. Displays of naval force in their harbors resulted in the most pliable kind of response. The next few years saw an increasing surge of free American commerce on the Mediterranean as the Barbary menace eased and died. Hamet was smuggled onto an American warship off Tripoli and the United States Government later pensioned him off with a small stipend. Hamet's place in history was guaranteed in Article III of the treaty the United States signed with his brother. Yussuf had agreed in writing to release Hamet's wife and children from the custody in which they had been held, but it took four years before he did so. When pressured by the American consul, Yussuf said that a secret article in the treaty had given him the right to delay implementation. Jefferson told the Senate in 1807 that the reason for the secrecy of the article "could not with certainty be said." Much about the Barbary War "cannot with certainty be said." The phrase "millions for defense, not one cent for tribute" is hallowed in the apocrypha of war along with the "Nuts!" later attributed to General McAuliffe when the Germans demanded his surrender during the Battle of the Bulge in World War II. The issue of Who Makes War tends to fade into the background when the drums beat. But it is that issue with which we are concerned.

Thomas Jefferson was the first President to send a naval force abroad without congressional consent. He was the first President to intervene in the internal affairs of a foreign country. Jefferson obviously hoped to turn a dispute between despots into a civil war that would result in American advantage. In neither case did he approach Congress even for its "advice and consent," until long after the fact. He was criticized severely by his political enemies for breaking with the Constitution, but his party's dominance was such and his administration was so successful that his executive ventures turned into precedent for the greater presidential incursions of the twentieth century.

Perhaps the key to Jefferson's ability to accomplish his ends without considerably more resistance from a peace-minded Congress lies in an observation made by one of the country's leading students of presidential power. Professor Edward S. Corwin observed:

> The tone of his messages is uniformly deferential to Congress. His first one ends "nothing shall be wanting on my part to inform, as far as in my power, the legislative judgment. Nor to carry that judgment into faithful execution." His actual guidance of Congress' judgment was nonetheless constant and unremitting even while often secretive and sometimes furtive.

Professor Corwin also noted that Jefferson was the first "President who is primarily a party leader, only secondarily a Chief Executive." The President manifested that party leadership in his ability to restrain criticism of a message delivered on December 8, 1801. It was the first time that he reported officially on the Tripolitan War, a war that had begun *nine months earlier*. After fighting a series of naval engagements, Jefferson bowed in the direction of the Constitution.

The legislature will doubtless consider whether, by authorizing measures of offense also, they will place our force on an equal footing with that of our adversaries. I communicate all material information on this subject, that in the exercise of this important function confided by the Constitution to the legislature exclusively their judgment may form itself on a knowledge and consideration of every circumstance of weight.

The President never did "advise" with the Senate as to the propriety of dealing with the hapless Hamet. It was only after the fact that the legislators were given the background of an alliance that foreshadowed similar "arrangements" made down to the present day. The aid to the rulers of South Vietnam and Cambodia in the twentieth century differs from what went to Hamet in Jefferson's day certainly in quantity but hardly in purpose.

There were those who took exception to the extension of presidential power. Following his first message to Congress, in which the members learned of the war, a resolution was introduced to the effect that "the President be authorized by law, *further and more effectively* to protect the commerce of the United States against the Barbary Powers." A member of the opposition noted that Jefferson had sent a naval squadron to the Mediterranean without consulting with Congress. This might have been wise, the Congressman said, but he did not wish "the House to commit itself until fully informed." Much of the debate centered on whether or not Jefferson had been carrying on a defensive action and whether or not Congress would be giving up its power in passing the resolution. The President won on the motion before the House and he was enabled to pursue his Mediterranean policy with increased vigor. But public opinion, as expressed in letters to the press, was divided and fully aware of the question of the war power.

The *Gazette of the United States,* financed in part by Hamilton, published these bitter words:

> The Constitution, which by the way he is under solemn oath to support . . . declares that making of war shall be a legislative act. Nevertheless we see the executive—*because it is popular*—can make war when it pleases . . .

Hamilton, ironically, took Jefferson to task for not acting with sufficient dispatch. He viewed the President's indirect approach as an abdication of authority. The subtle Jefferson could point to his enemy's words as evidence of the rectitude of his intentions. But there were those who saw through the immediate issue of piracy and tribute into the basic constitutional question.

An article in the *Columbian Centinel* appeared the summer after Dale had sailed for the Mediterranean. The writer observed that the Administration was under considerable pressure as a result of piratical acts. He denied any intent to "obstruct" but was determined to examine Jefferson's acts with "fairness and candor." Congress's right to declare war and grant letters of marque (commissions to seize enemy shipping) was then recalled, and the writer asked whether the legislature had actually done so. If not, he asked (about Dale's expedition), "Where are the laws and authority under which it has been planned and dispatched?"

Jefferson was charged with delegating to Dale "plenary powers to make war or commit hostilities should he be so inclined." The writer noted that congressional authority to declare war *cannot be delegated or vested,* and he then asked a question which has since been raised in the context of later hostilities. Why is it "lawful and constitutional to do that against any or all of the Barbary Powers, which it would be unlawful or unconstitutional to do against Great Britain, France or any of the other states or nations?" Jefferson's actions in Barbary were "a direct violation of the Constitution."

Given the standards of conduct of the twentieth century, Thomas Jefferson's use of presidential power appears in some ways to be almost timid. He was careful to observe the courtesies with Congress. Papers and messages were supplied them in profusion. They were repeatedly assured of their constitutional authority and of Jefferson's deference to that authority. He was careful to engage in no rearmament program without congressional authorization, but he slipped through loopholes in the law in order to strengthen those forces at his disposal. Jefferson knew the way to power and how to keep it. He had wanted a Navy for twenty-five years and he used the Barbary pirates as an excuse for wrenching one from an unwilling legislature. He was a master of timing and during congressional recesses he turned the distance between himself and legislators scattered to distant homes, to the advantage of presidential power. He acted, at least in part, because there was no one else to do so. Thereby he set a precedent that haunts us in an era of instant communication. His treatment of relations with Barbary *did* differ from the manner which he treated the European powers. The *Gazette* writer may well have sensed the beginning of an American attitude that sharply differentiates between Occidental values and those of the other cultures with whom we have had contact.

One is almost apologetic in assessing Jefferson the Republican as the first great violator of the right of Congress to exercise the war power. He was, after all, treading on new ground. The Constitution's tissue had yet to be tested. Jefferson's approach to its text and its spirit reflected his energy and the inherent lassitude imposed on a divided and dispersed legislature. It is a pattern that we have seen frequently repeated, but one that needs to be changed.

If Jefferson eroded the congressional war power, we can be sure he had no inkling of the horror of modern war; his writing indicates that the powers of the modern Presidency would have dismayed him. He was, moreover, fighting in a good cause. Nobody likes a bully and the Barbary pirates were bullies. Americans thrilled when they learned of the impressive blow their fledgling Marine Corps and Navy had delivered to the Mediterranean enemy. Thomas Jefferson's victories belonged to his countrymen and they were not too inclined to nit-pick about a strict observance of the rules.

In the years immediately following Jefferson's administration that indifference to fundamental law was to be vividly dramatized in the differing careers of two Presidents and a General who was to become both a President and a legend.

VI

Mr. Madison
Defers to Congress

THE conflict between the President and Congress over war power flared significantly during the successive administrations of James Madison and James Monroe. These two very different men were the last links to the generation that made the American Revolution.

In the early nineteenth century the country already sensed its "manifest destiny" to link the Atlantic and Pacific coasts and to extend its domain to all that lay between. Indians might have thought "manifest destiny" to be "manifest theft" or "the Great Land Grab," but Indians didn't write the history books.

Monroe, who was sometimes called the "last of the cockades" (he wore the tricornered hat of the late eighteenth century), was also America's first professional politician. His predecessor, Madison, was the only active participant in political life to have played a role in writing the Constitution. The alliterative quality of their names and the overlap of men and events during their terms in office tend to stamp them in the popular memory with a common quality. But their approach to public affairs rose from contrary sources. Madison was a great statesman who had come, over a long period in public life, to believe in the supremacy of the legislative will. He was saddled in the political wars with a written record of carefully formulated argument that during an earlier period in his career had placed him on the other side of the question. This is a risk with which politicians must live if they are capable of growth.

Monroe, on the other hand, earned his place in politics by attaching himself to the fortunes of his great predecessors with exquisitely precise timing. He switched sides several times during the factional disputes between Washington and Hamilton and Jefferson and Madison. Monroe never stayed to dinner too long to eat dessert across the political street. But he survived to become the President who presided during a period that has been labeled "The Era of Good Feeling." Madison and Monroe were both wary of congressional sensibility on the question of the power to make war. Whatever their motivations, their convictions were tested in the crucible of contact with a new kind of American.

Andrew Jackson first rose to prominence during Madison's administration and his conduct during Monroe's Presidency offers a frightening example of contention between the civil and military power.

Jackson was an Indian fighter and land speculator with a reputation for a hot temper, a keen eye and a killer instinct. He once fatally shot a man in a duel for insulting his wife, and had engaged in more than one frontier brawl during his days as a law student. The Jackson virtues and weaknesses belonged to the frontier on which he spent his early and middle years. In his case they were written larger than life because his spare frame often shook under the violence of his emotions. The nickname "Old Hickory" signified a toughness of character and competitive spirit unique even at the height of an era that exemplified social Darwinism before it had been conceived. But that character enabled him to survive in the American West and it brought him a hero's laurels in America's first formally declared war against England. He fought and won the Battle of New Orleans after the peace treaty had been signed. Jackson's victory had no effect on the provisions of the Treaty of Ghent, but it gave American spirits a badly needed lift. For war had been mishandled from the start and the young Republic was lucky to get out of it literally in one piece.

Legend has had it that America has never lost a war, but the one fought in 1812 was in many ways too close to call. It was also a factor in determining the attitudes of future Presidents and Congresses as to how the war powers were to be divided.

Madison began the War of 1812 as Commander in Chief of the forces of a divided country. With the exception of the Civil War, which is the great exception to all the issues on which we touch, only the wars in Mexico and Vietnam have caused such bitter domestic dissent. We fought in 1812 ostensibly to resist British impressment of American sailors, and to assure the rights of neutrals on the high seas during a war between Great Britain and Napoleonic France. But there were other issues perhaps more relevant to the actual outbreak of hostilities. The frontier fed on land hunger and a growing United States Congress reflected the increasing power of representatives from the frontier states.

The "War Hawk" Congressmen from the frontier states of Kentucky, Georgia and Tennessee looked to Canada to appease their constituents' increasing appetite for land. One Congressman said on the House floor that the war, if properly fought, would have its advantages. He expressed a willingness to welcome the Canadians as "adopted brethren." Jefferson wrote that Canada was ready to fall and the House of Representatives was willing to shake the tree. There was also considerable anger with the British for their support of Indian hostility toward the frontier settlements in the West. The opportunity to strike back at the British pocketbook appeared too good to resist.

But such sentiment was only occasionally avowed. The defense of the rights of American seamen provided a mantle of rectitude, and the British had certainly given us all the excuse we needed to take offense. Hundreds of sailors had been impressed during England's war with France and dozens of ships had been seized. A look at the division in both Senate and House reveals however that on the question of war and peace, a majority of Congressmen and Senators from the New England States were opposed to the conflict. It was New England where the ships were built. New England sailors took their chances with the warring powers. It was New England commerce that continued to prosper during that war despite the "inconvenience" of British intrusion.

The "War Hawks" under Speaker Henry Clay of Kentucky controlled the divided House, and they shaped the policies that brought us to war, on behalf of the interests of their section of the country. President Madison, though he hesitated as to whether or not the country was required to fight, was firm in his conviction that Congress must take the initiative. His conduct during his presidential term is remarkable for the consistency of his attitude. When Congress was in recess Madison intensified his activities on the diplomatic front. He attempted to negotiate differences with Britain and France and, generally, to set the tone for United States policy. But when Congress was in session the President assumed the guise of deference that had been worn by Jefferson. The difference was that Jefferson's approach disguised his more authoritarian relationship to the legislature. Madison's attitude was consonant with the reality of the power situation and his conception of what that relationship ought to be. He treated with Speaker Henry Clay almost as one would treat with a foreign ambassador. For, prior to the War of 1812, Clay had picked up the reins dropped by Jefferson. The division of the war power as prescribed by the Constitution, was, this time, *preempted by the legislature with the acquiescence of the President.*

Madison's principled deference was so complete as to annoy one of its recipients. "This message, in point of obscurity," said Senator Crawford of Georgia, "comes nearer my idea of a delphic oracle than any state paper which has come under my inspection. It is for war, it is for peace. It is so cautiously expressed that every man can put what construction on it he pleases." Crawford's displeasure was compounded by his memory of Madison as an active statesman in all of his prior public service. The Georgian could not conceive that the President's commitment to the Constitution as he understood it required him to remain aloof while Congress made the decision for peace or for war.

When war did come, President Madison gave a literal reading to the Constitution's Commander in Chief phrase. He took active charge of military and naval dispositions and made strategic and tactical decisions. The results were almost disastrous. Whatever Madison was, he was no great captain.

American arms, expected to triumph easily along the sparsely defended Canadian border, fled in confusion to Detroit and lower New York. The British threatened to cut off New England from the rest of the country, and to dismember the frontier that had been so vigorously in favor of war. The enemy even sailed into the Chesapeake and burned Washington, forcing the President to flee the capital. Only an England at war with Napoleon could have failed to pick up the pieces of a broken American union.

The raging European conflict and several United States naval victories in the Great Lakes combined to preserve the young Republic from its own folly. During the negotiations for the Treaty of Ghent, American negotiators were actually arguing among themselves as to which portion of territory they should surrender to Britain when word of Commodore Perry's successful capture of the British ship *Detroit* saved the day. But the treaty conferred no glory on either of the parties. It merely restored the *status quo*. The United States was lucky to get off with its territory intact and Britain was happy to turn her full energies to the European continent. That is why Jackson's "postwar" victory at New Orleans was of such enormous consequence. The communication gap between Ghent and New Orleans had led to the British assault, notwithstanding the official end of hostilities.

Five thousand troops under the English General Packenham advanced on New Orleans; from there they were to march through the Floridas and to take as much territory as they could, before bringing the war to an "amicable" end at the "negotiating table." Jackson's men stood firm, inflicting two thousand casualties on the assaulting British and killing their commanding general. Old Hickory had saved the day. While it is true that the war was already over, Jackson also *saved the face* of the American frontier. His character and his courage marked that frontier at its best and luckiest.

Jackson was an instant folk hero. Americans could look on the War of 1812 as a war we had "won." The General symbolized rejuvenation of the American westward thrust and even President Madison was enabled to bask in the glow of "victory." Only Henry Clay, the driving congressional force in the move to war, was to lose the political stakes on which he was gambling. In creating a situation in which Jackson could become a war hero, Clay had also produced a personal rival who would block his road to the Presidency. At the same time he created the elements for a confrontation between the executive and legislative branches that would embrace a struggle to keep the military subordinate to the civil power. That struggle grew from a mix of the characters and ambitions of the contestants and the growing tendency to "read" the Constitution in the light of those ambitions.

The bitterness of the conflict to come was remarkable in the context from which it sprang. President Madison, after all, had created what could have been a precedent for presidential behavior in relation to the question of the war powers. A number of factors intervened to prevent that precedent from taking hold.

Madison, in the first instance, offered literally *no leadership* to Congress on the issue before them. The Constitution empowers the President to conduct the foreign policy of the United States. Inasmuch as such direction necessarily impinges on the war power, the President is obliged to make assessments of foreign relations that will assist Congress in making its ultimate decision. Madison made little or no attempt to do so. The early days of his administration were marked by congressional sniping at his Cabinet selections. Such episodes placed him on the defensive and tended to restrain him from pointing a direction.

The President also knew full well that this war would exacerbate internal dissension. Many of the New England States were so violently opposed to it that more than one of their Governors disputed Madison's powers as Commander in Chief *after* the declaration. There was talk of treason and secession. A war fought under such circumstances is not likely to establish a happy precedent in the popular mind. Madison's own conception of his powers embraced the obligation to preserve the Union. He rejected the advice of his friend Jefferson to give the New Englanders a "dose of hemp" and embarked on a course of conciliation at home combined with coercion abroad. The President at one point even took pains to comment on the remarkable display of unanimity offered by the United States at war. He told Congress that "the Union is strengthened by every occasion that puts it to the test. [There are] daily testimonies of increasing harmony throughout the nation."

The President was fully aware that his words bore little relation to the contemporary reality. He could only have hoped that a satisfactory result in the field would make them come true; that hope was realized. When a group of New England Governors came to Washington to protest the war and its conduct, they arrived on the day of the announcement of the results of the Battle of New Orleans. The New Englanders had described themselves as "ambassadors" to the United States Government. They were laughed out of town and their mission marked the end of the founding Federalist party as a factor in American politics.

Congressional unwillingness to follow through on its commitment to hostilities was another factor that mitigated against the War of 1812 as a precedent for future governmental behavior. The War Hawks were all for shooting it out. Despite that fact they refused to appropriate money for a conflict with the world's greatest naval power. Madison's Secretary of the Treasury asked for twenty-five million dollars in order to strengthen the Navy. He was instead authorized to float a loan of eleven million. Although there was a readier will to strengthen the land armies, here too the ways and means provided were ludicrously inadequate. The nation observed that despite congressional footdragging on the naval appropriations, the only American victories before the treaty was signed came at sea against overwhelming odds.

A final element in the war's antecedents and in its conduct must be weighed in terms of its effect on future power relationships. Madison's assertion of authority as Commander in Chief (however ineptly executed) was accompanied by *congressional withdrawal from the policy scene*. Henry Clay, as Speaker of the House, had executed enormous influence on the decision to make war. (Some historians insist that he literally threatened Madison with the loss of a second term if he failed to ask Congress for a declaration.) From the moment hostilities were authorized, Clay and his congressional cohorts receded into the background. They made no institutional attempt to influence the course of the fighting or the management of the war. That failure, combined with

Madison's sudden push to the forefront of activity, established, once and for all, the principle of executive dominance *after* hostilities are under way.

It should be noted that nothing in the Constitution precludes Congress from actively participating in the details of a war's activity. The congressional war powers are extremely broad, but since 1812 they have not often been vigorously enforced. In those cases in which they have been fully exploited, their usage has usually corresponded to a violent policy split between the President and the Congress. (Such was the case with the Stevens Committee during the Civil War, which we will examine later.) One exception to the lapse of congressional authority occurred during World War II when Senator Harry Truman came to national prominence as chairman of a committee organized to uncover inefficiencies and inequities in the organization and use of the giant American war machine. That committee's work was of such significant assistance in the effective prosecution of the war that Truman's name was attached to it and he was afforded the public recognition necessary for his eventual rise to the Presidency.

But in 1812 there was no Truman Committee. The sharp contrast between strong congressional leadership *prior* to the outbreak of war and the almost literal disappearance of Congress as war policy maker *after* the guns began to fire offered no satisfactory clue as to effective constitutional procedure.

John Adams did comment in later years that "Mr. Madison has proved great points long disputed in Europe and America . . . that an administration *under our present Constitution* can declare war and that it can make peace." But no proper balance between executive and legislative branches had been established; the way was open once more for either of the two branches to step in whenever a new power vacuum was perceived.

The American people, then as now, were concerned with results. The War of 1812 became universally popular, *after the fact,* because Jackson's victory at New Orleans gave symbolic expression to the pioneer determination to move west. There was no time for the consideration of grave constitutional questions. Incursions on the powers of the legislature tend to have an abstract sound unless the ox that's gored is your own. If Americans are today aware of the importance of those incursions, it is because the nature of American power has changed and because we have seen the popular will repeatedly flouted by successive Presidents at the same time as Congress has manifested an inability to unshackle legislative hands that have been tied by historic precedent. These precedents were established in some cases, as in 1812, because one branch acted out of principle while the other acted out of constituent interest; in other situations, as in the case of the Barbary hostilities, the constitutional violation went unseen by its victim (Congress) and in still other situations, the national security was judged by at least some legislators and Presidents to be considerably more important than questions of constitutional principle. We have been fortunate in the past to escape the consequences of acts committed in our name and in violation of our laws. Such was the case of the House of Representatives versus General Andrew Jackson.

VII

General Jackson
Comes to Washington

THE United States Government had long had the "eagle's eye" on Florida, and if possible, on the island of Cuba. Only a series of historic flukes prevented this piece of manifest destiny from being swept into our national domain along with most of the other Spanish possessions in the area.

The Spaniards were plagued by rebellion in South America and war in Europe. There was little or no national will to maintain sovereignty despite American pressure, over possessions in the immediate vicinity of the young and growing Yankee Republic. But the Spanish court had every intention of getting as much as it could in return for the vestiges of its imperial past. The Americans, more often than not, were willing to play along with Spanish pretension as a counter in the struggle to keep *real* European power from asserting itself on the continent. Jefferson had written to the effect that Spanish Florida was preferable to British *anything* in the Western Hemisphere. Aware of the realities of power, the Spaniards turned their eyes from American infiltration into their territory and yielded special trading privileges to United States commerce in waters ostensibly dominated by Spanish forces.

Some Americans, nevertheless, were still dissatisfied with the pace of events. In 1810 President Madison arranged for a successful rebellion against Spanish authority by residents of West

Florida. When the new republic applied for annexation to the United States it was graciously accepted. Spain barely protested. American hunger for land and control of the inland waterways now focused on the eastern part of Florida. It was in this theater that the first great explosion occurred over the constitutional war power.

General Andrew Jackson, the hero of New Orleans, stood at the center of the storm to come. Jackson has come down through the pages of history as the first President to be a true democrat, a representative of the little man. But George Dangerfield has written of Jackson that he "was more responsive to the imperialism than to the democracy of the frontier." If that goes against the grain of the myth, it is substantiated by more than one student of the period. Jackson embraced an "odd jumble" of occupations: horsebreeder, lawyer, entrepreneur, soldier and, finally, slaveholder and gentleman. He was the epitome of the self-made man of the early nineteenth century; like most of his neighbors, he was the frontier arriviste incarnate. With the intensity that marked his character, "he hated both the Spaniard and the Red Man with all the venom of a Westerner." It could very well be that the inherent weakness expressed in Spanish decadence repelled the frontiersman in Jackson. For strength was the cardinal virtue in the lexicon of Tennessee survival and the relentless acquisition of property was one of its manifestations.

We know that close friends of Jackson made enormous profits on land taken from the Indians. These fortunes came to twenty-one million acres, or three fifths of Alabama and one quarter of Georgia. The General himself once remarked that he didn't understand all the fuss about whether or not the United States "was keeping treaty" with the Indians. During his own term as President, Jackson ordered the Cherokee nation removed from their homes in the Appalachian Mountains and marched one thousand miles beyond the Mississippi, along the Trail of Tears.

But in 1817 Jackson was a national hero as well as a General subject to the call to active duty. That call came when President Monroe asked the frontier fighter to assist in dispersing a group of Seminole Indians who were raiding border communities from their sanctuary in Spanish Florida. In the aftermath of a treaty with the United States that had required them to leave their lands, they had taken shelter in the Spanish fort of St. Marks and in a series of nearby villages.

The word Seminole means "they who live alone." Just across the border from their tribal home they now shared a dismal shelter with some eight hundred runaway slaves. (This Spanish asylum for blacks added to the American impulse to seize the territory.) They harassed American traders making their way down the Apalachicola River. On one occasion they killed a party of twenty-four United States soldiers on their way to reinforce troops at Fort Scott on the Georgia side of the river. Both blacks and Indians repeatedly provided the excuse for aggressive American action. A boatman had been captured, burned and tarred. A mother and her two-year-old daughter were scalped and the Indians had clubbed four other children to death.

These atrocities infuriated the frontier population, and Monroe ordered General Gaines to put an end to them. Then, after removing Gaines to another scene of Indian trouble, the President replaced him with Andrew Jackson. Nothing could have pleased the "Don Hater" more. He had long counseled the seizure of Pensacola and all of Eastern Florida, and this appeared to the General to be the occasion for action.

James Monroe knew with whom he was dealing. The President was fully aware of Jackson's reputation for behaving rashly. His own previous correspondence with him offered evidence of the Tennesseean's disregard for authority and the fine points of the law. The President's orders to Gaines specified that he was to pacify the Georgia border and to pursue the Indian enemy across the Florida border. Monroe added that Gaines was not to besiege a Spanish fort. If the Indians withdrew to the protection of those forts, Gaines was ordered by the Secretary of War to wait for further instructions before taking action. In transferring the mission to Andrew Jackson, Secretary Calhoun told him to follow the orders transmitted to his predecessor. The letter to Jackson was dated December 26, 1817.

On January 6, 1818, Andrew Jackson wrote the following to President Monroe:

The executive government has ordered, and as I conceive, very properly, Amelia Island to be taken possession of. This order ought to be carried into execution at all hazards, and simultaneously the whole of East Florida seized, and held as an indemnity for the outrages of Spain upon the property of our citizens. . . . *This can be done without implicating the government.* Let it be signified to me through any channel (say Mr. J. Rhea) that the possession of the Floridas would be desirable to the United States, *and in sixty days it will be accomplished.*

That correspondence (later notorious as The Rhea Letter) and its ostensible reply from the President, are at the core of the events that followed and at the heart of the constitutional dilemma faced by every administration to hold the reins of power. Jackson claimed, more than ten years later, that he had received an affirmative reply from the President through Congressman Rhea. He justified his actions on that claim.

The General struck savagely from Fort Scott across the border into Spanish territory. In the course of twelve weeks his troops had laid waste to three hundred miles of territory, killed hundreds of Indians and forced the rest to surrender. There was never any question of Indians taking shelter in the Spanish forts. The savagery of Jackson's assault overwhelmed them before they were able to rally their defenses. At this point Old Hickory turned west and demanded that the Spanish Governor surrender Pensacola. When the Spaniards refused, Jackson's troops invested the city and took it without difficulty. Prior to the victorious march on Pensacola, the Americans captured the Spanish forts that Monroe's official orders had explicitly put beyond their reach. Here, Jackson's hatred of Indians and of those who gave them succor manifested itself in a wanton act that could easily have precipitated us into war with Great Britain.

Behind the walls of the Spanish fort were two Englishmen who had stayed after the Spanish defenders fled. One of them was Alexander Arbuthnot, a seventy-year-old Scottish merchant. He had established himself as a friend to the Indians and built a profitable trade among them. Their affection for Arbuthnot brought him little credit among his fellow traders. The prevailing ethic was to pay as little for Indian goods as possible and to ignore their interests in any transaction. Forbes & Company, a rival commercial enterprise, had begun to establish connections with American interests across the border, including several men known to be close to General Jackson. That connection did Arbuthnot no good when the Spanish position was captured. He made no attempt to conceal his opinion that the Americans had always treated the Indians shabbily and would continue to do so as long as it was profitable.

Arbuthnot's only friends in the Florida wilderness were Indians. They had given him their power of attorney and on one of his journeys asked him to intervene with the British Governor at Nassau on their behalf. Arbuthnot was gentle in manner and dignified in appearance. The record of his diary testifies to the sincerity of his concern for his Indian associates. "They have been ill treated by the English and robbed by the Americans," he wrote. Such words did little to win him affection among the American officers. If Indians saw Arbuthnot as a friend and a counselor, Jackson saw the British subject as a renegade and an enemy. He ordered the old man court-martialed along with a youthful adventurer, Robert Armbrister. Both men were sentenced to die by a military court on charges of spying, giving aid to the enemy and inciting Indians to war.

Armbrister was a professional soldier who had guarded Napoleon at St. Helena. Wounded at Waterloo, he came to Nassau as a guest of the British Governor. There he fell in with George Woodbine, a semi-official agent of the British government who encouraged the Indians in their battles against the United States. Armbrister pleaded "gulty with justification" to the charges against him. He was ordered to be shot by the court-martial board, but his professional background appealed to his American captors and the board reduced the sentence. But General Jackson, on learning of the act of clemency, *ordered the original sentence reinstated*. The seventy-year-old Arbuthnot was hanged from the mast of his own trading ship, and Armbrister, who thought he had been rescued by fate, was shot to death.

General Andrew Jackson did nothing by halves. He had invaded Spanish territory and British citizens had been murdered. James Parton, an early Jackson biographer, called the execution of Arbuthnot "an act of such complicated and unmitigated atrocity that to call it murder would be to defame all ordinary murderers. He was put to death for acts every one of which were innocent, and some of which were eminently praiseworthy." Parton goes on to point out that Jackson himself might have committed the offense charged against Armbrister. He was a soldier in command of a party sent out to defend the province against an invading force. Jackson's bitterness against the two Englishmen was an outgrowth of the War of 1812 when British agents stirred the Creek Indians to do vicious battle against his troops and he found it difficult to still the memory.

But Jackson's swift incursion into Florida also expressed his personal vigor and an unspoken national will. Most of his political superiors in Washington evidenced no such strength. Nor did they sense anything but trouble coming out of his startling victories. Only the Secretary of State, John Quincy Adams, was ready to defend the General's actions. He regarded the news of American successes in Spanish Florida as an excellent trump card in his ongoing negotiations with Spain for the purchase of the territory now in American hands.

On March 25, 1818, as Jackson moved on the Spanish fort, President Monroe sent a message to Congress in which he attacked Spain for its failure to restrain the Indians in her territory from attacks on American positions. The President observed that the Treaty of 1793 with the Spanish Empire required her to regulate her own territories. Inasmuch as Spain had failed to do so, the United States was justified in taking up the task. Monroe cast American military operations in entirely defensive terms. At this point in time, the President assumed a public posture similar to the position John Quincy Adams later adopted in Cabinet discussion. But in mid-July Andrew Jackson's official dispatches arrived in Washington.

The President and his people found it difficult to absorb the extent and the nature of Jackson's success. Monroe met with his Cabinet for five hours on the afternoon of July 15, to consider what had happened and what was to be done in its aftermath. According to John Quincy Adams, the President and all of his advisers (Adams excepted), felt that Jackson had not only violated his orders to refrain from attacking Spanish forts but that he had put the Administration into the position of making war without congressional approval. Here, we are obliged to examine the President's public response in the context of his own actions.

On the same day that Jackson got his military orders he also received a private letter from Monroe. The President wrote, in part, that Jackson would now move "on a theater, where possibly, you may have other services to perform . . . until our cause is carried through triumphantly, and every species of danger to which it is exposed is settled, *on the most solid foundation,* you ought not to withdraw your active support from it." Monroe was careful to qualify his encouragement with references to possible Indian trouble in other places. The tone of his communication, nevertheless, indicates that the Chief Executive acquiesced in Jackson's outline for action against Florida suggested in the notorious Rhea Letter to Monroe.

Years later, during his own campaign for the Presidency, Jackson's conduct was again challenged and he insisted that the President had indeed authorized him, through Congressman Rhea, to take the offensive against Spanish interests. Rhea, whose faculties had declined with age, substantiated Jackson's recollection. Even in the prime of his life, it should be noted, Rhea was not regarded as a great thinker. John Randolph once observed of the House of Representatives that it sheltered "A. Wright always wrong, and a Rhea [pronounced Ray] without light." Whatever the strength of Rhea's beacon it does shed inadvertent light on the way Congress is often kept in the dark. For whether or not Jackson had received a secret directive from the President, he was himself a principal agent of the executive power. He took military action, for whatever reason, that enhanced the foreign policy objectives of the President and his Secretary of State. Only Congress was left out of the decision-making process.

The controversy that rose within the Cabinet over Jackson's actions reveals a great concern with the reaction of the legislative branch and with public opinion. Later Presidents were to learn, in part because of the Florida episode, that the weight of congressional opposition to breaches of the Constitution could often safely be disregarded. This would be true, particularly, in the aftermath of a military victory. Therefore, it would sometimes be worth gambling on such a success. President Monroe, however, had no such precedent to guide him. He expressed dismay at Jackson's action and wished to disavow the results of his military assault on the forts. Cabinet debate turned on the question of whether or not to return Pensacola to the Spaniards and how to placate Great Britain. At no time, however, did the Executive consider the question of disciplining Jackson for a major breach of military law. His popularity was already of such a high order that it would have taken more strength than Monroe could muster to bring Jackson to order. But the Cabinet felt, almost unanimously, that the General had been insubordinate. Perception, perhaps, was clouded by personal ambition. Each member of Monroe's Cabinet, at a later time, was to be a President or a presidential candidate; every one of them used the Rhea Letter to make claims against their opposition. The Jackson episode thus joins a torrent of events in which long-range policy evolves from short-range politics.

During the six-month period between July, 1817, and January, 1818, neither Jackson nor Monroe mentioned the existence of the Rhea Letter that Jackson had written to the President. Neither of them made reference to Congressman Rhea's intermediary role. That element of the controversy burst into the open many years later. Monroe, on his deathbed, made a formal denial that he had communicated with Rhea. The former President stated that he was seriously ill when Jackson's letter was given to him. Monroe recalled that when Secretary of War Calhoun came to call, he gave it to Calhoun to consider and asked him to respond. Monroe said that he himself didn't even read the letter until much later. In any case, no one but Jackson seems to have seen the presidential reply. Old Hickory said during the later controversy that in 1819 he had destroyed the President's written response at Monroe's own request.

We do not know which of the two men was telling the truth.

Jackson, however, made his first public mention of the letter during a period when he was at the center of political controversy. He spoke at a time when the Presidency was within his reach. Monroe, on the other hand, offered his version long after his retirement and only a few weeks before his death. His account does reflect the possibility that Monroe knew he could use Jackson's audacity on behalf of presidential goals. Florida was there. Jackson wanted to take it. Silence, Monroe might have thought, would inevitably be taken as assent.

Whatever the truth of the matter, the facts about the Florida adventure were deliberately obscured by the President and his agents. An article was planted in the *National Intelligencer* in which the military actions in Florida were explained and justified. Adams, responding to bitter British criticism of the executions of Arbuthnot and Armbrister, took a conciliatory note and the British, who had come within "a hair of war" with the United States, were effectively calmed.

Spain, too, was the recipient of diplomatic gesture. Here the tone was aggressive. Adams informed the Spanish Foreign Minister that the United States would return the captured forts and the city of Pensacola to Spain. The Secretary of State criticized Spain for failing to police her own territory, and asserted that Jackson had acted in simple self-defense. Adams even threatened that if Spain, by failing to maintain order, forced the United States to invade her territory again, she need not expect another "unconditional return" of her territory.

President Monroe was apparently more worried about Jackson's reaction to the return of the conquered territory than he was about the United States Congress or reaction from abroad. In a series of letters to the General he explained the need to disavow Jackson's territorial acquisitions. The two men exchanged communications in which Jackson firmly asserted that he had acted pursuant to presidential instruction. Making no reference to the later famous Rhea Letter, he said that the orders of December 26 authorized him to "adopt the necessary measures to terminate the conflict which it has ever been the desire of the President, from motives of humanity, to avoid."

The President attempted to assuage Jackson with the observation that even though Spain would get her territory back, the military action might well "furnish a strong inducement to Spain to cede the territory, provided we do not wound too deeply her pride by holding it." But Monroe continued to assert that while Jackson might have misconstrued his own orders from the War Department, he had acted on his own responsibility. The President's attempt to lift the burden of "responsibility" from his own shoulders to those of a military subordinate demonstrated a realization that constitutional questions were at issue. In one of his letters to Jackson he had remarked that *"if the Executive refused to evacuate the posts, especially Pensacola, it would amount to a declaration of war, to which it is incompetent. It would be accused of usurping the authority of Congress and giving a deep and fatal wound to the Constitution."*

It is difficult to judge, a century and a half later, the exact nature of Monroe's role in the events that had transpired, although the subtle character of his political manipulations provide us with significant clues. One thing is certain. He was right about the accusations that would be brought against his administration. They came in the guise of formal inquiries in both the House of Representatives and the United States Senate.

John Quincy Adams had taken strong exception to the Administration's determination to repudiate the acquisition of Jackson's conquest. He noted in his diary that he "strenuously . . . objected to a paragraph declaring that the President thought that he had no constitutional power to have authorized General Jackson to have taken Pensacola." Adams reluctantly acquiesced in the presidential decision to offer Congress a full explanation of the affair, along with the decision to return to Spain her conquered lands. His initial response was far more in tune with what turned out to be the prevailing tide of public opinion. In this he differed from Speaker Henry Clay, who set into motion the wheels of congressional investigation. Clay's motives were also tangled up with his own presidential ambitions. But the twenty-seven-day hearing he launched was a landmark in the history of the ongoing debate over the war power. He took his cue, in part, from a

Baltimore newspaper that observed that General Jackson appeared "unaware of the necessity of strict discipline and subordination."

The House, sitting as a Committee of the Whole, centered much of its attention on the question of the executions of Armbrister and Arbuthnot. But the entire country realized that the two Britons were only the focus of an inquiry into the whole nature of the Florida expedition. Press coverage was extraordinary for the time, and, predictably, divided along sectional lines. The western newspapers looked to General Jackson as the American of the Future. Much of the published opinion in the North reflected a view of Jackson as a potential tyrant.

Not since Aaron Burr's trial for treason had the country witnessed a spectacle such as this. Its most astonishing element was the appearance of General Jackson in Washington. On the morning of January 23, 1819, Andrew Jackson rode on horseback across the Potomac. He remained in the capital during the entire course of the hearings. Jackson made his headquarters at Strater's Hotel, where he received large numbers of callers who came to wish him well. It was there that he consulted with his lieutenants on the House floor who were determined to defeat the "hellish machinations" of Clay and his cohorts.

Well over a century later another military hero, General Douglas MacArthur, made a similar entrance into the capital. Washington became, for the second time in its history, the scene of an overt tension between the civil and the military powers. President Truman's brusque assertion of the supremacy of presidential authority, which by then had grown far greater, was followed by an address in which General MacArthur wrote his own political obituary. He "faded away" from the political mainstream. Andrew Jackson made no dramatic speeches during the hearings on his conduct. Neither did he fade away.

The aisles of the House were packed when Clay rose to speak to the issue of Who Makes War. One observer worried that the building (in temporary use since the British burned the Capitol four years before) would collapse because of the weight of the crowds. But Clay's concern, he said, was with the possible collapse of constitutional government.

The tall Kentuckian, only a few years ago in the forefront of the legislature's fight to assert its right to make war, now spoke against an executive and military power that had blatantly usurped that right. He lashed Jackson for the execution of Arbuthnot and Armbrister; demanded to know on what grounds the men had been sentenced to die, and proceeded to demonstrate that both were killed only in retaliation for their assistance to the Indian tribes. Here Clay pinned Jackson with the usurpation of congressional authority. "The right of retaliation is an attribute of sovereignty," he said. The decision to retaliate belongs to the Congress, inasmuch as the Constitution empowered the legislature to raise armies *and to make the rules that govern them.* "No Commander in Chief in this country has absolute power over life and death at his sole discretion." Such power would be "contrary to the laws and genius of our laws and institutions."

Clay noted that the House Military Committee, in response to President Monroe's message, had disavowed the executions of Arbuthnot and Armbrister. The Committee also expressed its disapproval of the seizure of Spanish forts, as contrary to presidential order *and a violation of the Constitution.* The Speaker asked that the Committee's actions be upheld by the House and that a law be passed forbidding United States troops to enter foreign territory without the previous authorization of Congress, except it be in fresh pursuit of a defeated enemy. Clay recalled that Monroe had assured Congress, in his first message on the campaign against the Seminoles, that our troops would be restricted in their mission across the border. No forts could be taken, the Congress was assured. Jackson's action "was a great abuse of the confidence of Congress in the assurances of the Chief Executive." (Every Congress must learn that lesson for itself.)

Of all the powers conferred by the Constitution, Clay observed, none is more expressly and *exclusively* granted than that as to Congress of declaring war. He told his colleagues that "it was to guard against precisely that species of rashness which has been manifested in Florida that the Constitution was so framed."

The Kentuckian's attack was two-pronged. Monroe was guilty of telling Congress one thing and doing another; Jackson was a prime example of what could happen if unlimited discretion is given a military commander. Clay warned that it would be "dangerous to permit this kind of conduct to pass without comment by the House. Precedents, if bad, are fraught with the most dangerous consequences."

With uncanny prescience Clay remarked that *"incidents were the habits of government and a single instance can fix them and determine the direction of government."* He acknowledged Jackson's great popularity and wondered if the General's exoneration would be a triumph of the military over the civil authority and "a triumph over the powers of this House and over the Constitution of the land." Clay concluded that such an outcome might also be a victory over "the liberties of the people."

There is no question that Henry Clay spoke eloquently. Representative Johnson, who spoke in rebuttal, could barely be heard in the hubbub that broke out when Clay had concluded. But if Clay had the eloquence, Jackson and Monroe had the divisions of public opinion. In Congress that opinion was expressed by those who claimed that a "defensive war" need not be declared. Others felt that Indians were not entitled to receive the benefits of the practice of "civilized warfare." A new principle was invoked on behalf of presidential prerogative. Inasmuch as the military repeatedly crossed Indian lands during hostilities at home, the same course of action was justified in Spanish territory. Ignoring the Constitution in one place became justification for ignoring it in another.

The attitude that Indians were outside the pale of civilized warfare was illustrated by one Congressman's rationalization of the invasion of foreign and ostensibly neutral territory. John Holmes of Massachusetts proposed the same kind of approach that, in our own time, resulted in the so-called DMZ of Vietnam turning into a major point of military conflict. We must not permit our enemies to make war upon us and then "to take refuge behind an ideal line where the law of nations forbids our approach. . . . Why shouldn't Jackson's army cross the line? No clause in the Constitution or the laws forbids it," according to the Jackson defender.

A "Free Fire Zone" approach was justified when a Representative commented that every means of hostility must be wrested from enemy hands. *"It is the misfortune or folly of the neutral,"* if he is found in *"association with the enemy or in a suspicious situation,"* one Representative remarked.

If military excesses found their apologists then as now, others listened and came to views about the need for constitutional support that have their equivalents in the discussion of the protection of congressional war powers in the 1970's. Senator Thomas Nelson proposed that Congress "enact other laws which cannot be misconstrued. I fear even this remedy will prove insufficient; the Constitution, to my mind, is so plain and explicit on this point, that he who runs may read." With anything so explicit, and so misread, Nelson asked whether new laws would be useless.

But the constitutional issue, as always, was only part of the story. One Representative remarked that a President was obliged to "protect American rights" *short of war.* He ignored the fact that the commission of acts of war was the very issue at stake. A Senator, speaking to that question in his own chamber, was so overwhelmed by the implications of the crisis that he "feels that the Executive has not gone so far as to justify" the attack on Pensacola. If he was wrong, Senator Storrs observed, "then the powers of Congress are double jeopardized." The Senator must have been reassured by the vote of a majority of his colleagues. They tabled the anti-Jackson resolutions.

In the House, Henry Clay saw his presidential ambitions receive a major setback. His colleagues had applauded him with enthusiasm. But when it came to a vote they rejected all of their own Military Committee resolutions by substantial majorities. The opinion of the country at large was best expressed by the editor who wrote that he could not understand all the "legalities" of the debate, but he understood what Jackson had done and he approved the results. Biographer Marquis James has called the House vote Jackson's greatest victory since the Battle of New Orleans.

Although some newspapers, during the Jackson affair, focused on the issue, many more did not. The Richmond *Enquirer* recorded its view that the proceedings in Congress were directed not at Jackson but at the "executive usurpation of power." Yet the majority of the people probably agreed with those who called the investigation "legal hair-splitting" and sneered at citizens who would "go to some learned treatise" to inquire what was right, rather than trust to "a General to inflict the heaviest damage upon such lawless offenders."

The failure of Congress to assert its constitutional authority in the Florida incident stamped on American policy the first of a series of precedents whereby executive authority was enhanced at the expense of congressional power. The issue was partially obscured because of the dramatic personality conflict that dominated public attention. Clay and Jackson were both dynamic figures. They would be described by today's political observers as men with charisma. That certainly was not the case with Monroe and yet it was, ultimately, the authority of *his* office that was vindicated. Jackson, the General, stood surrogate for Monroe, the President. Future Chief Executives profited from a situation in which a military leader, from the force of his personality and as an expression of his age, provided cover for a President to whom he was nominally subordinate. The paradox was further underlined by Monroe's insistence that Jackson's actions were taken on his own "responsibility." He responded almost as if the military were a fourth branch of the government. By 1972 when General Lavelle apparently acted in defiance of his orders in bombing North Vietnam, the President as Commander in Chief had long since become the embodiment of the country's military as well as civil authority. While Congress again raised questions as to the implications of the breach, the legislature eventually returned the responsibility for discipline back to the executive branch. Whatever the efficacy of the penalty, only a halfhearted challenge was issued to the immunity of the Commander in Chief and his principal agents from legislative accountability. General Lavelle was certainly no Andrew Jackson, but President Nixon and generations of his predecessors had reaped Monroe's harvest.

Unqualified military responsibility to the Executive alone further enlarges the presidential war-making power. But to all intents and purposes, that has become the unwritten rule. The only substantive question raised in the Lavelle case was whether anybody else was involved and what the Administration could or would do about it. Congress played a useful inquisitorial role, but its collective voice accepted the dictum that this was a matter to be decided between the generals and the President. Congress is too often perceived, not as one of the masters in making war, but as an intruder. If many among us have been perhaps too ready to accept that judgment, we can appeal only to the logic of history. The American people today, as in 1818, continue to admire the "strong" President.

It was "manifest destiny" (a phrase coined a few years later) that Eastern Florida belong to the United States. Andrew Jackson hastened its acquisition and he was rewarded by ever-increasing popularity and the Presidency itself. That acquisition fueled a national appetite that set the stage for a great flaring up of bitter division that was to be played out in the Mexican War.

VIII

The Mexican War: "MORE MORE MORE"

THE Mexican War exploded in a spasm of national greed when the United States entered her neighbor's territory, dared the Mexicans to defend their own country, and, when they bungled the job, made sure that a heavy price was paid in blood and soil. An expanded Texas and a California territory from which we carved three new states were joined to the Union, but the picture of the United States as an international bully made Americans uneasy in victory. Fortunately, the conflict also gave us material for true tales of battlefield valor and intrigues involving great men and beautiful women; the heroes and villains who have served as models for thousands of Hollywood actors ever since film became the repository of our national folklore.

But the war was more than a giant movie epic played against the magnificent background of southwestern desert, rugged Mexican mountain terrain and along the California coast. The epics and the novels have never caught the essence of the war in terms of the scar it left on the American spirit. There were war crimes on both sides. But the major casualty was that sense of national rectitude, later recaptured in the blood-letting of the great Civil War, and, many think, lost once more in Indochina.

The Mexican War was alternately popular and unpopular, in keeping with the rhythm of its battles and the length of its casualty lists. It also was our first major presidential war in which a divided Congress found itself faced with disingenuous reports from the Commander in Chief and the bitter alternative of voting support to troops in the field or abandoning an American army on foreign soil. The anguished debate on the floor of Senate and House had no parallel until the days of the Tonkin Gulf Resolution, McGovern-Hatfield, Cooper-Church and all of the other congressional attempts to extricate us from the war in Indochina. Analogies, it is true, can be stretched beyond the uses of truth. There were vast differences between the origins of the Mexican War and the conflict in Vietnam. Those differences, in part at least, reflect the qualitative difference in American power. The similarities, nevertheless, are both striking and chilling. Both wars were fought over national security.

For decades the United States had been troubled by the possibility of French or British commercial and political interests reestablishing themselves in areas adjacent to the American Republic. Concern with control of inland waterways was a vital factor in most of the westward movement. The explorers, surveyors and sailors who sketched for the public imagination the possibilities of the Pacific trade, new routes to India, to China, to Japan, were Pied Pipers to the American entrepreneurial spirit. Finally, we had driven Spain from the lands she had occupied for some three centuries. The island possessions and continental domain the Spaniards left behind had all of the attraction of fruit ready to drop from the tree. If anyone was to eat the fruit, Americans were determined it would be the United States. National pride alone, without all of the genuine interests at stake, would have prevented us from accepting the rivalry of another European power in the place of Spain's Empire Manqué. We were, indeed, prepared to force British interests from the Columbia River in the Oregon country. "Fifty-four forty or fight" was the slogan adopted by President James Polk's adherents. The British somehow sensed the impetus behind the American drive, and, wherever possible, compromised with the newest star on the horizon of empire. In the case of Oregon, Britain moved gracefully north of the Columbia River and there was no need to fight.

But Mexico could not compromise. Mexico was nobody's possession. To Yankee cheers she had fought and won her independence from Spain. In the eyes of her governors and her people there was nothing she could give without giving herself. England could balance one commercial interest against the other. She could judge one set of political values in terms of the values to be achieved by their abandonment and replacement. A threat to the territory of newly independent Mexico, however, was a threat to her dearly won sovereignty. But the United States was in no mood to pay more than the most cursory attention to Mexico's sensibilities. We had our destiny to worry about and we took it into our own hands.

When Mexico achieved independence in 1821, her North American neighbor was warm and friendly. Mexico at first encouraged American settlers to cross into Texas and settle as Mexican citizens under Mexican law. Land grants were made with generosity and, sometimes, withdrawn in the arbitrary manner of governments that rise and fall by arms rather than ballots. Adherence to the Catholic Church was required by the Mexican government. The new settlers acquiesced with pragmatic indifference. The protestations of loyalty made by Stephen Austin and his fellow "Empresarios," as the real estate tycoons of the day were called, were almost completely disingenuous and the time soon came when the settlers from the north were no longer willing to submit to the rule of the governments in distant Mexico City.

To the settlers, the quixotic strain in Mexican law sometimes seemed to mean no law at all. At the same time Mexico became aware that the United States was establishing an unofficial presence on Mexican soil in the guise of migration and settlement. Regulations were imposed to reduce the impact of that presence. Here was the first test of the Anglo-Saxons' "loyalty." By Mexican standards, the settlers flunked the test. The Texans resisted the new rules. Skirmishes were fought. Grisly massacres occurred. A Declaration of Independence was issued; a Republic was proclaimed, and the settlers, with organized, if unofficial, support from the United States, were able to maintain its integrity.

At the Battle of San Jacinto, Sam Houston's forces defeated a great Mexican army and compounded the triumph with the capture of a man in the uniform of a common soldier who turned out to be Santa Anna, the Mexican dictator. With the Mexican chief in their hands, the Texans had no trouble wresting recognition of their independence from the Mexican government. That recognition was withdrawn, of course, as soon as Santa Anna was permitted to go home. But the Mexicans made no further attempt to assert their authority. Although blustering statements issued from the capital with a fair degree of regularity, there was no organized thrust across the Nueces River in force. Texas claimed all of the territory south of the Nueces to the Rio Grande. But the new republic kept its troops on its own side of the disputed boundary line and few of the settlers from the United States lived in the area between the two rivers. The territory had not risen against the Mexico City government during Texas' War for Independence and the Catholic population continued to demonstrate its loyalty to Mexico up to the time when the Lone Star Republic was formally annexed to the United States. That annexation, and the controversy which surrounded it, poisoned relations between James Polk, the expansionist-minded President, and a Congress that embodied the national divisions over "manifest destiny" and slavery.

Polk's run for the Presidency in 1844 had been keyed to the theme that Texas must inevitably be part of the Union, that Oregon country was American country and that California must someday (the sooner the better) be American too. His victory demonstrated the strength of the expansionists and focused the resentment of the anti-slavery Whigs on the new Chief Executive; for Texas was slave territory and her accession to the Union had long been resisted in the struggle for power between the free states and the slave states. Polk's predecessor, John Tyler, had negotiated a treaty of annexation with Texas. He sent American soldiers into the "sister republic" to protect her against Mexican reprisals as the Texans voted on the proposal. The Mexican government, which had conditioned its recent and reluctant acceptance of Texas independence on her maintaining her separate status, was furious at American duplicity. Still, Mexico avoided a challenge to the United States military contingent. After the Texans accepted the treaty, the United States Senate rejected it because of the fear of spreading slavery.

Tyler, at that point, introduced a device which was to be used by later Presidents when they failed to muster a constitutional majority. The bill for annexation was reintroduced as a *joint congressional resolution,* and passed by simple majority in both houses. Whatever the legality of the measure, it was signed by the President. In December, 1845, Texas happily entered the Federal Union as a slave state and the Mexican ambassador picked up his passport and went home.

The United States was now on the verge of a war that might extend the boundaries of Texas to the Rio Grande and open up the possibility for immense westward expansion. An embarrassing clue to the long-range intentions of the executive branch had come in 1842 when Commander Thomas Ap Catesby Jones sailed up Monterey Bay, bombarded the Mexican position, and forced the garrison to surrender. The Navy Commander ran the United States colors up a flagpole overlooking the Pacific Ocean, as a symbol of things to come. Jones acted because of a false rumor that the United States and Mexico were at war. His quick response to the rumor and the decisive nature of his action were solid evidence of what the United States had in mind for Mexican territory when the conflict did begin. Catesby Jones was informed by his superiors that he had made an error; that the two neighbors were in a state of peace. He made handsome amends by attending a party given by his erstwhile prisoners at which he apologized profusely before sailing away. A half dozen years later, Catesby Jones's successors on land and sea were to fight over California once more. By that time the war was no rumor and the victory was permanent.

War was inevitable because Mexico had been repeatedly provoked to action. To Polk, however, it must have appeared that the Mexicans would never defend themselves. They went through all of the preliminaries. They broke off relations and issued a statement that Mexico considered itself in a state of "defensive war"; but no Mexican fired a gun in anger.

The fury at the Texans' unification with the United States

was real enough, but the memory of the War for Independence in which Texas had won her freedom without Yankee help gave the insecure Mexican government pause. She vented her anger by refusing to receive Polk's emissary to discuss the issues between the two countries. No Mexican government could have survived after receiving a "Minister Plenipotentiary" from the hated North Americans. If John Slidell, the President's envoy, had agreed to present himself as a "commissioner" from Washington, the Mexicans would have talked. He was also informed that negotiations could not be held with a United States warship cruising off Vera Cruz.

Slidell had been instructed to negotiate the Texas boundary dispute and the "purchase" of California. Polk, for good measure, threw in the question of claims by American citizens against Mexico in connection with her actions during the bloody conflict with Texas. For Mexico, there was only one question to be discussed—annexation. Both sides stood firm. Slidell was not received. As a matter of fact, he boarded the very warship to which Mexico had objected and conducted his business from a battle station in Mexican waters.

The President was ready to use Mexico's refusal to receive his minister as an insult that required war. But Polk's political antennae told him that Congress would not readily respond to a request for a declaration on such tenuous grounds. Even while Slidell bargained over the ground rules for negotiations, our troops dug themselves in on the bank of the Rio Grande. In the months of preparation for annexation, American forces under General Zachary Taylor had entered Texas with an eye to instant action. President Tyler, who carried the annexation fight until Polk took office, began the move south. He justified military intervention with the observation that Texas belonged to the United States from the moment her citizens voted to join the Union, referring to the "inchoate interests" of the United States. But a large majority of the Senate had rejected the treaty of annexation *after* our troops had occupied the territory. Events followed so quickly, one after another, that the constitutional implications of Tyler's actions were mentioned only in passing.

Polk, who came to office in March of 1845, believed in "negotiating from strength." Although the bill to admit Texas to the Union was not passed until December of 1845, General Taylor's troops were under presidential orders to defend the "republic" as far south as the Rio Grande. Polk covered his political flank by telling Taylor to stay "near" the Nueces River. Taylor took the word *near* literally. He kept the Americans at Corpus Christi for the rest of the year, despite a series of communications from the War Department that told him in considerable detail about what he could expect to happen.

In July, Taylor was told not to attack Mexican military establishments east of the Rio Grande unless a state of war should exist. In August, he was reinforced with four thousand regulars and troops from Alabama, Mississippi, Louisiana and Kentucky. Secretary of War Marcy hinted quite explicitly at the executive strategy when he wrote to Taylor that "the emergency rendering such assistance [necessary] does not appear to have been foreseen by Congress, and consequently no appropriation was made for paying them." The President, in other words, was taking into his own hands the means of making war and the decision as to how and when to bring it about. The fact that Congress was excluded from the process is evidenced by a series of Polk's military orders.

On August 30, *some four months before Texas became part of the Union,* Polk issued a remarkable directive to his Whig General. (Taylor's political party was later to provoke the violent distrust of his Commander in Chief.) The President said that the assemblage of a large Mexican army on the borders of Texas (which Polk established by executive fiat as the bank of the Rio Grande) would be regarded by the executive branch *as an invasion of the United States.* In that case, Taylor was told, such an assemblage would constitute the commencement of war. The General was informed that he was to regard the protection of Texas as his primary mission, but that he could cross the river and take as much territory as seemed "practical and expedient." Even if the Mexicans failed to fire a single shot, Taylor was thus empowered "at your discretion" to wage an aggressive war in territory to which neither the United States nor Texas itself had established an acceptable claim.

Some two months later, with Taylor's men still at Corpus Christi, the General was informed by the War Department that Washington had serious reason to believe that Mexico would *not* invade Texas. Taylor replied that, under the circumstances, he did not "feel at liberty to make a forward movement to the Rio Grande" without authority from the War Department. Taylor, too, was interested in protecting himself from the domestic fallout of an aggressive war fought without congressional sanction. The President and General failed to force on each other a replay of Jackson's Florida invasion.

In January, 1846, after annexation had become law, Taylor got specific instructions to move to the Rio Grande. Over the next two months his troops established themselves on a line that included a gun position in which cannons were pointed directly at the Mexican town of Matamoros. General Taylor accurately summed up the situation in a dispatch to Washington:

These guns bear directly upon the public square of Matamoros, and within good range for demolishing the town. Their object cannot be mistaken by the enemy . . . the Mexican authorities persist in considering our march as an act of war in itself, and I believe they would so treat it, and attempt to drive us from our position if they felt sufficient confidence in their strength.

But the Mexicans still failed to respond with gunfire. Slidell, our "peace emissary," informed the President that force alone would achieve American ends. Polk was frustrated by what appeared to be the inadequacy of armed provocation as a tactic to ensure war. The President and his Cabinet decided on May 9, 1846, to ask Congress for a declaration on the ground that President Herrera had refused to receive Slidell, and to enforce the financial claims of American citizens against the Mexican government. Although it was not the ground Polk would have chosen, it appeared to be the best he could do. The Cabinet meeting broke up with its participants unaware that Polk's provocation had finally paid off in a shooting fracas on the Rio Grande.

In late April, a small party of Americans had entered the

premises of a Mexican ranchero where they exchanged fire with Mexican troops. Taylor's army struck back and hostilities commenced in earnest. Polk, who had hoped for an act of aggression by Mexico, received the news on the night before his projected message to Congress. He discarded the statement that had been drafted for the occasion and went before Congress to ask for a declaration that war, "having begun by an act of the Republic of Mexico," the funds would be provided to assure victory over those who had "shed American blood on American soil." That phrase earned the President the nickname of "mendacious Polk." It was to haunt him for the rest of his life.

Polk was the first American President who had to contend with an improving system of mass communications and the activities of a mobile free press, even as he attempted to conduct the business of the executive branch in comparative secrecy. American activity in Texas was emblazoned across the front pages of newspapers throughout the country. Pro- and anti-war factions were prepared for the political explosions that hostilities would set off. The President had no way of controlling "leaks," and the vast Texas country had been the scene of intense political reconnaissance. Even the Commanding General was a member of the opposing political party and he never failed to remember it during the battles to come. Neither did the President. Polk's conduct of the war was conditioned in large degree by the unpleasant fact that all of his leading commanders were potential rivals for his own office.

Circumstances had changed considerably since Jefferson was able to conduct an essentially private war with the Barbary Powers. Even Jackson's foray into Florida was covered to some degree by a time lag in communication and the absence of on-the-scene reportage.

But Polk was forced to face immediately the domestic consequences of his war policy. While American armies and naval expeditions fought sometimes bitter and usually victorious engagements on enemy soil, the battle over the war's morality and the United States Constitution was fought at home.

Congress was the principal arena for the domestic conflict. No legislator wishes to be put into the position of cutting off his country's troops without supplies. Many of us, while disapproving of presidential actions in Vietnam, felt bound by our duty to American troops, thousands of miles from home. Our dilemma was nothing new. A good number of those who were opposed to the Mexican adventure wished to vote the necessary appropriations if the President did not insist that war had begun because of "acts by the Republic of Mexico." Appeals were made from the floor to separate the supply bill from the war resolution. Senator John Calhoun of South Carolina emphasized that "the President has *announced* that there is war," but that, according to the Constitution there is no war unless Congress makes war, "and it is for us to determine whether war shall be declared or not." Calhoun and others were speaking for the record. They knew that the appropriations bill would be passed.

Polk's insistence on linking military supplies to a congressional resolution that blamed Mexico for starting the war exacerbated tensions within Congress and throughout the country. The President's insistence on such a linkage was similar to President Johnson's use of the Tonkin Gulf Resolution as justification for heating up the Vietnam war. In the case of the Mexican War an unwilling Congress was forced into acceptance of presidential hostilities on the basis of assertions later proven to be false. The Tonkin Gulf Resolution was also passed on the basis of information about North Vietnamese naval attacks that later investigation put into question; yet it was used to carry on an extensive war, rather than to retaliate for a single incident. In both cases, Congress felt compelled to ratify actions that had already taken place.

Helplessness against presidential initiative was a theme sounded again and again during the Mexican conflict. Three days after Polk's war message, the *National Intelligencer* called the imminent passage of the Military Supplies Bill the "beginning of an unnecessary war." But the *Intelligencer* added, the manner in which the conflict came about was to be far more deplored, because it "exposed the feebleness of the Constitution. It has already become a dead letter whenever it comes in conflict with executive power."

The *New York Tribune* asserted that only Congress could

decide whether the collision that had taken place "was of such a character as to justify the assertion that a state of war existed." The *Tribune*'s Washington correspondent commented venomously on "the mysterious and imbecile course of President Polk." That fairly well established the tone of the dialogue between the hawks and the doves of the 1840's. Americans who have grown weary of the extreme language of the 1960's and 1970's have something to learn from their predecessors.

"America wants no friends, acknowledges the fidelity of no citizen, who after war is declared, condemns the justice of her cause, or sympathizes with the enemy. All such are traitors in their hearts, and would to God that they would commit such overt act for which they could be dealt with according to their deserts." That accolade was bestowed on some of his fellow citizens by the Little Giant, Stephen Douglas.

A Congressman from Douglas' home state of Illinois took a very different position. Abraham Lincoln accused the President of "sheerest deception." The first acts of war, he told the House, were committed by American troops in the "midst of a Mexican cotton field, in country that had never submitted to either American or Texan authority." Lincoln said he suspected that Polk was "deeply conscious of being in the wrong; that he feels that the blood of this war, like the blood of Abel, is crying to heaven again him."

Whatever the state of the presidential soul, his armies were making impressive progress. The fighting was hard and sometimes desperate, but United States troops made steady and convincing gains as they marched south, deep into Mexico itself and west to golden California. While our interest is principally in the conflict between President and Congress and in the dissent of large numbers of Americans from national policy, there is irony in the fact that the Mexican War, from a military viewpoint, was one of this country's most notable successes. Although there had been considerable fear that our troops would be trapped and destroyed in Mexican mountain country, it soon became apparent that the volunteers from the frontier states and the tens of thousands of Regulars could take care of themselves. The issue that bitterly divided Americans was whether their soldiers had any business being where they were in the first place. That question was debated in terms that seem as fresh as this year's television news reports.

Polk himself appeared to have no doubts. As Americans advanced in Mexico, he took the offensive on the domestic front. Like later Presidents, he denied that his war was unjust and aggressive. His detractors were scorned as a small minority with exotic views that "were widely and extensively circulated not only at home, but have been spread throughout Mexico and the whole world." He charged the dissenters with protracting the war, encouraging the enemy and contended that his opponents might just as well have joined the Mexican cause in order to "give them aid and comfort."

Polk's use of the "aid and comfort" phrase was lifted from the United States Constitution. Indeed, it is the only constitutional definition of treason. Polk knew it and so did the opponents of the war. One observer wrote that the President's speech was an attempt to "intimidate his opponents" by impeaching their patriotism. Opposition to the war was in keeping with the constitutional right to free speech and such opposition was not "inconsistent with patriotism," the same observer remarked. Many of the war's supporters felt differently.

A Washington newspaper suggested a "War Register," to be kept in every town, on which the names and sentiments of "those who plead the cause of the enemy" would be recorded for posterity. The same paper labeled any Congressmen who voted against the continuation of war supplies as "Mexican Whigs." A Senate vote to which the President was opposed was described as "another Mexican victory."

Most of the substantive arguments were keyed, however, to the question of who, rightfully, is authorized to make war. It was noted that the President's first war message came "*after* the blow had been struck." Polk's timing of the war message, his handling of the Slidell mission, the movement of troops across Texas, all came under constant fire as expressions of unconstitutional behavior.

Some legislators were torn with doubt. Senator Butler of South Carolina thought it unwise to examine the origins of the war. He couldn't "see what good would come of it." Butler was worried that a decision to quit the war "would be to apparent dishonour." Yet, he went on, to stay in the fight would subject the country to much mischief. "The truth is," Butler said, "we're like the shepherd who has got the wolf by the ear. It is hazardous to let go. It is worse to hold on."

John Calhoun contended that "the President had no more right to determine on his own will what the boundary was than I had, or any other Senator." In the House, more than a year later, as the war still raged, Abraham Lincoln remarked that "if the Senate had been left free to decide on the question, not one third of the body would have been found in favour of war." Whether Lincoln's count was accurate or not, his assessment reflects the resentment that ran through the Senate's consideration of Polk's first war message and all of those to follow.

Senator Davis of Massachusetts was willing to support the President in repelling an invasion, but he felt that it was up to the Senate to determine whether or not "American blood had been shed on American soil." Others disparaged the President as a boundary maker, and Texans as land grabbers, while still others asked what American troops had been doing in foreign territory when the Senate had already refused to annex Texas to the Union.

Polk had his staunch supporters in both houses. Much of that support came from western country. Lewis Cass of Michigan told the Senate that he considered America's response to be "a test of the country's fortitude and determination." Senator Cass repeated the essence of Hamilton's argument with Jefferson during the Barbary War. Once an offensive war is begun, the Senator asserted, the President must prosecute it to the fullest extent. But the question in the minds of many in Congress was whether or not Mexico had actually been guilty of aggression at all. Daniel Webster, long an elder statesman, summed up the position of the "doves" in his analysis of the events prior to the conflict. Polk, according to Webster, forced the United States into an unconstitutional war when he ordered Taylor's forces into disputed territory without congressional authorization. (It was one of the few times Webster and Calhoun found themselves on the same side of a policy issue.) "What is the value," Webster asked, "of this constitutional provision, if the President, of his own authority may make such military movements as must bring on war?"

The answer to Webster's great question has in the past seemed to turn on the character of the men who have occupied the Presidency. Polk was a man so dedicated to the achievement of his policy ends that he gave short shrift even to the appearance of constitutional procedure. His actions are a case study of almost unbridled executive activism. In his view, Congress was there to implement executive decisions. He was the first President to leave behind a written record that demonstrates the principle of complete executive dominance. In September of 1845 he wrote in his diary that he considered Texas to be "virtually a part of the United States." In the privacy of his chamber the President substantiated the best part of the arguments to be made against him by his opponents. "We had so treated Texas by sending our squadron to the Gulf and our Army to her Western border," he wrote. Polk was, at the time, concerned with whether or not he should receive a minister from the Texan Republic. If he did, he feared, "it would be difficult to justify our sending our Army into her territories . . . claiming it to be a part of our country."

The important thing about the President's words is in their timing. He was thinking those thoughts and taking those actions many months before the annexation resolution was rammed through Congress. Texas, if it was to be considered part of the United States, was to be so considered on the sole authority of the American President. There is no record that Polk was uncomfortable with the concept. The irony is that he had served seven terms as a Tennessee Congressman and had even been Speaker of the House of Representatives. Like others before him and many who followed him to the Presidency, the change in the perspective of power seemed to erase his political past.

Historian Justin Smith, wholly sympathetic to Polk's claim that Mexico started the war, described the President as obstinately

partisan in his approach to the great questions and deeply convinced of his own importance and the fullness of his responsibility. Alexander Stephens, later to become Vice President of
the Confederacy, is the man who named the President "Polk
the Mendacious." Stephens claimed that James Polk was a man
whom none could believe. He called the President a model for
"duplicity and equivocation."

Much of the anti-Polk feeling was an expression of resentment at Polk's sudden political success. The President was the
first dark horse candidate to win his party's nomination and then
to take the Presidency itself. The fact that his victory was an
expression of the national enthusiasm for expansion did nothing
to endear him to his Whig opposition. The Whigs, destined to
die on the eve of the Civil War, were an aggregate of men and
women opposed to expansion on grounds of conscience, balance
of power and commercial interest. To be confronted with a relatively new face at the White House door and to see him pursue
his aims, with little or no regard for established procedure, was
bound to infuriate them. The fact that Americans were dying in
Polk's war lent moral fervor to political expediency.

Polk's own political expediency was related to his conception
of national need. It is difficult to escape the conclusion that he
forced war on Mexico to fulfill what he believed to be the nation's
"manifest destiny." In so doing he failed to take into account
the ultimate cost of the Mexican War to the whole concept of the
Federal Union. Polk's vision was limited. But within that limitation he conducted the war at home with tenacity and the war
abroad with skill.

American troops, many of them contingents from the Deep
South, fought ably under men who became legendary as officers
and officials in the Civil War. Jefferson Davis' Mississippi Rifles
played a key role in breaking Mexican resistance at the Battle
of Buena Vista. Both Captains Ulysses Grant and Robert E. Lee
were first exposed to major combat during the Mexican War.
Grant hated every bit of it. He seriously considered resigning
because he was so distraught at what he considered the injustice
of the American cause. But battles are usually won by firepower.
The Americans demonstrated their superiority on that score in

almost every encounter on Mexican soil, for that's where most of the war was fought.

Taylor drove deep into the heart of the enemy's country. General Scott, the Chief of Staff, took the field in an expedition that was to land him at Vera Cruz, at the tip of the Mexican Peninsula, and bring him through a series of engagements to a brilliantly conceived campaign in which Mexico City itself fell to American troops. In the West, a combination of American naval and military forces, under men like Kearny, Stockton and Frémont, fought and won California, lost it and then won it once again. It was a war in which brilliant moments were matched by glaring errors and incredible incompetence. It was, in other words, like most wars. But the pot of gold at the end of the rainbow was well worth the sacrifice to those who believed in "manifest destiny."

A good portion of the American people, perhaps a majority, took "manifest destiny" quite seriously. One Whig publication, heartily opposed to the entrance of any slave states, looked on the potential acquisition of California as a God-willed extension of the area of freedom. In the South, a somewhat cooler eye was cast on national expansion. Beleaguered by the trauma of slavery, southern leaders were not at all anxious for territories in the Northwest or Alaska where there would be no opportunity to plant the seeds of their region's "Peculiar Institution." The southerners foresaw that in a continental union they would be weakened in the political struggles that were bound to intensify.

The Mexican War, however, was a different matter. In Mexico slavery might well take root. But some southerners (John Calhoun is a good example) were opposed to this war, too. Calhoun's views were conditioned by a vision of the cataclysm to come. He also represented a certain strain of racism that has been an endemic factor in American life. Many Americans were opposed to the annexation of country in which large numbers of non-Anglo Saxons made their homes. It was feared that the Republic would be unable to survive if its bloodstream was polluted by an influx of Mexicans into the body politic.

The war brought to the surface a feeling of superiority that has troubled American relationships with people of different cultures. The loathsome words "greaser" and "breed" were part of the lexicon of the conflict, just as the word "gook" emerged from the vocabulary of war in Asia. The grotesque attitude of some of those trapped in the Vietnam conflict was foreshadowed by James Russell Lowell when he wrote a verse ascribed to an American fighting in Mexico.

> Afor I cum away from hum I hed a
>   strong persuasion
> Thet Mexicans worn't human beans,
>   an orang outang nation
> A sort of folks a chap could kill
>   an never dream on't after,
> No more 'n a feller 'd dream o' pigs
>   thet he hed led to slarter.

There were, on the other hand, those who thought we had a mission to claim the lost souls to the south. We made war, it was said, "to civilize an inferior people." If we managed to incorporate their territory in the process, that too was manifest destiny.

Not all of the expansionists were so palpably self-serving. Naïveté could best describe the postures struck by some of the country's leading artists and intellectuals. Walt Whitman, the "Poet of Democracy," wrote that it was ordained by Providence that the United States "take territory from other nations because it was its destiny by the will of God, to spread happiness far and wide." The Spanish minister wrote to his foreign office that the Americans considered themselves to be superior to any other people on earth and that they expected that they "would one day become the most sublime colossus of human power, and the wonder of the universe."

If it was difficult to deny Mexico's rightful title to California, it was easy enough to say that she didn't deserve to continue to hold it. The United States was entitled to wrest California from her owners because the Mexicans were too lazy and inept to develop it, according to a leading northern newspaper, the Hartford *Times*. The United States, the same newspaper declaimed, would make it "a paradise on earth." Perhaps the crux of the American impulse to expansion was best expressed by John

O'Sullivan, who coined the phrase "manifest destiny," when he wrote defiantly, "Yes, *more more more* . . . till our national destiny is fulfilled and the whole boundless continent is ours."

Albert Gallatin, in a call for peace with Mexico, struck savagely at the expansionist philosophy. Jefferson's Secretary of the Treasury was an old man by the time of the Mexican War, but his incisive mind was at the service of an angry conscience. He noted that much of the pro-war opinion was based on the assumption that Mexicans were our inferiors, that they were degraded and that, ultimately, American ministrations would "increase the happiness of the masses." Then Gallatin asked the question that we should ask ourselves today: "If we, in the name of Democracy, deny the hereditary superiority of individuals, how can we uphold that of races?"

Gallatin thought he knew at least part of the answer. Denying our enemies their common humanity was simply a "shallow attempt to disguise cupidity and ambition."

The battle about the war raged all during its prosecution. As late as 1848 a resolution passed the Senate giving thanks to General Taylor for his successes in "a war unnecessarily and unconstitutionally begun by the President of the United States." The clause was later deleted but its initial success reflects the temper of the time. The Mexican War was an illuminating example of the bitterness engendered when a President insists on engaging in a foreign adventure in the face of deep divisions among his own people. Not all citizens were expansionists. Many members of Polk's own party opposed the territorial grab. The experience of Thomas Hart Benton is a case in point.

Benton, the Democratic Senator from Missouri, made it clear to Polk that he opposed the war message because he thought that the United States had begun hostilities. He asked Polk to eliminate the preamble in which Mexico was accused of starting the conflict. White House pressure was applied and like many a Senator who was given the President's confidence during later crises, Benton chose to believe the President. When Polk asked for his support in the Senate, the Missourian went along. Afterwards, he drew the rueful conclusion that he had been right in the first place.

A good deal of antiwar and anti-expansion feeling was closely related to the slavery question. Some of the northeastern Whig opposition took their stand on simple moral grounds, thereby earning the not altogether complimentary sobriquet of "conscience Whigs." They were more vehement in debate than any of the other legislators. But *all* of the opposition felt handcuffed by executive power.

Resolution after resolution was passed in which Polk was called to account. At one point the question of impeachment was raised and quickly dropped. Only the fact that reports of victories were coming in from the front prevented the country from being torn apart. Polk's eye was on territory in Texas and California. He cast hardly a glance at what was happening to the people who lived in the territory back home. To the cries of "Peace, Peace," the President's reply was that his troops would "conquer a peace." He was, in the words of a later Commander in Chief, Lyndon Johnson, determined "to nail the coonskin to the door."

The President's critics examined his account of the war's origins and found it wanting. When Stephens named him "mendacious Polk," the label achieved wide circulation, not because the President had deliberately lied. Rather, he was charged with misleading Congress and the people. "He passed over in silence half of what it was essential to know . . . and what he did say he said in such a form that all the essential facts appeared reversed." Previous Presidents had been accused of deceptive practices in their relations with Congress, but Polk was the first to suffer a full-scale "credibility gap."

The President, whatever his faults, wished to end the war when he had achieved his purpose. Americans were astride the Rio Grande and far beyond. Military and naval contingents were entrenched in California and any reasonable people would have known that they were defeated. But the Mexicans, somehow, didn't get that message. They kept losing battles and they kept fighting the war. Polk, who told his Cabinet and confidants that the war would be over in ninety to one hundred and twenty days was taken aback. His initial intent had been to apply pressure only on the periphery of northern Mexico. He was in no mood to give Generals Scott and Taylor any room for glory in the heart of enemy country. As for Taylor, he wrote to his son that he would enjoy hearing of the death of Polk more than anything else he could think of!

Polk was sucked deeper and deeper into the morass. He agreed to launch an expedition to Vera Cruz, where the Army would head for the interior and the capital. If there was no other way to make the Mexicans surrender, we would simply occupy the whole country. But Polk began to parley as United States troops continued to fight. He sent out several unofficial peace missions to Mexico, with varying degrees of hope. Failure lay at the end of each of the false trails but some of the "unofficial feelers" were of considerable interest.

Moses Beach, the editor of the New York *Sun*, had been approached by two Texas entrepreneurs with connections inside the Mexican Army. At least one General and some high-ranking members of the Mexican clergy were ready to reach an accommodation with the Americans. Beach received authorization from the Secretary of State to act as "confidential agent" and to stir up as much trouble in Mexico as possible. Polk confided to his diary that it would be a "good joke" if Beach was able to surprise the whole country and negotiate a satisfactory treaty.

Polk, in an earlier attempt to buy peace, had permitted himself to be convinced by the exiled Santa Anna that he would make peace with the United States if he were to be returned to power. The President saw to it that Santa Anna was convoyed safely to Mexican shores, only to find that the Dictator, as soon as he arrived on Mexican soil, turned savagely on the invading Americans. It was up to Beach to persuade enough of the Mexican dissidents to rise against Santa Anna as soon as he lost a battle with General Scott. The dissidents would then take over the reins of government and sign on America's dotted line.

Beach did not go to Mexico alone. He was accompanied by an American lady with a colorful past. In 1833 Jane McManus Storms had been named corespondent in the seventy-seven-year-old Aaron Burr's divorce case. Rumor had it that she agreed to serve that useful function in order to get a sufficient stake to settle in Texas. For some years she traveled through the Southwest writing articles for the New York press and increasing her wide circle of acquaintances. She teamed up with Beach on his Mexican junket, as a potential liaison with General Scott. Polk, however, had neglected to inform the General of Beach's role and when Jane Storms arrived at Scott's camp he refused to believe her story.

Beach's hope was that Scott would time his encounter with Santa Anna to give the rebels their best chance for success. But Scott, apparently oblivious to Miss Storms's charms, ignored her! Santa Anna, meanwhile, had discovered Beach's role in the plot to overthrow him. The American newspaperman hastily retreated to Tampico and Jane Storms went on to other tropical adventures when the war was over. The President meanwhile was left to look for more orthodox approaches to the peace table. He was encouraged in that direction by Congress and the American electorate.

Polk was faced with a remarkable political dilemma. American armies were successful in the field, but the Democratic party was absorbing a series of defeats at the polls. The voters had responded to Whig glorification of their party's generals who were winning great victories, while at the same time they denounced Polk for carrying on the war. House and Senate passed from Democratic control and the bitter criticism of the President was intensified. The Whigs were certain that their gains meant the war had lost its appeal. They appropriated three million dollars for the President to use in negotiating a boundary with the enemy. The bill was recommended as "an important measure for securing a speedy peace." But the Mexicans did not seem to think so. Even as they retreated south, even as they were encircled and driven north, even as their California fortresses fell, they refused to talk to the Yankee invader.

The *New York Tribune* in December of 1846, after a year of relentless fighting, demanded that Congress refuse to "vote one dollar or man more until the President tells what his terms of peace are." The *Tribune* and others charged that Polk would not make peace until Mexico gave up California and that he intended the new territory to be a slave state. One observer remarked that "honor has already been satisfied" by the American troops who had conquered as much territory as the Senate could consent to keep.

A story made the rounds in Washington that a mother who had lost her son in the war asked the President's wife, "if you can, for no one seems to be able to answer me, tell me for what was this wicked war brought upon our country? Why was my son murdered in that barbarous country?" Mrs. Polk's answer went unrecorded, but the tale illustrates the futility and anguish over the war felt by many of the people on the winning side. The war's adherents were just as vehement. One argument heard on the political soapboxes of the day was that the acquisition of California would "help to defray the expense" of the conflict that had been forced upon us. Others called for "all of Mexico." Our troops were in possession of much of it, and, in any case, the Mexicans would be better off under American rule.

Contemporary historians, while differing in emphasis, generally agree that the acquisition of California was almost as much on President Polk's mind as the Texas boundary dispute, when he set out on the road that led to war. It was becoming increasingly difficult to achieve that end, and a Congress awakened to deep hostility by his arbitrary actions gave him only the grudging support necessary to sustain the troops in the field.

Our armies, strung across hundreds of miles of enemy territory, were harassed by constant guerrilla warfare. Their supply lines were thin and they were threatened with disease. The spoils of war had yet to be carried off and there was considerable question whether we would ever be able to absorb our victory. If the war continued much longer, Polk's difficulties with Congress would increase in intensity.

The President, in a desperate attempt to end the fighting, sent Nicholas P. Trist, the State Department's chief clerk, to join Scott's forces. Trist was commissioned to negotiate a treaty with whatever was left of the Mexican government as soon as Mexico City fell. Polk, unfortunately, had now fallen into a comic-opera version of the conflict between the military and civilian authorities. Scott felt that it was *his* prerogative to make the peace. He bitterly resented Trist's arrival on the scene and his disdain for the civilian "clerk" was compounded by Trist's refusal to show him the message Secretary Buchanan had given him for discussion with the Mexican authorities.

The squabble between the two men assumed the form of unpleasant letters to each other and reports of the rift reached Washington. By the time the General and his civilian companion had made it up, Polk had become so disabused of Trist's conduct that he was prepared to recall him. Whatever doubt Polk had about Trist's ineptitude was resolved when he learned that just before Scott reached Mexico City, Trist had arranged an armistice. The terms of the agreement horrified the President. Trist had agreed with the Mexicans to return San Francisco to their authority and to establish the region between the Nueces River and the Rio Grande *as a neutral zone.* Inasmuch as that piece of territory was the reason for fighting the Mexicans to begin with, the whole rationale for Polk's conduct, his speech about "American blood on American soil," was cast as grotesque chicanery. How could the United States surrender American soil after fighting a successful war over that very issue? Polk decided that commissioning Trist had been a serious error and he ordered his recall.

The President's lot, in those final days of war, was not an easy one. Victory after victory and still no peace was the refrain across the country. The situation had reached a point where most Americans were ready for any kind of agreement. Horace Greeley, no friend of the President, cried out that he hoped the Senate would "ratify anything Mr. Polk would send them . . . sign anything, ratify anything, pay anything, to end the guilt, the bloodshed, the shame, the enormous waste of this horrible contest."

Polk was ready to do just that if the Mexicans would only cooperate. He was finally, and much against his wishes, extricated from his dilemma by two men he had come to dislike intensely. Scott's capture of Mexico City resulted in the abdication of Santa Anna and the formation of a provisional government that was ready to discuss ending hostilities with the battle-weary American. Trist, although aware of the President's recall, was pressured to stay by his erstwhile enemy, the Commanding General. Even the British minister got in on the act. He told Trist that if a treaty was not signed immediately, all government would disintegrate, anarchy would prevail, and United States forces would be faced with a guerrilla conflict that could last for years. Trist, a man without a commission, took the situation into his own hands. The time lag in communications with Washington permitted him to proceed.

At a small town outside Mexico City called Guadalupe Hidalgo, the Mexicans agreed to accept the Rio Grande as the southern boundary of a now-American Texas. The Mexicans accepted fifteen million dollars in return for the bitter pill of ceding California, Arizona and New Mexico to the United States. Polk, who had called Trist "an impudent, unqualified scoundrel," sent his repudiated minister's treaty to the Senate, where it was ratified on March 10, 1848.

A ninety-day expedition had turned into a two-year war and inflamed the passions of a divided people, earning us in passing an enmity from our southern neighbor that it took years to overcome. In return we got our window on the sea and, it has been noted in other places, no one has suggested we give any of it back.

President Polk's conflict with Congress and the impassioned dissent from his war policies were unequaled until the war in Vietnam. If television and radio had covered that earlier war and its implications, the United States might well have been racked with disorders that would have made our most recent trauma seem pale by comparison. The issues were much the same as those we have confronted in our own time. They differed only because Polk and his enemies fought out their differences on essentially virgin terrain. Presidents today have the constitutional and historical ground well reconnoitered. Polk was the first Commander in Chief to fully implement President Madison's early attempt to direct strategy from the White House. Only his distance from the theater of war prevented an even more active engagement.

The attempts of Congress to impose restraints on the Commander in Chief ended in dismal failure. They refused to allow the President to install a Lieutenant General over Scott's head, but it was a pale victory. The President simply concentrated more personal attention on the military situation than he had before. His obsession with validating his position led him to a series of self-serving statements that rarely reflected the complete truth of the American situation. He was so concerned with his own vindication that he could not see that the war was planting seeds which would choke the country in the blood of its own people. The admission of Texas intensified the controversy over slavery, and the sectional differences over the prosecution of the war eventually resulted in such rancor that a Civil War that might have been avoided became almost inevitable. But the President had gained his point in respect of the executive power over war. One may ask whether he would have pursued it with such vigor if he could have seen the eventual outcome.

His own contemporaries argued with him that war was not necessary to achieve the cession of California. Time and relentless American migration would have brought us to the same places where we stand today. All of that, of course, is conjecture. But it relates directly to our own situation in which the Constitution is too often abused so as to meet the views of a single President.

In 1847 a politician, commenting on the unconstitutionality of the President's action, expressed amazement at congressional acquiescence. He failed to understand how men who were against annexation and opposed to conquest could be "bound to adopt the view of the President to sustain him in his course and to grant him all of the money and the men he requires." Many have asked that same question in the 1960's and 1970's. The answers have not changed very much. I noted earlier that loyalty to our men in the field sometimes comes into conflict with loyalty to constitutional principle. The men in the field have their lives at stake.

Another question raised in the 1970's has to do with national priorities and the expenditure of men and treasure in places far from home, in a cause not all of us have been ready to embrace. As the Mexican War drew to its conclusion, the Administration was charged by newspapers across the country with neglecting problems here at home.

"Every man engaged in making war supplies is diverted from

the manufacture of domestic products of enduring value." The country's supply of capital is limited, Americans were told, and "further appropriations for aggression and subjugation" should be withheld. Domestic needs were sadly neglected, it was said, and President and Congress were obliged to turn their heads to internal improvements instead of foreign war.

But the most prescient comment to be made, one which we cannot fail to ponder with at least a hint of precognition, came from the editorialist who asked that Congress give Mr. Polk anything at all so long "as he give us peace; *and then for the reckoning*."

IX

President Pierce
Avenges Solon Borland's
Injured Nose

THE conflict over presidential use of the war power was secondary during the 1850's to the issue of the nature of the Union itself. Was the Union a compact or a contract? Could it survive as an amalgam of slave and free states? Was it doomed to unravel with a whimper or a bang?

In Congress and in the country as a whole, the question of slavery dominated the conversation, the debates and the headlines, until finally, in 1861, Confederate guns at Fort Sumter signaled the beginning of America's greatest tragedy. But before that climax tore at the country's vitals, the Government, almost reflexively, continued to do its everyday business. In 1854 an incident occurred in Greytown on Central America's Mosquito Coast, that, although it has not received much attention, was described by at least one historian as the most significant use of presidential war power in the nineteenth century.

In the light of what was to come, I am not at all sure that I fully agree with that assessment. But Greytown does mark a turning point in the attitude of the President toward congressional authority, and a signpost on the road to increasing congressional surrender of the war power.

History has not been kind to Franklin Pierce. He was one of those Presidents who get a college or two named after them in their home states and become one more bust gathering dust in the national pantheon. But while he served, Pierce wanted to make a record that would match those of Jackson and Polk. The Democrats had put him up as a compromise candidate, and he was going to demonstrate that he was qualified to hold the office.

Pierce was an expansionist in the tradition of those who came before him. He was a good-looking, backslapping veteran of the Mexican War, whose wife made him return to New Hampshire after he had served a couple of terms in Congress. Washington, as far as she was concerned, was too encouraging to his natural conviviality. Little did Mrs. Pierce or her husband know that he would turn out to be the only politician whom Democrats from both slave and free states could agree on as their candidate for the Presidency. Pierce's self-image was at least partially responsible for the aggressive tone of his administration's foreign policy. The President's belligerency almost resulted in war with England and, at Greytown, gave early hints of later and more complicated American interventions in Latin America.

Greytown was a free port, recognized as such by prior American administrations and the British Foreign Office. Its population of some five hundred people was a motley collection of Americans, British, and Dutch traders, along with a large number of Jamaican Negroes. The town's principal importance was as a point of transit between the Atlantic and Pacific Oceans. For Americans, Central America was the easiest way of reaching the new California territory. U.S. Highway Number 1 was a long way in the future and so were the railroads that would later span the continent. A trans-isthmus canal seemed to be the best way of assuring a steady stream of traffic to and from the new American West. The Mosquito Coast line near Nicaragua was a logical place to try to build it. Meanwhile, travelers sailed to Greytown, disembarked, were hauled across by train to the Pacific and reembarked on other steamships to complete the trip to California.

The system was in the hands of the Accessory Transit Company, a venture owned in large part by Commodore Vanderbilt. Accessory Transit was chartered by the Nicaraguan government, although most of its stockholders were Americans. It was Pierce's view that Commodore Vanderbilt's friends, since they were Americans, were entitled to protection wherever they were. And that is why Greytown literally exploded.

The Transit Company had been feuding with Greytown's civil authorities over property leased from the municipality as a steamship coaling station. When the Greytown officials realized that the station was rapidly expanding into a city in itself, they felt threatened and demanded that the company destroy facilities that were unrelated to the fueling operation.

The company's refusal resulted in a row in which a house was destroyed by the town's agents. A United States Navy ship under the command of Commander George S. Hollins was in the area. At the request of accessory transit officials, Hollins led a party of Marines ashore and prevented the continued destruction of company property. Inasmuch as they were outgunned, the civil power retreated and resentment of company immunity intensified among the townspeople. Hollins' "demonstration" was a standard diplomatic technique at the time, and aroused little notice back home. But the affair was to take on serious dimensions a few months later, when an American official named Solon Borland was passing through on his way to Washington. Borland was United States minister to Central America. He had been charged with straightening out our relations with other governments in the area, and, as far as the Administration was concerned, he had botched the job. His resignation accepted, Borland, still steaming, stirred the pot one more time.

The American diplomat was a passenger on the steamship *Routh,* captained by a man named Smith. Newspaper accounts differ on what transpired during the voyage, but a consensus indicates that Borland was at the center of an argument during which Smith shot and killed a black boatman who was paddling a canoe alongside the *Routh.* Words were exchanged between the two "officers" and Borland was said to have told Smith he should "have shot the damned nigger." The Captain then backed up the steamer, picked up his rifle and did exactly that. Much shaken, Smith told passengers that he "never would have done it," if Borland had not egged him on.

The canoe and its surviving passengers scurried for Greytown as fast as they could make it. There, a posse of enraged residents accompanied the marshal when he tried to arrest Smith for murder. A struggle ensued when the Transit Company's ship docked and Smith, with Borland's support, resisted arrest. Borland told the marshal that the United States did not recognize the right of Greytown authorities to arrest a United States citizen for any crime whatsoever. Washington and London had previously agreed to accord Greytown authorities *de facto* recognition so as to encourage a "police power" in the Central American political flux.

But the Greytown people, at that point, were not interested in the legal niceties. When Borland threatened to shoot the first man to try to board the ship, the crowd grew angrier and a bottle was thrown that cut the minister's nose. That cut on Solon Borland's nose was to provide President Pierce with a *casus belli*. It was a cause for war that he could never have gotten through Congress, but it fit in nicely with the plans of the Accessory Transit Company and its Washington representative.

Commodore Vanderbilt's man in the nation's capital was Joseph B. White. He and the President had discussed the Transit Company's situation in Greytown and he had also talked at length with Secretary of State William Marcy. Although the Transit Company initially accepted the town's authority, the "interference" of the municipal officials with company activity had become more of a nuisance than it was worth. When a disgruntled black employee stole some flour from a company warehouse, he was attacked by Transit personnel and the police once again intervened.

The insistence of the town on enforcing its lease, and the destruction of the company house before Captain Hollins arrived on the scene, had provided a good beginning for the escalation of a conflict that could have only one ending. Now the Borland affair brought the situation to a head.

When Borland, who had continued his journey home, arrived in Washington, he conferred with his superiors and with Transit Company representative White. Borland described in dramatic detail the imbroglio in which he had been attacked. He failed to mention that the Greytown authorities had "apologized" for the bottle-throwing episode and that Smith had been let off without investigation into the murder charge. The people of Greytown knew they were dealing with irresistible power. The town's mayor and council had resigned in the aftermath of the challenge to their authority but it was too late for the small coastal village to avoid a confrontation with the armed might of the United States. Commander George Hollins was again instructed to intervene. This time he had orders from the Secretary of the Navy that would cause a national uproar and end in the total destruction of Greytown.

Although Secretary of State Marcy referred in all of his public correspondence to the "pretended authorities" at Greytown, he took the trouble to keep an official American representative named Joseph Fabens on the scene. If there was no duly constituted authority in Greytown, the presence of an American "commercial agent" or consul, was anomalous. But Fabens had enough to keep him busy. He and White, the Transit Company man, maintained a steady correspondence and Fabens' recommendations to his superiors in Washington were remarkably similar to those remedies sought by the Accessory Transit Company.

In a directive to Fabens, the Secretary of State ordered him to demand of the town's "pretended authorities" an apology for their conduct to Borland along with an "indemnity" of $24,000 for damages done to the Accessory Transit Company's property. The sum was determined after consultation between the State Department and Mr. White. There is one letter extant from White to Fabens, which implies an extra-governmental agreement between them. White, writing about Navy Commander Hollins' anticipated visit to Greytown, mentions the demands to be made, and closes with the ominous phrase ". . . and you know the rest." Newspaper reports, in the aftermath of the Greytown incident, estimated that the house for which the Transit Company was asking $8,000 had a value closer to $250. The value assigned to a boatload of stolen flour was similarly disproportionate.

When Commander Hollins arrived on the warship *Cyane,* he conferred with Fabens who told him that the citizens of Greytown had refused the United States Government's demand for an apology. Some residents, he remarked, had gone so far as to use foul language when they referred to Minister Borland. They also had refused to make "restitution" to the Accessory Transit Company for the damages due them. The instructions Commander Hollins received from the Navy Department were intentionally ambiguous about the action to be taken in such a situation. They were written so as to give the ship's captain the widest latitude, while at the same time qualifying that latitude with references to his "prudence and good sense." Commander Hollins was told by his superior that "these people should be taught that the United States will not tolerate these outrages, and that they have the power and the determination to check them. It is, however, very much to be hoped that you can effect the purposes of your visit without a resort to violence and destruction of property and loss of life."

On July 12, 1854, Hollins, after consulting with Fabens, decided to give the Greytowners one more chance to apologize and make restitution. He dispatched a party of Marines to post a "proclamation" at strategic points throughout the community. Hollins announced that if the "authorities" (his quotation marks) failed to submit to the American demands, he would, at 9 A.M. of the following day, July 13, 1854, "proceed to bombard the town . . . to the end that the rights of our country and citizens may be vindicated, and as a guarantee for future protection."

The Accessory Transit Company meanwhile made its own humanitarian arrangements. Its agent announced that residents who wished to do so could board a Transit steamer with any possessions they could carry and watch the bombardment of their homes. Only a dozen or so frightened Greytowners took advantage of what Fabens later called the company's "generous offer."

Commander Hollins was as good as his word. At nine o'clock the ship's batteries opened up on the defenseless town with a barrage that lasted forty-five minutes. After a forty-five-minute intermission the guns fired again for thirty minutes, and after a second intermission of three hours, they laid on a final barrage that lasted twenty minutes. Hollins, in his dispatch to Washington, commented that he had ordered the intervals in gunfire so as to give the inhabitants an opportunity to "satisfactorily arrange matters." There is a petulant tone to the Commander's observation about the people of Greytown, that "no advantage was taken of the consideration shown them."

Although the town was almost completely destroyed, Hollins felt it essential "to satisfy the whole world that the United States has the power and determination to enforce that reparation and respect due them . . . in whatever quarter the outrage may be committed." He therefore landed the Marines once more and put to the torch those few pathetic structures left standing. The town was literally wiped from the map.

The Greytown affair caused instant uproar. The British were both offended and astonished at the American action. A British officer had asked Hollins to desist and was roundly snubbed. The press at first expressed general disbelief at what had taken place, and then, almost gleefully, examined the incident and its implications in full detail.

The *New York Tribune* struck a common note when it called the bombardment "a needless, unjustifiable, inhuman exercise of warlike force." The event that had triggered President Pierce's warlike response had fallen into the background. But now a correspondent of *The New York Times* discussed the killing of the black boatman with on-the-spot witnesses. One man called it "a deliberate cold-blooded murder without a shadow of palliation." *The Times,* after recounting a number of stories that substantiated that view, thrust to the heart of the entire situation. If there was cause for executive intervention, and if that failed to secure redress, the country "should have been appealed to *through Congress,* to take such steps as its honor and rights might demand." *The Times* in its most cutting tones observed that the Pierce Administration had behaved as though it "had not the faintest recollection that there is such a body as Congress in existence." The newspaper expressed doubt that American history "can show an instance of more glaring usurpation than that of which General Pierce has here been guilty." The use of the President's military title was hardly inadvertent. Pierce's martial ardor had long expressed itself in a tone of bellicosity toward Great Britain, as well as a willingness to assert American authority over the neighboring states to the south. Historians of a later day have concluded that without William Marcy's restraining influence as Secretary of State, the President could easily have plunged the country into war with England over the issue of the yet to be constructed isthmian canal.

Two years before Pierce became President the United States and Great Britain had agreed to the Clayton-Bulwer Treaty, whereby the two countries agreed to participate in the construction of a canal that would be neutral and open to all international shipping. Inasmuch as the agreement recognized by implication that Britain had established interests in the area, it was fairly unpopular among a large segment of the American public. Much of Pierce's activity in Central America, including the act of war at Greytown, was aimed at diluting the effect of the Clayton-Bulwer Treaty and telling the British that the Caribbean was essentially an American sea.

Greytown, one of the earliest examples of what later came to be called "gunboat diplomacy," was also a blatant example of the Executive's unrestrained use of war power without even *pro forma* congressional consultation. An early critic noted that it was highly unlikely that the President would have dared to bomb Le Havre or Liverpool in a similar situation without going to Congress. Historian James Schouler, writing in 1904, called the bombardment a "base and bullying exploit, unworthy of a dignified government." He commented with asperity that "this swaggering contempt of black and mixed races to the south of us was a phase of the American character in this degenerate age, of which Greytown's bombardment afforded no solitary instance."

Pierce erected a wall of silence against the growing criticism that mounted in the summer and fall of 1854. A group of New York merchants with property interests in Nicaragua accused him of a "violation of the Constitution." Their petition to the President reminded him that under Article 1, Section 8 "Congress alone has the power to declare war . . . and make rules concerning captures on land and water."

One newspaper said that "the whole transaction was the act of the American executive and for it that executive must account." Another publication called the presidential intervention a "violation of the great Charter." But it was the asperity of the *New York Post* that bitterly underlined the principal issue.

> The American Constitution is justly thought to be a masterpiece of wisdom, but after this event let no one deny it has serious faults . . . chief among these is the power of evil that is conferred on a weak and wicked Executive. The ashes of [Greytown] attest that in this respect our forefathers of the Revolution committed a deplorable error.

That angry editorial illustrates a flaw in our political thinking and practice that goes far to explain one of the principal reasons that the President has been able to successfully expand his powers at congressional expense. The writer implicitly accepts the *right* of the Executive to take vicious action, simply because it is within his physical power to do so. The blame is cast not on the President as an individual but on the Constitution from which he derives his power. No one can dispute that executive authority is derived from the Constitution. But it does not follow that the illegitimate exercise of that authority also derives from the Constitution. The repeated failure of Congress to draw the line when the Executive exceeds his authority further sanctions the extra-constitutional power that has accrued to the Presidency over the course of time. The affair at Greytown was a particularly blatant example of a congressional abdication of responsibility that resulted in another precedent for later Commander in Chief forays on the high seas and in foreign territory. Congress must accept the blame if only because the executive branch under Pierce was divided, weak and would have been susceptible to the exercise of determined action by the Congress.

Although the Administration tried to keep a low profile, the *Washington Union,* regarded as a Pierce "house organ," betrayed a considerable disarray in the ranks. A reply to the attacks on the President contended that Commander Hollins' course was not dictated by his orders. The editorialist at the same time refused to condemn the officer, suggesting that an assessment be delayed until he returned to report in person to his superiors. Ivan Spenser, a biographer of Secretary of State Marcy, also suggests that the Administration was playing for time in the hope that an adequate scapegoat could be found and that the furor would die down when the Congress returned in December. The event fulfilled the hope.

The President's message to Congress was read on December 4, some six months after the bombardment of Greytown. It was his first direct reply to the criticism that had dominated the summer months. The President stated that documents relating to the Hollins mission, now in the possession of the House, fully justified the naval attack on Greytown. Pierce referred to the course of events as stated by Borland and took note of the "known character" of the town's population. He replied to "complaint on the part of some foreign powers," that it would have been "submissive acquiescence to national indignity" to permit the Greytowners to go unpunished. Pierce, in backing Hollins up, told Congress that the people of Greytown themselves had frustrated "all the possible mild measures for obtaining satisfaction." To allay any doubt that the blame lay elsewhere, the President chastised the captain of the small British schooner that had been in port during the affair. If he had remonstrated with the population, they would in all likelihood have acquiesced in Hollins' ultimatum. That, the President noted, would have avoided the town's devastation. Not once in his message did Franklin Pierce acknowledge that there was any question as to the propriety of his actions. He made no reference to the possibility that congressional authorization might be required for the Executive to take offensive action against foreign territory. If there was to be a contest over the nature of the war power the initiative would have to come from Congress.

In some ways, the business conducted in the House on December 11, 1854, was a watershed in the history of relations between the executive and legislative branches. A New York Congressman named John Wheeler presented a resolution to the House that embodied all of the questions relating to the execution of war powers. Wheeler observed that no declaration of war had been made and that no authorization of "warlike hostilities" had been authorized by Congress at Greytown. He called for the establishment of a Committee of 13 "to investigate whether the

Constitution of the United States had been violated by any officer of the government in the said transactions." A stream of parliamentary maneuvers succeeded in getting Wheeler's resolution amended beyond recognition. When it finally reached the floor it received a relative handful of affirmative votes. Only fifty-four Congressmen could be rallied even to ask the question as to whether or not the President had the right to use such force and in such a manner as he had at Greytown. One lawmaker, his words dressed in sarcasm, asked "under what clause of the Constitution the power is found to enable the President to judge the case, pass sentence, and execute it himself." In the Senate a similar attempt to bring Greytown to the floor for debate was smothered with even greater parliamentary dispatch. Pierce had waited for the adverse public opinion to die down, he had found a scapegoat in the always handy British Navy, and he had successfully avoided constitutional confrontation. An awkward and ugly situation was turned into a strong affirmation, *without congressional reply*, of the seemingly untrammeled right of the Executive to read the war powers clause as he wished.

Pierce's victory may be understood in the light of the distractions offered Congress and the people it represented. House and Senate were racked by debate over issues that were to divide the Union. Venom and hatred, as well as considerable intellectual power, were expended on ways to exploit the national divisions to the advantage of one or another sectional party. To those involved in the preliminaries to the Civil War the bombardment of a predominantly "black town" situated in an "uncivilized" part of the world must have seemed of minor consequence. In the minds of the legislative leaders, the real question was whether the Constitution was a contract or a compact. Questions as to its individual parts were subordinate to the great question of its fate as a whole. It was in this context that the power of the President was upheld by legislative *refusal to consider the issue*.

Commander Hollins was sued in United States District Court by an unhappy Greytown property owner. The Judge, in denying the plaintiff's suit, noted that Hollins was a presidential agent. He cited Marbury v. Madison in ruling that the propriety of the bombardment was a "public political question," within the discretion of the executive power. Judge Samuel Nelson's contention that there "exists and can exist no power to control [that] discretion," was not appealed to a higher court.

The decision linked two elements of the executive power that are of particular interest. The presidential obligation to insure that "the laws are faithfully executed" was tied directly to the duties of the Commander in Chief. Within the next few years a great President was to cite the same linkage as justification for reading the Constitution and its war powers clause in an entirely new light. Abraham Lincoln is sanctified by history as the Great Emancipator. But on the issue of the war powers, he may also have been the Great Violator.

X

Lincoln:
The Great Violator?

THE mythic quality of the American Civil War was established even as the nation was rent by the grim reality of one of the greatest struggles so far recorded in human history. The names of battles, and of the men and women who participated as combatants or observers and victims, have come down to us as landscapes and figures from a much larger than life American Tragedy. One finds it difficult, even at more than a century's remove, to weigh the conduct of Lincoln and Grant, Davis and Lee, on the same scales used to assess the consequences of actions taken by other national leaders in other times.

Lincoln, in particular, has achieved a status analogous to political sainthood. His successful preservation of the Union through the national agony over which he presided is in American history the great triumph of the national political will. Lincoln was, in his bones, the essence of the political man. His battles were fought within the arena of the American system and the very magnitude of the dilemma with which he contended requires close analysis of the solution he applied.

The historic conflict over the war power was resolved during the early years of the Civil War in such dramatic style and with such quickness of execution as to make one wonder that there is any room for doubt as to the question today. For, in 1861 and the years immediately following, the President assumed a series of powers relating to the conduct of the war and of the national life that were constitutionally unwarranted. But was this the "war" the Constitution contemplated? This was a war for the preservation of the Union. There can be no question as to motive. Nor can there be doubt that the historically unique emergency confronting the new President when he took office required extraordinary measures. We were then in another twilight zone respecting the war power—domestic insurrection. The emergency, however, confronted the entire body politic as it was constructed by the founders and that body very much included Congress and the Judiciary. Lincoln, nevertheless, decided he had to go it alone.

On April 12, 1861, Confederate batteries opened fire on Fort Sumter. Three days later the President proclaimed a state of insurrection and called Congress into special session. His proclamation is noteworthy on two counts. He called for the State to provide 75,000 militiamen inasmuch as the rebellion was supported by "private combinations . . . too powerful to be suppressed by the ordinary course of judicial proceedings." Although there is no question of Lincoln's constitutional authority to call out the militia, his reference to the inadequacy of "the ordinary course of judicial proceedings" was to be the underlying theme of repeated executive initiatives, which even under the extraordinary impact of Civil War raised serious constitutional questions. Even more striking was the date the President set for the special session. He convened Congress for July 4, *fully three months later.*

The pace of Lincoln's activities during the interval gives clear evidence of his intention and ability to prosecute the war with vigor, and also of his determination to preempt total authority in the exercise of the war powers. If Congress was to be held off for three months, the rebels weren't. With the Union in genuine peril, the President was enabled to take such action as *he* deemed necessary without legislative consent before the fact. Lincoln didn't hesitate. He issued a series of directives as Commander in Chief that went far toward casting him in the role of "a single body legislature."

Almost immediately, he drew on treasury funds to pay for

military and naval equipment that would be required to put down the rebellion. Despite the constitutional prohibition that no money shall be drawn from the treasury except "in consequence of appropriations made by law," Lincoln ordered the Secretary of the Treasury to disburse two million dollars to a group of private citizens he had delegated to purchase supplies. The money was expended, he later asserted, "for military measures necessary for the defense and support of the government." Nineteen naval vessels were purchased by presidential order, in clear opposition to the constitutional precept that Congress alone will regulate the size of the armed forces.

On April 19 and April 27, 1861, the President ordered a blockade of all southern ports. In international law such an order is an act of war and the President's action was said by many to have exceeded his constitutional authority. He could and did, however, point to his obligation under the same Constitution to put down rebellion and repel invasion as justification for his action. Some critics replied that inasmuch as no invasion was threatened, a blockade measure was not necessary to "put down" the rebellion, and that if it became necessary, Congress could and would have authorized it. That appears to have been the heart of the matter. Lincoln was willing to face up to the enormous burdens of the Presidency in the crisis of national dissolution; he was not willing to risk increasing the intensity of the crisis by inviting a division of the authority to break it.

One element in Lincoln's attitude at war's outbreak was the historical record. Presidents in that age assumed office in March of the calendar year. Congress, by custom, did not normally go into session until the following December. This gave each new administration an opportunity to set its course by the time the legislature began its deliberations. In those cases in which Congress had come into early session, the administration in power usually took a disastrous course. A piece of the political folk wisdom of the day was to "avoid Congress in May." If such had been the case in the past, under conditions much less dangerous than those obtaining in civil war, it was hardly remarkable that Lincoln preferred to put his own stamp on events for as long as he could.

The President followed his initial militia proclamation and the imposition of blockade with an order increasing the size of the Regular Army and a call for nearly 50,000 volunteers. The high emotion of the period was reflected in a lyric sung to the tune of an old folk melody—"We are coming Father Abraham three hundred thousand strong." The men rushing to preserve the Union weren't about to leaf through the Constitution to see whether or not Father Abraham had the right to ask them to join up. Much of Lincoln's initial action was calculated to elicit the kind of support that civil war engenders on both sides of the barricades between brothers. He got that support from the American people. The Constitution of the United States certainly didn't give it.

Article 1, Section 8 reads: "Congress shall . . . declare war . . . *raise and support* armies . . . make all laws which shall be necessary to carry into execution the foregoing powers and all other powers vested in the Government of the United States."

Nowhere in the Constitution is there any indication that the President is entitled under any circumstances to expand the size of the regular military forces beyond the numbers fixed by Congress. Writing over a hundred years later, one is almost diffident in applying retroactively such a constitutional test to our greatest President. This is particularly true for a member of the United States Senate during a period when the Executive has assumed even broader decision-making war powers with little or no effective congressional protest. But it must be remembered, by the writer as well as the reader, that the reason for today's easy incursions are those that came before. Lincoln's assumption of war power was on so huge a scale as to change historically the nature of the constitutional structure. In rapid succession, a series of stunning executive actions upset all the old modes of transacting the national business. The President quickly asserted the right to suspend the writ of *habeas corpus*, the right to order summary arrest (arrest without warrant, solely on executive authority), the right to confiscate private property and the right to suppress free expression. For good measure he barred from the mails materials he deemed inimical to the national interest and he changed custom-hallowed practice by executive proclamation rather than through the legislative process. The President displayed iron nerve and a deep concern for the country's peril in each of the actions cited above. He was in no mood to give more than a passing glance to the long-range implications of his acts. In his view there would be no chance for the Republic's survival into a distant future if the executive power faltered in its will to run the entire apparatus of government without restraint.

There was rational explanation for every extra-constitutional measure taken by the President. Although we may regret the actions because of the precedents they established, we can be grateful that they had the desired effect. But, what if another man had been President? The question, and it is perhaps unanswerable, is whether the republic would have survived its Civil War notwithstanding. Many of those who opposed the sweeping nature of presidential government fully recognized the nature of the national crisis. They asked simply for discrimination in the application of blatantly unconstitutional measures. But the country at large, that is to say, Union country, was on the side of the President. That mood was reflected in the reluctant acquiescence of Congress in the measures taken by the President before they met in July's belated "emergency session." Lincoln's message was extraordinary in its frankness. It also provides us with a benchmark from which we can see the development of his own attitude toward constitutional law as the war continued. After describing to the legislature the executive actions that had been taken in their absence, the President said:

> These measures, whether strictly legal or not, were ventured upon, under what appeared to be a popular demand and a public necessity; trusting then, as now, that Congress would readily ratify them. It is believed that *nothing has been done beyond the constitutional competency of Congress.*

The President himself, almost explicitly, at this point in the war, thus recognized that he had appropriated the legislative function. He cites "popular demand and a public necessity" as his justification. The voice of the people is substituted for the voice of the law. Even though, in Lincoln's case, a good argument was made that survival was the issue, many Congressmen were unhappy in their submission. Two of Lincoln's closest associates, John Hay and John Nicolay, wrote after his death that acts taken on presidential authority were ratified by Congress without the "grace" that Lincoln's secretaries apparently thought should have accompanied the abdication. All acts of the President affecting the Army, the Navy and the militia were approved "as if they had been issued and done under the previous express authority and direction of the Congress of the United States."

Senator John Sherman of Ohio underlined the prevalent belief that Lincoln had violated the law when he asserted that "I am going to vote for that resolution and I am going to vote for it on the assumption that the different acts of the Administration recited in this preamble were illegal." But Lincoln initially did not ask Congress to validate some of his administration's early actions. Only as necessity revealed itself did he ask for legislative sanction. It was a full year before Congress endorsed the right of the Executive to suspend *habeas corpus* and when it did so it stamped "approved" on a delegation of its own constitutional authority.

The Lincoln Administration was faced with an unprecedented emergency. With considerable justification the entire North was regarded as a potential asylum for Confederate sympathizers. In such a situation, it was felt, "the enemy is all around us." A kind of Fifth Column psychology prevailed, and, too often, the concern for security provided cover for acts of vendetta perpetrated by Lincoln's agents against their personal enemies. The suspension of *habeas corpus* was an efficient weapon to silence those who dissented from national policy and who might have crossed swords with War Secretary Stanton or Secretary of State Seward earlier in their careers.

Habeas corpus is that legal protection entitling any person under arrest to be brought before a judge and charged with a crime. (History's dungeons were filled with men who rotted their lives away without cause or hearing.) The men who made the Constitution established *habeas corpus* as one of the principal safeguards against the tyranny of unrestrained power. They required that it be suspended only "when in cases of Rebellion or invasion the public safety may require it." That clause was written into Article 1, the section which describes *the powers to be granted to Congress.* But on April 27 it had been suspended, at first in a limited area, by President Lincoln. The suspension provided the fuel for a major clash between the judiciary and the executive branches. The case, *ex parte Merryman,* underlines the potential for conflict within a government of divided powers when one or the other branch of that government finds it necessary to disobey the law. This is particularly true when the violator is the executive branch, in which resides all of the power of enforcement. It was Andrew Jackson who said, "the Supreme Court has made its decision. Now let it enforce it." But it was Commander in Chief Abraham Lincoln who meant it.

In order to understand the pressures under which Lincoln labored it is necessary to remember that the seat of the Federal Government was located on the very borders of "enemy country." In April of 1861 it was still uncertain as to whether the Maryland legislature would attempt to secede from the Union. The President had ordered Lieutenant General Scott to prepare to bombard Baltimore if the need arose. It was in that context that John Merryman, a Marylander serving as an officer in a secessionist drill company, was arrested by the military and thrown into a prison cell at Fort McHenry.

On May 25, Merryman's attorney petitioned for a writ of *habeas corpus.* He presented his case to Roger Taney, the Chief Justice of the United States. Taney issued the writ in which he ordered Fort McHenry's Commanding General to bring Merryman before the Chief Justice on the following day. General George Cadwallader failed to appear as instructed. An aide entered the Chief Justice's courtroom and read a statement on behalf of his commander to the effect that the President had suspended *habeas corpus* in Maryland. Cadwallader asked for a postponement of the case until he could consult personally with the Commander in Chief. Chief Justice Taney refused and ordered a United States marshal to bring General Cadwallader before him twenty-four hours later. When the marshal attempted to serve his order on the General he was refused admittance to Fort McHenry. In this case too, "combinations too powerful to be suppressed by ordinary judicial proceedings" were in control. When General Cadwallader failed to appear before Taney, the Chief Justice read an opinion that legal scholars consider a classic defense of civil liberties against presidential usurpation carried out by military power.

The opinion expressed surprise that the President had suspended the writ because he had never publicly declared such a suspension. Taney, going to the issue itself, contended all constitutional authorities were in agreement that "the privilege of the writ could not be suspended except by act of Congress." The Chief Justice reminded the Executive that it was his duty to "faithfully execute the laws of the land." He observed that in the Merryman case the President's military subordinates were violating the law they were sworn to uphold. The writ of *habeas corpus* was not merely in illegal suspension but the judiciary itself had been brusquely prevented from doing its duty. The Chief Justice pointed out that the civil courts in Maryland were sitting, that no rebellious faction was engaged in keeping the civil power from going about its duties and that there was therefore not even a facade of necessity to cover the abrogation of the writ and the handcuffing of the courts. Warning against the tyranny of military control, the Chief Justice noted that the Constitution prohibited the taking of life, liberty and property without "due process of law." He said that "these great and fundamental laws have been disregarded and suspended . . . if the authority which the Constitution has confided to the judiciary department and judicial officers may thus, upon any pretext or any circumstances be usurped by the military power, at its discretion, the people of the United States are no longer living under a government of laws, but every citizen holds his life, liberty and property at the will and pleasure of the Army officer."

The Chief Justice noted that he had done everything within his power to fulfill his constitutional function. He had been prevented from exercising that function by a power too great for him to overcome, and, forwarding his opinion to the President of the United States, he observed that "it will then remain for that high officer, in fulfillment of his constitutional obligation to take care that the laws be faithfully executed, to determine what measures he will take to cause the civil process of the United States to be respected and enforced."

Lincoln's conception of his obligation to enforce the law's faithful execution was different from that of the Chief Justice. In his message to the newly convened Congress in the summer of 1861, he took note of the Chief Justice's opinion and responded with one of his own. "The whole of the laws which were required to be faithfully executed were being resisted and failing of execution in nearly one third of the states." He called concern over the *habeas corpus* issue "extreme tenderness of the citizen's liberty" and asked the great question: "Are all the laws *but one* to go unexecuted and the government itself go to pieces lest that one be violated?" He failed to note that just such an "extreme tenderness" of liberty was one of the motivating forces for making the Constitution into the national instrument of government.

Lincoln was solicitous also of offending congressional sensibility. He remarked that the matter was in their hands, and that if they thought it necessary, they could enact legislation with regard to *habeas corpus*. But he did not urge them to do so, and no immediate action was taken. The President, on the other hand, expanded the use of suspension as an executive tool as it suited the convenience of his Secretaries of War and State. The latter, William Seward, is reported to have remarked to a friend that if he picked up a bell in his right hand and tinkled it, two people would be placed under arrest in New York. "If I ring the bell to my left, a man will be arrested in Pennsylvania," he said with a smile.

The growth of the executive war power in the area of *habeas corpus* was given legislative approval a year later. The law as drafted hinted at congressional discomfort over granting the President such complete license. It required that any citizen in jail was to be released at the end of a grand jury session in that district if no indictment was brought against him. The limitation was apparently never taken seriously, and the Administration went about its business of seeing that the laws were faithfully executed.

The "faithful execution" clause and the Commander in Chief function were united during the Civil War. Lincoln's conception of the Commander in Chief role was signally enlarged by that unification. Only ten years before the war broke out, the Supreme Court had unanimously held that the Commander in Chief had no power beyond the realm of military action against an armed enemy. He was the Chief General and Admiral and was subordinate to the will of Congress in the execution of the war power.

Lincoln's outlook was quite different. In 1863, he underlined his view of the breadth of his war powers when he promulgated General Order 100 to the armed forces. An elaborate code of rules and regulations as to military laws was established by the Commander in Chief, although the Constitution states clearly that Congress will "make Rules for the Government and Regulation of the land and naval forces." The President, in issuing "Instructions for the Government of the Armies of the United States in the Field," thus expanded the Commander in Chief role, while at the same time he assumed the congressional power to legislate.

In government, as we have seen before, law often follows policy. William Whiting, the War Department's solicitor during the Civil War, supplied much of the legal rationale for presidential action. That structure reared an impressive edifice of logic on a foundation built on the words "amidst the clash of arms the laws are silent." Professor Corwin has noted that Whiting applied the rule specifically to the Bill of Rights of the Constitution. The War Department solicitor contended that the Constitution prescribed no territorial limitations to the President's military operations, which he conducted as Commander in Chief. Further, as President, the Constitution mandates him to see that the laws of "war" as well as peace are faithfully executed. In Whiting's view the laws of war were whatever the military exigency required. Inasmuch as the President was the Commander in Chief who determined those requirements, he, to all intents and purposes, determined the law.

Lincoln, who in one sense needs no defenders, has had an army of them. One, acknowledging the abrogation of written constitutional guarantees, justified them, not in terms of the document itself, but as being in accord with "the spirit of the Constitution."

James Randall, who wrote extensively on constitutional problems under Lincoln, expressed another view. He remarked that before the Civil War the weight of judicial precedent fell on the side of a government restrained by the "rule of law" even when at war; there was no legal basis, according to Randall, for the imposition of martial law and the use of summary procedures without restraint. That, however, is exactly what happened as the Lincoln Administration expanded its conception of the Executive's war power.

In the fall of 1862, the President proclaimed martial law throughout the United States. He justified his action on the grounds that those Americans who were suspected of disloyalty were not "adequately restrained by the ordinary processes of the law." Lincoln enumerated in his proclamation a number of offenses that were not in violation of any statute of the United States. Dissent from administration policy and expressions of unhappiness with the draft law, along with discouragement of enlistment in the armed forces, were now to subject the perpetrator to trial by court-martial or military commission, without recourse to the still functioning civil courts. Chief Justice Taney's warning that civilians would be at the mercy or the whim of the military commanders in their area was quickly proven in the event. The President had extended by proclamation a system of martial law to be applied to *persons* rather than areas. It is worth noting that during World War II both the Civil War suspension of *habeas corpus* and the use of presidential authority for martial law were cited as precedent for the internment in concentration camps of American citizens of Japanese extraction.

Lincoln himself exercised considerable restraint in the use of the powers he had drawn to the Executive. This was not always true of his subordinates. During the spring and summer of 1861 so many newspapers with Confederate sympathies or with anti-Administration views were harassed out of existence that one pro-Administration journal felt called upon to observe that "there is no opposition press to speak of." Perhaps it was a sign of the violent temper of the time that no editor of Union sympathy protested against the quick suppression of freedom of the press. Many have been angered in recent years about government attempts to limit dissent during the Vietnam War. Whatever the merits of each particular case, the historical record provides a different perspective on that issue. Life for a dissenter was far more difficult when the Great Emancipator was President of the United States.

The case of Clement L. Vallandigham illustrates the point. Vallandigham was an Ohio Congressman, a Democrat with strong sympathies for southern views. In May of 1863 he made a speech in which he charged the Administration with prolonging the war by its refusal to negotiate and refusing to accept a French offer of mediation. Vallandigham professed to wish for the preservation of the Union, but he saw war as no way to accomplish the end. He was bitter in his denunciation of Lincoln and called the struggle an attempt to enslave southern white men and to free the blacks. General Burnside ordered Vallandigham arrested immediately. He had issued an order threatening punishment by military courts to all who "declared sympathy for the enemy." Vallandigham, denied *habeas corpus*, refused to enter a plea before a military court which he claimed had no jurisdiction. An "innocent" plea was entered by the military Judge and the Congressman was found guilty and sentenced to imprisonment for the war's duration.

The incident somehow triggered a wave of protest against the system. Lincoln had turned to summary arrest in the first place, in order to avoid causes célébres. A trial usually meant publicity. Simple imprisonment hushed the victim for as long as he was held behind the prison walls. Now Burnside's action had focused the spotlight on the arbitrary nature of the Commander in Chief power when it is exercised without recourse to the legislative will or judicial restraint.

New York's Governor, Horatio Seymour, was himself a Democrat. He spoke scornfully of the Vallandigham arrest. "We pause to see what kind of government it is for which we are asked to pour out our blood and treasure." Ohio Democrats challenged the institution of summary procedures "subject to the will of the President." There was bitter complaint at the arbitrary definition of treason made by military judges without reference to the provisions of the Constitution. Lincoln, above all an astute politician, turned away the wrath by releasing Vallandigham from imprisonment and ordering him to "exile" behind the Confederate lines.

The Ohio Congressman, however, refused to oblige the President. He successfully ran the federal blockade of southern ports and reentered Ohio via Canada. In 1863 he was nominated for Governor and in 1864 he played an active role in the presidential campaign against Lincoln. Not a hand was raised against him. It is of considerable significance, however, that in February, 1864, the Supreme Court refused to review the Vallandigham case, declaring that it had no authority to review the actions of a military commission.

The political context in which the definition and expansion of the presidential war power took place is of primary importance in evaluating the significance of the presidential breakthrough and, also, its inherent limitations. Lincoln took office in the midst of a political hurricane that left a vacuum in its wake. The balance of power that had obtained in Congress between Free State Whigs and Republicans on the one hand and Southern Democrats on the other, was now a thing of the past. All of the antagonisms that had expressed themselves in legislative strife were now to be manifested on the battlefields. But in Congress, Republicans reigned supreme. In the wake of secession, the principal objective of that unchecked Republican leadership was to see that their brothers and enemies be punished as severely as possible. The last thing in the world that most members of the war Congresses were concerned with was any constitutional inhibition that would hinder the prosecution of a victorious war. The hostilities of decades were given free expression and the rule of law was a rhetorical device rather than a living reality. In that respect the presidential decision to enact as many war measures as possible *before* Congress convened turned out to be the essence of political wisdom. There was no way a Congress so strongly opposed to secession could have engaged in a struggle with the President to reverse his "legislative" course. To do so on the high ground of principle would have seemed to the radicals among them to be the work of the devil.

Historians have conjectured that if Congress had been in session many of the same enactments would have been made, but a struggle would have evolved for leadership of the effort to chastise the South. On that level it was a game of political one-upmanship and Lincoln was determined to win. The congressional leadership was nevertheless uneasy that it was thus cast in a subordinate role and when the results on the front lines were less than happy, the effort was quickly made to restore the balance of power between the Executive and the Legislature.

A Joint Committee on the Conduct of the War was set up under the leadership of Thaddeus Stevens, Senators Wade, Chandler and Sumner, and Representative Davis. The Committee brought its weight to bear on strategy, tactics and military organization. Lincoln, in still another expression of his political genius, absorbed the Committee into the executive apparatus. He paid great attention to its recommendations and at one point replaced his Secretary of War with a political figure recommended by the legislative gadflies. Lincoln's subordinates, however, felt that the Committee was an albatross around the executive neck. The President himself was able to handle the situation only as long as there was agreement on questions of policy. When that agreement began to unravel over the question of reconstruction, the lines were drawn for bitter conflict between the Executive and Congress.

The assassination of Abraham Lincoln resulted in a revulsion against the executive dominance of the war years. Congress, with the Committee leaders in the vanguard, asserted its supremacy with a vengeance. President Andrew Johnson's impeachment was the symbolic expression of rebellion against the fallen Commander in Chief. But the powers established by that Commander in Chief before his death have colored our perceptions of the Constitution to the time of this writing.

Lincoln took an increasingly broad view of the Executive's war power as the struggle with the Confederacy increased in its scope and in its cost in blood and treasure. "I think the Constitution invests its Commander in Chief with the *laws of war in time of war*," he wrote to a critic of the Emancipation Proclamation.

It is difficult for us, more than a century later, to conceive of the Emancipation Proclamation as anything other than a human necessity. The war, after all, was fought primarily over the issue of slavery. What was more natural than freeing those held to bondage? But, examined in the time frame of the 1860's and in the context of our concern with the war power, the proclamation presents a somewhat different picture. Although Lincoln felt that slavery was abhorrent, he believed that those enslaved were legally the property of their masters. The Emancipation Proclamation was intended to be an act of permanent expropriation without compensation of private property. It was understood to be exactly that by the President and Congress. But it was the *President* who acted under the "laws of war." Congress had already placed the telegraph and railroad lines under executive control. Although the Emancipation Proclamation was fervently endorsed by almost all shades of public opinion as an expression of moral rectitude, it was issued to facilitate the presidential war power. Only a year earlier the President had told John Charles Frémont, who had been the Republican party's first candidate for the Presidency, that he was constitutionally inhibited from emancipating the slaves. The pressures of the conflict had altered further Lincoln's already large perceptions of the President's inherent war power.

In a private moment with his Secretary of Treasury, Salmon P. Chase, he put the point with sorrow: "These rebels are violating the Constitution to destroy the Union. I will violate the Constitution, if necessary to save the Union, and I suspect, Chase, that our Constitution is going to have a rough time of it before we get done with this row."

The President was the kind of man who would have done anything that he felt necessary to accomplish the great end of preserving the Union, but his position was significantly bolstered by the Supreme Court in its decision on the Prize Cases of 1863. This litigation rose from a dispute over the legality of the blockade imposed on southern ports in the first days of the war. The owners contended that inasmuch as blockade is an act of war the President had acted beyond his constitutional powers when he seized their property. Only Congress, it was contended, could declare war and without such a declaration all acts of war were null and void. The Court, in a 5 to 4 decision, upheld the President.

The majority reasoned that the proclamation itself was a recognition that war already existed by action of the other side. A congressional declaration in such a case was not required in order for the President to pursue his duties as Commander in Chief. This was particularly true in the case of rebellion, when war is never declared. But the Court went further. It noted that Congress, during its first session, had retroactively validated all of the President's war acts. Justice Grier's opinion said that if Lincoln's actions did in fact have a constitutional defect it had been cured by the legislative acquiescence of that first wartime Congress.

Grier explicitly denied the need for such validation. But his reference implies an underlying uneasiness at the broad powers the President had arrogated to himself. The Court's minority held that the blockade was legal only from the time Congress had declared its existence. Thus, the thin margin of a single judicial vote saved the Administration from a severe constitutional confrontation in the midst of a major civil war.

The Prize Case decision supplied Lincoln with legal justification for his own increasingly broad interpretation of the presidential war power. By 1864, he had moved to a point where he could write that "I may in an emergency do things on military grounds which cannot constitutionally be done by the Congress." The President's view, after three years of war, presents a remarkable contrast to his 1861 speech before Congress when he appealed for legislative support. At that time, it will be recalled, Lincoln had said that nothing he had done was *beyond the constitutional competency of Congress.*

There was no disagreement of substance between Congress and the President about the nature and extent of the war power. They both returned, in that time of stress, to the primitive attitude that when blood is shed and life is at stake, the objective is to survive at any cost. The differences that did emerge between

Lincoln and Congress were embedded in questions of power. The Constitution was used, to the extent that the matter came up, as a weapon rather than a writ.

Charles Sumner, the Senator from Massachusetts, was the most articulate spokesman for congressional supremacy in the exercise of war powers under the Constitution. He displayed, throughout his career, a remarkably consistent view of the relationship between Congress and the President; in the years following the Civil War it was to come to flower in something approaching a constitutional crisis; now, in the early days of the conflict, Sumner sounded this theme on the Senate floor:

> The President, it is said, as Commander in Chief, may seize, confiscate and liberate under the Rights of war, but Congress cannot direct these things to be done. Pray, Sir, where is the limitation upon Congress? Read the text of the Constitution, and you will find its powers vast as all the requirements of war . . . I do not mean to question the powers of the President in his sphere . . . but I claim for Congress all that belongs to any government in the exercise of the rights of War. The Government of the United States appears most completely in an Act of Congress. It is by Act of Congress that the War Powers are all put in motion. When once put in motion, the President must execute them. But he is only the instrument of Congress, under the Constitution.

Professor Corwin has argued that Sumner ignored the simple fact that Lincoln had grasped the levers of huge areas of authority that had never before been used as part of the war power and that Congress had passively accepted the presidential requisition. It was that acceptance, and the nature of the emergency that brought it about, that continues to shadow the debate over the war powers in relation to the Constitution. One historian noted that Congress, whenever possible, declined to legislate with regard to presidential prerogative. There appeared to be a feeling that if Congress did not specifically give the sanction of law to Lincoln's actions, some of the power that he had assumed might be retrieved when the emergency was over. Inasmuch as we have since been inundated with "emergencies," it would have been well for Congress to place statutory limits on the presidential war power whenever the opportunity presented itself. The absence of almost anything except "after the fact" validation of presidential authority has provided sanction for the actions of later executives who were no Lincolns and who confronted no crises of the dimensions of the Civil War.

A decision of the Supreme Court, taken in the immediate aftermath of the war, cast a cold constitutional eye on much of the executive activity of the Lincoln era. The decision in *ex parte Milligan* was written, ironically, by Justice David Davis, an old friend from Illinois who had played a key role in getting Lincoln the Republican nomination.

Lambdin Milligan was a citizen of Indiana who had plotted to free a group of Confederate prisoners of war. He and his associates then planned to march with the escaped prisoners to Kentucky and Missouri, where they would make war against the Union forces. Unlike the Vallandigham case, the military were in this instance confronted with a direct operational threat. The plot was discovered and a military commission sentenced Milligan to be hanged. A technicality in the law made it possible for him to take an appeal to the Supreme Court. That technicality was also reinforced by the Union victory. Countervailing forces that previously had failed to assert themselves against the Executive were now coming into play. The Court had refused to review Vallandigham, declaring itself without authority to judge the actions of a military commission. The new climate provided a setting for a reassertion of constitutional principle.

Justice Davis, speaking for a unanimous court, acknowledged that "during the late wicked rebellion the temper of the times did not allow that calmness in deliberation and discussion so necessary to the correct conclusions of a purely judicial question." He went on to note that when "considerations of safety were mixed with the exercise of power" it was not possible to adequately form a legal judgment. Having cleared the ground of the past, Davis ordered Milligan's release on a variety of constitutional grounds. The Court found that martial law could not be applied arbitrarily. A threat of invasion itself was not sufficient. "The necessity must be actual and present; the invasion real, such as effectually closes the courts and deposes the civil administration."

The Court noted that Indiana's courts and civil institutions were in full operation when Milligan had been arrested. This, of course, had been true in thousands of other cases decided by executive fiat. In ordering Milligan's release, the majority laid down the rule that "martial law can never exist where the courts are open and in the proper and unobstructed exercise of their jurisdiction." A four-man minority led by Chief Justice Chase held that although Milligan must be released, there might be occasions when it would be incumbent upon the Government to institute the use of military tribunals to assure the public safety.

"When the nation is involved in war . . . *it is within the power of Congress* to determine to what states or districts . . . public danger exists as justifies the authorization of military tribunals."

Thus, only one year after the close of the Civil War, the Court affirmed that the Executive had usurped the war power, while a strong minority noted that such a power, when it is enforced, is the constitutional prerogative of the Congress. But judicial decisions notwithstanding, it is Abraham Lincoln who is rightly credited with saving the Union. The precedents of his conduct are those with which each succeeding administration and each new Congress has been obliged to wrestle.

Lincoln was the first President to marshal the country for what has come to be called "total war." In so doing, he set the pattern for the actions of Presidents Wilson and Roosevelt in the great conflicts to come. Public opinion, too, had been molded to anticipate an executive leadership that would assert itself across the entire fabric of the national life during periods of emergency. That opinion made it easier for later Congresses to submit to executive authority during time of war, with little or no question as to the proprieties. But other lessons had been learned. Congress, in the future, would legislate by statute all of the broad authority needed to wage modern war. Congressional action would give constitutional credence to presidential authority during both of the great world wars.

Power, nevertheless, feeds on itself, and extra-constitutional extension of the presidential war power has continued to manifest itself as American international interests have exploded across the globe. Even today we confront the issue raised by James Randall when he wrote, "If Lincoln was a dictator, it must be admitted that he was a benevolent Dictator. Yet in a Democracy it is a serious question how far even a benevolent dictatorship should be encouraged."

XI

"Too Grave for Silence"

". . . the employment of the Navy without the authority of Congress in acts of hostility against a friendly nation, or in belligerent intervention in the affairs of a foreign nation, is an infraction of the Constitution of the United States and a usurpation of power not conferred upon the President."

ON March 24, 1871, Charles Sumner spoke those words to the United States Senate. His scorching indictment of the Chief Executive's abuse of his authority came at the height of a dispute over war power that accompanied President Ulysses Grant's drive to annex the Dominican Republic to the United States. Sumner's resolutions of censure were a direct challenge to an assertion of executive will that had fueled a feud between the President and the Chairman of the Senate Foreign Relations Committee.

Along with a now-indivisible nation, Lincoln's heritage included the need to reshape its institutions. When John Wilkes Booth killed the President, he had murdered the one man who might have been able to restore the Union without opening a new era of partisan strife. That strife was exemplified by the battle between President Andrew Johnson and the first Congress of the Reconstruction era. The "High Crimes and Misdemeanors" for which Johnson was impeached symbolized a legislative thrust at the executive preemption of power during four years of civil war. A revulsion against presidential authority had set in, clothed in the trappings of debate over the Reconstruction issue.

Charles Sumner was in the forefront of those who were most determined to demonstrate legislative supremacy over national affairs. Although the move against Andrew Johnson failed by a single vote, his effectiveness was destroyed and the power of Congress to make policy across the board was reestablished for the duration of his administration. Sumner emerged as the principal leader of the congressional radicals. His moral fervor, molded to one of the best minds in the Senate chamber, enabled him to wield a power over national affairs and international relations that placed him on an equal footing with the President and his principal agents. Not since Henry Clay had a legislator exercised such influence.

Sumner was entitled to his precedence on the basis of a record that had placed him in the forefront of the fight for abolition and made him a martyr to his convictions immediately before the Civil War. (He had been brutally assaulted by a southern Congressman as he sat in his Senate chair; it was three years before he could resume his seat at the height of the conflict.) But according to his biographer, David Donald, Sumner's strong conviction and brilliant intellect were marred by a self-righteousness and a lack of humor that prevented him from recognizing that other men could hold other views with equal conviction. One British diplomat who observed the quarrel between Grant and Sumner remarked that it was quite unnecessary. A proper deference, he thought, would have been sufficient to satisfy the Senator, inasmuch as "he is at this time the vainest of Americans." But the vanity had taken its toll of the tolerance of the President's principal aides. He was a marked man.

Sumner's attitudes blocked Grant's ambition to continue to expand the territory of the United States. His Puritan sensibilities were deeply offended by what he perceived as an abdication of the President's moral leadership. The Massachusetts Senator saw the corruption of Grant's administration long before any equivalent figure was willing to give it credence. When the former General used the war power to support his wish to annex Santo

Domingo to the United States, the two men came into open conflict.

Grant was convinced that the Dominican Republic was especially desirable territory for American acquisition. He had been particularly influenced by Secretary of State Seward's expansionist views; now, in his own administration, he determined to add luster to the Grant years with a tropical isle that would supply the United States with impressive coffee and sugar crops, and a fine naval base in Samana Bay. The need for a naval station, to Grant's way of thinking, was to guard Caribbean waters against threats to the isthmian canal that would someday link the two American coasts.

The President was encouraged in his wish to make an American possession of the Dominican Republic by newspaper articles that appeared in the New York *Sun* under the byline of Cora Montgomery. Miss Montgomery, it will be remembered, was the former Jane Storms of Mexican War notoriety. She was now the wife of General William L. Cazneau, an American promoter with large-scale interests in the island of Santo Domingo. The Montgomery articles stirred memories in Grant of America's manifest destiny. The fact that major financial interests were also involved did not disturb a President who was deeply impressed by the gambling millionaires of the day, Jay Gould and Jim Fisk. They might not have been popular in the reform press, but the President himself, it is now generally recognized, was impressed with the ability to turn a quick dollar. Though Grant was personally honest, he presided over a nest of aides who were interested principally in lining their own pockets.

The President of the Dominican Republic was himself hardly a figure to inspire confidence in a Senator like Charles Sumner. Buenaventura Báez had literally placed his country on the auction block. Dominican annexation to the United States was, in Báez's eyes, the only way he could save himself from the revolutionaries who had allied themselves with the new Haitian government. At the same time there was a profit to be made on the presidency that would enable him to lead a more than comfortable life under the protection of the American flag and under the muzzles of United States naval guns in Samana Bay.

It is important to remember, at this point, that the Dominican Republic shares the island of San Domingo with the Republic of Haiti. This proximity was a significant factor in events to come.

Sumner regarded the Haitian Republic as an important experiment in black self-government. Back in the 1840's he had argued in the Massachusetts courts against "separate but equal" school facilities. His activities on behalf of black civil rights have a contemporary ring. Sumner's participation in that early struggle convinced him that it was essential to permit black self-government to develop without interference from American interests. The annexation of the Dominican Republic, he felt, would lead inevitably to the acquisition of Haiti and the other black populated islands that dotted the Caribbean Sea.

That Sumner's view was shared by others, who were deeply involved in the annexation scheme, is evidenced by a conversation the Senator had with Joseph Fabens of Greytown fame. Fabens was now a partner of General Cazneau in his Dominican ventures. He appeared in Washington as an official emissary of President Báez in order to bring influence to bear on those who might have weight in the annexation fight to come. When Sumner questioned him, Fabens remarked enthusiastically that after the Dominican Republic, "you must have Haiti too." In the nature of things, he added, the United States would finally absorb all of the West Indies. If Sumner had had any doubts as to his position, the conversation with proselytizer Fabens must have done much to resolve them.

Secretary of State Hamilton Fish also had reservations about the Dominican annexation. But his loyalty to the President and his own dedication to the accomplishment of other foreign policy objectives kept him from arguing the point. In the rising conflict to come, it was the President himself who determined his course. Grant, the Civil War's great Union hero, was enormously popular. He was ready to use that popularity in an attempt to persuade Congress to yield to his views on the Dominican issue. Only a series of blunders and misplaced confidences prevented him from succeeding in his objective.

The President sent his principal aide, General Orville Babcock, to the Dominican Republic to confer with Foreign Minister

Gautler and to examine the ground on the spot. Grant wished to determine whether annexation was as popular among the Dominican people as he had been led to believe by Báez and those Americans who were interested in the project. When Babcock arrived on the scene, he immediately became an intimate of General Cazneau and Fabens. Under their guidance, Babcock was quickly converted to the absolute necessity of bringing the Dominican Republic under the sheltering wing of the United States. He suited his actions to his views.

Babcock negotiated two treaties with President Báez. The first was for the annexation of the Dominican Republic. Just in case that failed to pass in the United States Senate, the American consul, on November 29, 1869, put his signature to another document that called for the leasing of Samana Bay as an American naval base. Báez, who was hard-pressed for funds to fight against the revolutionaries, demanded and received a cash payment of $150,000 for the base facilities. The Dominican Republic was to be paid one and a half million dollars when the Senate approved the treaty of annexation.

The Babcock-Báez protocols were unusual on two counts. Article 2 of the treaty of annexation contained the written statement that President Grant would not present the treaty to the Senate until he was assured that a majority favored its passage, to which end the President pledged his "best efforts." No other treaty in American history embodies in writing a commitment by the Chief Executive to influence the Senate which is constitutionally obligated to give him its "advice and consent."

Article 6 was an assurance that no grants or concessions would be given by the Dominican Government to any private parties following the signing of the documents. Knowledge of just such concessions to the Cazneau group soon became widespread. President Báez had given, in return for a "geologic survey," some 200,000 acres of land and mineral rights to Cazneau and his partners. The information leaked into the American press along with gossip to the effect that plots of property along the waterfront on Samana Bay were marked with the names of Fabens, Báez, Cazneau and Grant. It is difficult to credit the latter story, but the widespread circulation it received illustrates the negative public opinion which began to build on the question of further extension of American territory.

President Grant ignored the rumors of misbehavior among his aides and their friends at the same time as he brushed aside the pleas of Dominican exiles who asserted that the Dominican people wished to maintain their independence. Grant pointed to the plebiscite that had endorsed annexation to the United States. That plebiscite was the occasion for the dispute over presidential abuse of the war powers.

Secretary Fish had informed Babcock officially that the President directed him "in case of the execution of such treaty and convention . . . as an Officer of the Army of the United States to take steps to carry out the agreement of the United States contained in said treaty *to protect the people of that Republic against foreign interference* while the nation is expressing its will and also *to protect the interests and rights which the United States may obtain under such convention.*" Grant had previously, in the summer of the year, ordered the American warship *Seminole* (an appropriate echo of past executive incursions) to drive a Dominican rebel ship from the seas. "This vessel has been interfering with American commerce . . . seize her and bring her into the port of Baltimore." The *Telegrafo* was commanded by General Luperon, one of President Báez's principal rivals for power. Now, with the sanction of an unratified treaty to support him, the President in his instructions to Babcock drew on the same "inchoate interest" asserted by President Tyler when he invaded Texas with American troops in order to "protect" the Texans when they voted for annexation. The precedent that had been established on our own continent was thus extended to the high seas. The theme was further strengthened when Secretary of the Navy Robeson ordered the U.S.S. *Tuscarora* into Dominican waters to provide Babcock with "the moral support of its guns," although no such support was necessary for the success of Babcock's mission. Báez, however, soon found himself under attack for having signed away his country's independence. A successful Haitian revolution on the other half of the island gave sanctuary to Dominican rebels and the outlook for Báez's political and personal survival became uncertain. He immediately demanded support from Washington. Grant, without consultation with Congress, dispatched a number of warships to the area. By the end of February, 1870, *before the treaty of annexation was submitted to Congress,* seven men-of-war cruised the Dominican waters to protect Báez from the consequences of domestic insurrection.

The most explicit warlike action was taken when the *Severn,* flagship of the United States North Atlantic fleet, sailed into port at the Haitian capital of Port-au-Prince. There, Rear Admiral Poor, at the instructions of General Grant, sent the following message to Haiti's President Saget:

Sir:
The undersigned avails himself of the arrival at this port of the *Severn,* flagship of the United States North Atlantic Fleet, accompanied by the monitor *Dictator* (an unintended irony) to inform His Excellency that he, the undersigned, has instructions from his Government to inform His Excellency that negotiations are now pending between the United States Government at Washington and the Government at Santo Domingo and that during the existence of such negotiations, the United States Government has determined, with all its power, to prevent any interference on the part of the Haitians, or any other power, with the Dominican Government.

Any interference or attack, therefore, by vessels under the Haitian or any other flag upon the Dominicans during the pendency of such negotiations will be considered an act of hostility to the flag of the United States and will provoke hostility in return.

The Haitian government uttered not a word of response to Admiral Poor's ultimatum. Any further hint of revolutionary interference or Haitian intervention disappeared from consideration and Báez held his annexation vote on an island surrounded by a protective circle of United States warships. The results were a stunning affirmation of popular support for selling the Dominican Republic to the highest (and the only) bidder. First reports from Santo Domingo said that only eleven voters out of sixteen thousand polled had disapproved. A recount raised the negative vote to approximately 2 percent. If Báez and his friends had won a victory with the support of American arms, Grant's battle was yet to begin.

The President knew that Charles Sumner was the key to Senate approval of the annexation treaty. He and Secretary of State Fish did everything in their power to convince Sumner that he should lend his weight to the pro-treaty forces. As Chairman of the Foreign Relations Committee, Sumner's views were likely to have a major influence on the outcome. But the relationship between the Senator and the Administration was complicated by the Radical Republican view that policy should be made by Congress and executed by the President. In the aftermath of Lincoln's death that power had been seized from a President whose political views were antipathetic to the Republican majority. Now, however, the Presidency was occupied by a man who stood for everything for which the Republican party had fought. Grant meant to seize the executive initiative that had been lost during the Johnson years. In his eyes, Sumner stood in the way of the restoration of what the President considered to be a desirable balance of power between the branches of government. On issue after issue the President felt that Sumner had delayed or prevented executive policies from full implementation. Fish later said that Sumner attempted to arrogate the powers of the Secretary of State to the Foreign Relations Committee, despite the constitutional mandate that the President is to direct the foreign policy of the United States. The battle over Dominican annexation was to be the breaking point; the abuse of the war powers was to be Sumner's point of attack.

On a winter evening in early 1870, the President called on Sumner at his home just across the park from the White House. Over a glass of wine he appealed, as a matter of party loyalty, for the Chairman's support. Witnesses to the encounter differed over Sumner's response. But the majority of those present were at one time or another under the impression that Sumner, who had described himself as "an administration man," was ready to go along. Looking back on the event, however, Sumner, who had a reputation for diligent examination of the issues before his committee, asked rhetorically how he could have acquiesced in the treaty when he had not yet examined a single document related to its inception.

Grant, thinking he had persuaded Sumner to agree to annexation, was shocked when he learned that the Foreign Relations Committee had reported negatively on the treaty by a vote of 5 to 2 and with the Chairman leading the majority. In the Senate as a whole the Administration was able to secure only 28 out of 56 votes, instead of the necessary two-thirds majority required by the Constitution.

Ulysses Grant had "[stuck] it out along this line all summer" in the battle for Richmond. He was ready to do as much on behalf of the annexation of Santo Domingo. He chose patronage as his weapon in this war against senatorial resistance, and although he was unable to succeed in his objective he did remove a friend of Senator Sumner from his position as United States minister to London. The relations between the President, his Secretary of State and the Massachusetts Senator deteriorated beyond repair. Sumner's determination to stand against the treaty was reinforced by the Committee's examination of the documents. In hearings held over the course of the ensuing months, Sumner's suspicions that corrupt influences had been brought to bear were supported by a number of responsible witnesses. And, vitally important, in the Senator's view, the Constitution had been deliberately violated when the Executive used armed force to assert American interests without congressional authorization.

Sumner, who had demanded congressional supremacy over war power at the height of the Lincoln era, was certainly in no mood to abandon the Constitution to Grant. When the President, in December of the same year, asked once again for congressional approval of the treaty, Sumner rose to speak to the issue. "The resolution before Congress commits Congress to a dance of blood . . . it is a new step in a measure of violence which so far as it has been maintained has been upheld by violence ever since." He scathingly recalled Admiral Poor's threat to the Haitian government to "blow the town down." If the Admiral had been ordered to "insult a sister Republic too weak to resist," he should "rather than carry out such instructions have thrown his sword into the sea."

The Senator asserted that no law of the United States, only "the law of force," could vindicate the President in his use of the United States Navy to protect Báez against his own people and to threaten the helpless Haitian Republic. Addressing Vice President Schuyler Colfax, he pleaded that he "counsel the President not to follow the example of Franklin Pierce . . . not to allow the oppression of a weak and humble people; ask him not to exercise war powers without authority of Congress."

Sumner became increasingly isolated in the Senate during the battle over annexation. He had spurned party discipline. Although his December speech was made in the midst of a debate that substantially ended all chance of an annexation of the Dominican Republic, for Sumner it was a Pyrrhic victory. The President was determined to assert his authority as party leader and the Republican majority, rallying behind the Administration, stripped Sumner of his committee chairmanship.

On March 27, 1871, after a serious illness, Sumner took the Senate floor to speak on behalf of a resolution censuring the President for using an American naval force to intervene in Santo Domingo. As he entered the chamber his admirers burst into applause. He earned their approval with a classic address on the power to make war. Ulysses Grant, he thundered, had disobeyed the law. The United States Navy, "acting under orders from Washington, has been engaged in measures of violence, and of belligerent interventions, being war . . . without the authority of Congress. Such a case cannot pass without inquiry. *It is too grave for silence.*"

Sumner noted that the treaty of annexation had been obtained under the duress of American guns. For the President of the Dominican Republic could not have been maintained in power without the assistance of the United States Navy. The treaty was therefore null and void under law. Sumner charged the duress was itself a violation of international law, inasmuch as it was an "interference in the internal affairs" of another country. The slogans of today's conflicts are not all freshly minted.

Declaring that Grant's use of naval force transgressed the Constitution, Sumner noted that the "Kingly prerogative" of war had not been confided by the Constitution's authors to a single individual. Rather, "it was placed under the safeguard of the people, as represented *in that highest form of national life, an act of Congress.* No other provision in the Constitution is more distinctive, or more worthy of veneration." He noted that Justice Joseph Story, one of the most famous of the commentators on the Constitution, had remarked that "it should be difficult in a Republic to declare war," and that such a declaration is "the highest act of *legislation.*"

If the President were a king, Sumner said, he could have done as he had done in the Dominican Republic. Inasmuch as the Constitution provided for no crown, "the Constitution has been dismissed out of sight like a discharged soldier."

Senator Oliver Morton of Indiana was one of those who replied on Grant's behalf. He noted that President Tyler had regarded a Mexican threat to Texas as "highly offensive to the United States" and that he had taken military action to prevent a Mexican move. Morton's citation of Tyler as precedent for Grant's action drew a scathing retort from Sumner's ally, Senator Carl Schurz. It was "absurd and audacious," Schurz said, to contend that "the President can, under the Constitution, steal the war-making power from Congress under the shallow pretense of having created by his own arbitrary act an inchoate right of the United States in a foreign country, thus creating for himself the power to use belligerent measures to enforce that inchoate right." The Senator from Missouri denied that bad precedent (like Greytown) made good principle. "An act of usurpation once submitted to without resistance," he told the Senate, "is no reason why its repetition should not be condemned, rebuked and resisted."

But Senator Schurz was speaking against a national tendency to look to past action as a guide for future conduct. This factor in the development of executive authority over the right to make war is exemplified by a comment made by Clarence Berdahl, who wrote in the 1920's one of the definitive works on presidential use of the war power.

Berdahl, referring to a series of American interventions in South American affairs, commented that "the use of Marines has been so common as to warrant the suggestion of *a new consti-*

tutional principle, that the landing of Marines may be considered as 'a mere local police measure,' while the use of regulars for the same purpose would be an act of war."

Senator Sumner would have disagreed with the premise that if the law is violated frequently enough, the violations are magically elevated into "constitutional principle." Ironically, he won the battle for Dominican independence. Congress refused to annex the island. But when the Senate tabled his resolutions reaffirming the congressional war power, Sumner lost the battle he had fought on behalf of the Senate's own authority under the Constitution. For the rest of the century American foreign policy was wedded to the virtually unchallenged power of the President to use the armed forces at his own discretion. The trend was even more firmly established as American commerce and the American flag penetrated for the first time into Pacific islands and Asian lands.

XII

Little Brown Brothers
and Harmonious Fists

"I KNOW of no way to come out but to get out." The words were spoken by William McKinley. Inasmuch as he was President of the United States, he was able to apply them to the situation in which twenty-five hundred American troops in China found themselves in the early part of this century. They *did* come out.

But the American people are still very much *in* Southeast Asia and McKinley himself must bear some of the historic responsibility. His Presidency spanned the period between America's effort to build a continental republic and an age in which the United States flag began to symbolize a presence in affairs of state in every part of the globe. A nation which was dedicated to "no entangling alliances" has forged a series of international relationships that dominate the business of our government, affecting the lives and deaths of our own sons as well as those of the millions of people of Indochina. America's outward thrust has put foreign policy in first place among the priorities of the most influential statesmen of the twentieth century. The exhilarating triumphs of that order of business have been replaced in our time with the agony of Vietnam and with a rising chorus of question as to the value of the system itself.

On March 18, 1971, the Senate Foreign Relations Committee began a series of hearings on a bill I introduced to reestablish the constitutional division of war powers between

Congress and the President. Professor Henry Steele Commager, speaking to that issue, put the question in its most significant context. He noted "twenty years of repeated, and almost routine, invasions by the Executive" of powers assigned under the Constitution to Congress. But Professor Commager's concern went beyond the legal implications.

> . . . we can see that more is at stake even than the constitutional principle of the separation of powers. At stake is the age-long effort of men to fix effective limits on government; at stake is the reconciliation of the claims of freedom and of security; at stake the fateful issue of peace or war, an issue fateful not for the American people alone, not alone for the stricken peoples of Southeast Asia, but for the whole of mankind.

Commager's words sharply define the problems we confront in the 1970's. But they were foreshadowed on the eve of this century, when the American flag began to fly beyond the bounds of the North American continent.

William McKinley got those American troops out. But it was his administration that put them there in the first place. From 1898 until shortly before his death in 1901, American forces took the Philippines during a successful war with Spain, then defeated the Filipino insurrectionists when they attempted to wrest independence from the United States, and simultaneously landed a contingent of Marines in China to help put down the Boxer Rebellion. President McKinley's actions, and those of his immediate successors, dramatized the inherent ability of the Executive to aggrandize his own prerogatives within the context of a perfectly legal exercise of constitutionally assigned authority. As the United States asserted itself on the international scene, the presidential role as sole executor of the foreign policy of the United States and Commander in Chief of the armed forces came to shadow and finally to dominate the processes that determine peace or war.

The events of the Spanish-American War are a part of the national folklore. "Remember the Maine" and "Dewey at Manila" were newspaper headlines that burned themselves into the history books. The impulses that swept us into that war and the consequences of our involvement are very much to the point of executive encroachment on the war powers. The conventional wisdom has it that the conflict with Spain was a product of yellow journalism, that it was, in reality, a war stimulated and forced on the United States by William Randolph Hearst in the days of his glory. Hearst's journalism, however, was a product of national impulse rather than its progenitor. Cuba, ninety miles from our shores, had always been a part of the American expansionist dream. The opportunity to remove Spain from the Western Hemisphere once and for all, while at the same time supporting the Cubans in their struggle for independence, was too much to resist.

A reluctant President McKinley (at least he presented the appearance of reluctance) permitted himself to be "guided" into the clash by the United States Congress. There is no question that the Spanish-American War opened as an expression of the will of a Congress responding to the wishes of its constituency. The consequences were fearful. A train of events that brought the United States into conflict with the very principles for which it fought in Cuba was set, perhaps inevitably, into motion. At the same time the loss of congressional power was sharply accelerated in the course of this popular war. Encouraging conflict with Spain, Congress helped to trigger the diminution of its own power.

There is, in the words of William Blake, a "fearful symmetry" to the events of the past seven decades. We began fighting for Cuban independence, and in short order, found ourselves putting down a fight for Filipino freedom. American intentions were "good," as they were in Vietnam. One Senator observed at the time that the road to Hell is paved with good intentions. The geography has not changed. Allied with us in the struggle against Spain, the Filipinos had relied on the generosity of American power to assure them of their liberty in the wake of Spain's inevitable defeat. They found themselves instead continuing against us the guerrilla war they had waged for years against their Spanish masters. But American firepower proved too much for Emilio Aguinaldo and his *insurrectos*.

After nearly four years of bloody conflict, the United States was able to make good its mastery of an archipelago only four hundred miles from the China coast. At the same time, American forces jumped off from the Philippines to join a "concert" of European powers in putting down the Boxer Rebellion. How had we moved so far from home? Who was at the controls?

The rapid movement beyond our own shores was the natural expression of a frontier people with no frontiers left to explore. It was the natural expression of the vitality of a burgeoning population with a sense of manifest destiny and a window on the Pacific. It was the natural expression of the trading impulses of a commercial people whose ships had sailed around the globe since the days before independence. The China trade was already a staple of New England myth and the foundation of a good many New England fortunes long before our Marines landed at Tientsin to protect American lives and property.

The European watchword that "the flag follows commerce" was preempted in the late nineteenth century by a vigorous United States, as it gradually abandoned the concept of a unified federation of states under the Constitution for a new nationalism that embraced colonial expansion to stimulate commercial growth. Events moved so rapidly and public opinion shifted with such dramatic force that Congress, for the first time, began to lose its institutional equilibrium. The pressures were so varied and so intense that it began to appear that only executive decision-makers had the information and the power to exercise adequate response. Grover Cleveland was the last American President to recognize explicitly that his power to acquire territory and to make war was constitutionally limited. In 1893 he sent Congress a message in which he withdrew a treaty for the annexation of the Hawaiian Islands. Cleveland's message is a masterpiece of narrative exposition. He clarified the impulses behind American expansionism and the ways in which executive power (when unhindered by self-restraint) can be abused beyond constitutional discretion.

Cleveland revealed to Congress that a group of insurgents, principally Americans, had decided to overthrow the Hawaiian Queen, Liliuokalani, to achieve the islands' annexation. They were convinced that their commercial interests, principally in sugar, would be best served if Hawaii was part of the American union. The only difficulty facing the growers was the fact that the large majority of the population was loyal to the Queen. Taking advantage of the great distance between Washington and Honolulu, John Stevens, the American minister, triggered a *coup d'état.*

The problem, from Cleveland's viewpoint, was that the *coup* was backed by the United States Marines. The "rebels" had absolutely no other armed force at their disposal. Stevens ordered a detachment of one hundred and sixty United States Marines to land and take possession of some of the city's key areas.

The Queen, in Cleveland's words, "knew that she could not withstand the power of the United States, but she believed that she might safely trust to its justice." Accordingly, she surrendered, in the hope that Washington would reject the "invasion" of its own forces on behalf of a small group of insurgents representing only their private interests.

Liliuokalani was fortunate. When President Cleveland assumed office he investigated the circumstances under which the treaty of annexation had been negotiated with Hawaii's provisional government and rejected it out of hand. Noting that "the Provisional Government owes its existence to an armed invasion by the United States," the President commented that he misunderstood the American people "if they favor the odious doctrine that there is one law for a strong nation and another for a weak one."

When he refused to negotiate with the provisional government, the President said that "by an act of war, committed with the participation of a diplomatic representative of the United States and without authority of Congress, the Government of a feeble but friendly and confiding people has been overthrown." He added his willingness to cooperate in any "legislative plan" that could help to solve the problem "consistent with American honor, integrity and morality." A short five years later the problem was solved. The United States annexed the Hawaiian Islands in connection with its need to support naval operations during the short-lived war with Spain.

Cleveland's response to usurpation of the war power from

within his own branch of the government was almost unique. Not since President James Buchanan's frustration at congressional refusal to authorize armed force in Central America had a President bowed specifically to the constitutional requirement that has become so vital in our own era. (Buchanan had remarked that without legislative authority, he had no right to fire a single gun or land a single Marine in any foreign port.) But, for the record, it must be observed that Democrat Cleveland's obeisance to congressional authority came in the wake of an action taken by a previous Republican administration. In the years to come, Presidents from both parties took an increasingly large view of their authority in situations analogous to the Hawaiian annexation plot.

The growing executive drive was encouraged by a new mood of national assertiveness that was closely related to the ambition for supremacy in international trade. Perhaps Senator Albert Beveridge best expressed the attitude in a speech that has come to be regarded as the anthem of American imperialism. Speaking in Boston, Beveridge sketched out the opportunities offered by the war with Spain. "We are a conquering race . . . we must obey our blood and occupy new markets, and, if necessary, new lands." Then, for the first time, Americans heard the demand for vigorous international trade as a substitute for domestic "overproduction." (This, before the year 1900!)

> American factories are making more than the American people can use; American soil is producing more than they can consume. Fate has written our policy for us; the trade of the world must and shall be ours . . . American law, American order, American civilization, and the American flag will plant themselves on shores hitherto bloody and benighted, but by those agencies of God henceforth to be made beautiful and bright.
>
> In the Pacific . . . Spain has an Island empire, the Philippine Archipelago. It is poorly defended . . . In the Pacific the United States has a powerful squadron. The Philippines are logically our first target.

Senator Beveridge's call to arms was widely heralded. More important, it was also acted upon. Brooks Adams, one of the country's leading intellectuals, impressed on Oliver Wendell Holmes the importance of the American overseas mission. Others, who would not have chosen to phrase their feelings in Beveridge's prose, felt essentially the same way.

Theodore Roosevelt and Henry Cabot Lodge, figures who later played large roles in the determination of American policy, responded to the settlement of the American continent with a determination to extend national power beyond its geographic limits. Their natural impulses were reinforced by the intellectual formulations of a brilliant naval theoretician, Captain Alfred Mahan. His principal work, *The Influence of Sea Power Upon History*, became the Bible of American imperialism. Mahan, thinking in terms of the history of maritime powers of the seventeenth and eighteenth centuries, argued that foreign commerce was the "life blood" of nations bordering on the sea. He contended that the United States had failed to match its capacity for industrial production with a maritime capacity that would carry that production round the world and return with an equivalent flow of goods and gold.

To Mahan, maritime capacity meant a strong navy, coaling stations to which it could repair for fuel when sailing great distances from the American continent and colonies as markets and defense sectors. National defense, Mahan believed, was best implemented "far away from our own coast." Thus, a new element had entered into the philosophy of those who would exercise major influence on the way the nation looked at its institutions and the way those institutions would function in the twentieth century. It was a long way from the era when the Constitution-makers had authorized the President to use the armed forces to "repel invasion." The phrase "national defense" was destined for repeated and bewildering redefinition.

Theodore Roosevelt, in many ways the first of our "modern" Chief Executives, was deeply influenced by Mahan's concept of the relationship between commerce and national mission. At the very beginning of the Spanish-American War, Roosevelt was an Assistant Secretary of the Navy. He took advantage of the absence of his superior, Secretary Long, to see to it that Admiral

George Dewey assumed command of the Navy's Asiatic Squadron. Roosevelt, poring over the Pacific maps, wanted the aggressive Dewey at the ready when the inevitable conflict came. The Philippine Archipelago and Manila Bay were there for the taking. (The war was to be fought for Cuban freedom.) Beveridge made the speeches, but TR placed the men who did the job.

Roosevelt's action, in a way, was symbolic of the increasing frustration of congressional authority. Even before his accession to presidential power, his position within the executive branch had enabled him to initiate action with an eye to further steps that would eventually violate the constitutional separation of powers. That *sub rosa* executive authority has, if anything, been increased in our day to a point where even anonymous White House assistants can wield such power. The concept of executive privilege has protected many a "shadowy" figure housed in the Executive Office Building from direct accountability to Congress and the people. Constitutional erosion proceeds on more than one front.

But Assistant Secretary of the Navy Roosevelt's action was at least the mark of a vigorous man with the ability and the daring to take large chances on behalf of his conception of national destiny. The fact remains, however, that no matter the size of the men or the convictions that impelled their decisions, the executive powers exercised during the Filipino insurrection and the Boxer Rebellion were, it seems to me, unconstitutional invasions of the congressional war powers.

There is irony in William McKinley's role as presidential ground-breaker. Historians have frequently pictured him as a "small-time politician," or a "tool" in the hands of "Boss Hanna." McKinley did have the manner of a Fourth of July orator; he was not graced with the wit or style of the giants of the Republic and he did have close relations with other politicians who belonged to the same political party and who shared many of his views. The record indicates that grace and wit are not necessarily requisite to strong political leadership, and that effective government results often from the effectiveness of one's political alliances. (Mark Hanna, incidentally, along with most of the leaders of the business community, was vehemently opposed to war with Spain. They saw the conflict as a threat to a recently revived prosperity under a pro-business Republican administration.)

But if McKinley was his own man, he was at the same time extraordinarily responsive to the political currents of his time. The acts of his administration do bear the mark of his views. But those views changed rapidly to reflect the sudden outburst of national self-awareness that swept across the United States. One newspaper, observing a phenomenon that was to become a commonplace of our later history, commented that "a flag over every schoolhouse door" seemed inappropriate in the context of "read-in', writin' and 'rithmetic." McKinley was able to respond to this quickening of the tempo of American ambition and power by using one of the principal tools of political survival: adaptation to reality. In his judgment that adaptation required that the executive branch of the government shift the national objectives of the war with Spain and that the United States fight an undeclared war with the Filipinos in order to assure America a large element of Pacific power.

The President was a transitional figure. He was torn by conflicting impulses. At the same time as he moved to act alone against the Filipinos, he did everything in his power to keep our involvement in the Boxer Rebellion as tentative as possible. Yet even here he acted alone. McKinley's hesitancies reflected a nineteenth-century commitment to older values. His assertions of executive authority came of an awareness that the country stood on the threshold of the twentieth century in which all of the Presidency's latent power would be fully exploited.

The war with Spain was a jingoist dream. In less than one hundred days American troops had taken San Juan Hill (and the rest of Cuba), destroyed the Spanish navy in Caribbean waters and driven Spain from her Philippine jewel. Admiral Dewey in the Battle of Manila Bay spoke the famous words, "Fire when ready, Gridley." When the smoke cleared in the aftermath of Gridley's fire, American seamen first looked on in awed silence and then broke into loud cheering. It was as though the spine of Spanish power had finally snapped, thousands of miles from the home shores of a centuries-old empire. Seven Spanish battleships were grounded, sunk or on the way to the bottom. Not one American vessel sustained serious damage and United States casualties numbered nine. The nation glowed.

Four years later the glow had worn off. Aguinaldo's *insurrectos* had inflicted eight thousand casualties on the Americans and twenty thousand Filipinos had died in battle. William McKinley, who told the American people in 1897 that annexation of a territory by force of arms would be "criminal aggression," had changed his mind. His astonishing claim that just before the war opened he could not have located the Philippines within two thousand miles did him less than justice. But the President was attempting to justify a change in political course on the basis of a higher morality. It was essential that no hint of national self-interest shadow the forcible acquisition of territory belonging to a foreign power. McKinley explained the reasons for American annexation to a group of visiting clergymen; "I walked the floor of the White House night after night . . . and I am not ashamed to tell you . . . that I went down on my knees and prayed to Almighty God for light and guidance more than one night."

The President went on to say that divine authority revealed to him that to give the islands back to Spain would be "cowardly and dishonorable," that to permit annexation by "our commercial rivals in the Orient—that would be bad business and discreditable," and that the Filipinos themselves were "unfit for self-government." Under the circumstances, the President concluded, "there was nothing left for us to do but to take them all, and to educate the Filipinos, and uplift and civilize and Christianize them, and by God's grace do the very best we could by them. . . ." Having reached that conclusion, Mr. McKinley "went to bed and went to sleep and slept soundly."

But the domestic opposition to a war with the Filipinos found no such rest. Many Americans remembered Aguinaldo's innocent rallying cry, "There where you see the American flag flying, assemble in number, they are our redeemers." To the anti-imperialists at home our insistence on taking the Philippines as an American outpost in Asian waters was a betrayal of the impulses that had initially brought us into the war with Spain. The American fighting men confronting the Filipinos on their home islands had other problems. Dewey himself had said in the halcyon days of alliance that the Filipinos were effective fighting men with distinctive qualities of leadership and intelligence that compared favorably to those of other Asian peoples. Now they had turned into "niggers" and "googoos." The President may have been interested in lifting them up, but the troops, confronted with savage opposition, wished to "civilize 'em with a Krag," the closest approximation of the B-52 bomber they had at their disposal.

As the fighting raged across the archipelago, the military instituted increasingly effective methods of repression. General Jake Smith ordered all civilians suspected of sympathy for the insurrection into a series of zones of concentration or camps that were remarkably similar to the pacification areas introduced into Vietnam. Anyone found outside these zones, the General ordered, was to be shot. He made the mistake of putting his orders down on paper. "I want you to kill and burn." Smith included boys of ten in the list of enemies to be eliminated and he told his troops that he wished the island to be made into a "howling wilderness." A court-martial "admonished" him for the severity of his instructions. But those instructions were in the spirit of a conflict in which American troops were rumored to have sliced the ears from fallen Filipinos as trophies of battle.

In order to get information on *insurrecto* movements the Americans frequently resorted to the "water cure," a form of torture in which the victim is forcibly filled with liquid until his body distends and he talks or dies. The treatment was charged against the French in Algeria and against Americans in pursuit of the elusive Viet Cong. During the guerrilla war in the Philippines, American generals instituted a "body count" procedure that showed a 20 to 1 "kill ratio" in our favor.

Not all observers on the scene were so sanguine as Generals Otis, Lawton and MacArthur. (The latter incidentally commented that the Filipinos required "ten years of bayonet rule" rather than any nonsense about civil government.) Despite a stringent censorship, introduced by the military in order to gloss over the difficulties of the fighting, correspondents managed to inform American readers that this was a war that was not going nearly as well as the conflict with Spain. The Kansas City *Times* said that "every day adds to the expenditure of lives and treasure in this war prosecuted for greed and territorial aggrandizement." A correspondent for *Harper's* magazine commented that in spite of a stream of "victories" the American position was weaker than it had been at the outbreak of the conflict. He noted that "the whole population sympathizes with the insurgents," and that the United States forces had been "floundering about" for months with little or no genuine accomplishment to their credit.

In Congress, Senator George Hoar spoke of the sacrifice of ten thousand American lives, the devastation of a countryside ten thousand miles from our own land, and of the President's *"refusal to talk or reason with a people with arms in their hands."* The military, in a practice that has come to be familiar over the last decade, looked to the "enemy" at home as the principal cause of the stubborn Philippine resistance. General Lawton wrote, shortly before he died in battle, that "the continuance of the fighting is due to reports that are sent out from America." President McKinley, it was reported, gave serious consideration to prosecuting the *Nation* and other magazines on charges of treason. Although McKinley resisted the impulse to engage the media in courtroom confrontation, he set the stage for further executive encroachment in the inaugural address that began his second term in office, when he stated, "The Philippines are ours and American authority must be supreme throughout the Archipelago. No outside interference blocks the way to peace and stable government. *The obstructionists are here,* not elsewhere."

Despite the President's confidence, the fighting continued for more than a year before the United States was able to crush the last remnants of the independence movement. At the same time a quiet war was conducted on the home front over the issue of congressional independence. McKinley moved quickly to combine "the executive power" with his authority as Commander in Chief during the treaty negotiations with the Spanish. It was during the course of those negotiations and in the way in which the treaty was implemented that congressional authority to legislate was nullified in areas where the President chose to exercise the authority himself.

The President first pointed to "right of conquest" as justification for the annexation of the Philippine Islands. Later, when subjected to a barrage of criticism by the anti-imperialists, he shifted his ground. He then asserted that Spain's "cession" of her colony legitimized American authority.

The President was in close touch with his negotiators in Paris. They had first been instructed to demand Luzon as a United States naval base. These requirements were then expanded to full possession and the hapless Spaniards had no choice but to give in. In the struggle that followed, a large number of Americans, anguished at their country's participation in a war of spoils, shared the views of the Anti-Imperialist League. "We earnestly condemn the policy of the present administration in the Philippines," the League platform proclaimed. "Much as we regret the war of criminal aggression in the Philippines . . . we more deeply resent," the platform continued, "the betrayal of American institutions at home."

Representative James Williams of Mississippi cried out on the House floor, "The declaration [of war] made no mention of the Philippines. How did we get there?" Williams asserted that "this is not our country's war . . . this is McKinley's war." But the President was not to be stymied by congressional handwringing. He asked for no authority for the fight against the insurrectionists; his generals were reinforced as quickly as troop ships could reach Manila Bay. As the pressure on the rag-clad Filipinos was increased, Carl Schurz, a veteran of the fight against Grant's usurpation, spoke out again.

We are engaged in a war with the Filipinos . . . a war of conquest. Now I ask any fair-minded man whether the President, before beginning that war, or while carrying it on, has ever taken any proper steps to get from the Congress, the representative of the people, any proper authority for making that war.

To those, like Henry Cabot Lodge, who had favored the war, the question of authorization was unimportant. There was no point, in his view, in reopening "questions of the past."

McKinley himself was struggling with some of the questions that would plague the future. In a proclamation that called for "benevolent assimilation," he placed the Philippines under military government on December 21, 1898. Congress was then in session and the treaty with Spain in which she ceded the islands to the United States had not yet been ratified. But the President proceeded, *without placing the issue before the legislature.* He refused to engage in "useless parley" with the Filipinos and he took it upon himself to determine the rules of government for the islands. All legislative enactments were signed by the military with the validating phrase "by authority of the President of the United States."

For three months a newly acquired foreign territory was governed as a possession *solely by a combination of the executive authority and the Commander in Chief power* of the President of the United States. In an editorial inserted into the *Congressional Record,* Charles Lummis wrote:

McKinley tells us that we have expanded and it is no longer a question. But it is not yet too late to ask . . . how? when? and who is *we*? What was the date and ceremony? Certainly to annul the Constitution of the United States must have taken a specific act by a specific person. If a thing can be so easily done without Congress and the people, we would like to know so we can see how we were wasting our time till now. This is no war *that menaces the country.* The only danger we're in is from citizens who think self-government means playing Blind Man's Buff and following the man who is "it" blindly.

But the President's victory over Congress was not finally assured until the Senate ratified the Treaty of Paris in February of 1899.

The integrity of congressional authority was dramatically diminished when William Jennings Bryan intervened in the Senate debate. Bryan, expecting to be the next Democratic presidential candidate, anticipated that American imperialism would be one of the principal issues in his favor. He persuaded a large number of Democratic Senators to vote in favor of McKinley's treaty with Spain. Bryan believed that the clause annexing the Philippines would be an albatross around the presidential neck, enabling the

Democrats to promise to free the Philippines and win the election. He was wrong. But his intervention assured McKinley's treaty of a slender margin of two votes over the necessary constitutional majority. Henry Cabot Lodge, who carried the President's case to the Senate, termed the debate "the hardest fight of my life." For the Filipinos, however, the fight had just started.

American military tactics grew increasingly severe and McKinley became anxious to place a civilian cast on the American governing power. He picked an Ohio judge named William Howard Taft to do the job. Taft attempted to reconcile the rebellious "Little Brown Brothers" to American rule. A popular military tune of the day was sung with a lyric that ran, "They may be little brown brothers to Big Bill Taft but they ain't no brothers of mine."

The Taft Commission, first an investigating body, rapidly became a governing council, and the Judge himself was eventually named Governor General of the Philippines. An entire structure of government for a United States territory was thus codified without the authority of the only legislative organ acknowledged by the Constitution. It was a stunning executive usurpation and it was achieved over the violent protests of editorialists and anti-imperialists but with the acquiescence of a prosperous electorate and a Congress and Supreme Court capable of reading the election returns. The Court had decided in a series of "insular cases," relating to Puerto Rico, that people living in territories under American rule were entitled to the protection of the "underlying principles" of the Constitution, but not the Constitution itself.

As the Filipino insurrection gradually succumbed to the force exerted by American arms, Congress also succumbed to the pressure of an insistent President. A bill offered by Senator John Spooner put the stamp of legislative approval on executive-made law. The Spooner amendment, tacked on to an army reorganization bill, gave the President a wide range of new powers. Pointing to the Court's "insular decisions" that the Constitution *does not follow the flag*, McKinley had asked for the flexibility afforded by executive lawmaking without congressional restraint. Congress, with little protest, passed a bill empowering the President to act *as the sole organ of government* in the Philippines. Taft had reported to the Senate Foreign Relations Committee that his work was handicapped by the limitations that were placed on his legislative function because he operated within the constraints of the executive war power. Confronted with this recognition that there were still some limitations on that power, Congress in effect struck the remaining shackles from the presidential hand.

The Spooner amendment provided that "all military, civil and judicial powers necessary to govern the Philippine Islands . . . shall, until otherwise provided by Congress, be vested in such manner as the President of the United States shall direct . . ."

To all intents and purposes this congressional abdication gave McKinley dictatorial powers over the Filipino people. Edward B. Whitney, a contributor to the *Columbia Law Review* of January, 1901, wrote that "the old maxim that the legislative power cannot be delegated, has very nearly been overthrown." The Boston *Post*, noting the language, objected that "the constitutional powers which Congress derives from the people are turned over to the President. The surrender is complete." Senator George Hoar, a leader of the Anti-Imperialist League, took the Senate floor to denounce the law as "pure, simple, undiluted, unchecked despotism."

Not all of the comment on this new approach to legislative responsibility was negative. The New York press contended that Congress could not legislate for the islands because of its great distance from the continent, and that its conditional grant of power to the President could be withdrawn at any time. But the vantage point of seven decades of hindsight leads me to believe that the Springfield *Republican* was almost prescient in its editorial judgment.

> This step marks the abdication by the American Congress of vast civil powers which the Executive takes up . . . circumstances will necessitate the continuance of a special government of more or less absolutist powers by the Executive and this is Imperialism.

The Massachusetts newspaper seized on the essence of the conflict between the Executive and the Congress as it exists in much aggravated form even at this late date.

The President compels Congress to assume responsibility for any untoward efforts of imperialism. He drives through a treaty annexing the Philippines and then, in prosecuting the War of Subjugation brought upon himself, he acts as one forced to execute the will and laws of Congress for which he is not responsible.

Another editor, observing the charade of McKinley's deference to Congress even as he asked it to divest itself of its constitutional responsibilities, worried over the future. He reported "much apprehension" among students of the political system, about the "growing powers of the President." As a result of the war with Spain, he noted that Congress had practically abdicated in favor of the President. *The Commoner*, edited by William Jennings Bryan, demanded that "the law making and war declaring power be exercised exclusively by the Congress; that the President resume his Constitutional place as an executive." *The Forum*, one of the country's leading magazines, summed it up most succinctly in an article by Henry West.

The lines along which the legislative, judicial and executive divisions of the government were laid down are no longer equal as to themselves nor parallel to each other! The legislative and judicial [branches] are merging toward the executive.

McKinley, the target for this constitutionalist wrath, was aware of the danger and was uncomfortable with its implications. But the new century carried him even further into the morass of Asian involvement. American assertion of authority in the Philippines made inevitable our active participation in the suppression of China's Boxer Rebellion. Here too, presidential authority to move American troops into hostile action was invoked without reference to congressional authority. McKinley in this case responded to a situation that clothed his action with constitutional cover. For the lives of American citizens were endangered by an outburst of Chinese resentment at foreign influence.

In the spring of 1900, a secret society called "The Fists of Righteous Harmony" exploded in rebellion against the European powers that were in the process of dismembering a decadent and helpless Chinese empire. The Dowager Empress Tz'u Hsi, while officially aghast at the "Boxer" excesses, secretly encouraged her subjects to vent their discontent by attacking isolated Christian missionaries and the diplomatic representatives of Europe's arrogant powers. (These "diplomats" actually claimed and exercised sovereign power on Chinese territory.) The Boxer assaults horrified Europe and the United States. But they were responses to an avaricious greed that had destroyed what was left of Chinese dignity in the aftermath of her disastrous war with Japan in 1895.

China's misfortunes began with her loss of the Opium War to Great Britain in the middle of the nineteenth century. The irony of Western self-righteousness is underlined by our current concern with the effects of the drug traffic on our own people. But a century ago there was little anger at British insistence on holding fast to the opium trade laid on Chinese backs. In 1895 the imperialist powers began a series of incursions on Chinese territories designed to assure special commercial concessions and sovereign powers in special areas of influence. Only America resisted the impulse to stuff the national coffers at Chinese expense. But that resistance was to give way to temptation during the battle for the Philippines. The expansionists viewed possession of the Philippines as an opportunity to extend American influence onto the Chinese coast. The Boxer Rebellion gave them the chance they had been waiting for.

In June of 1900 Washington was informed that the Boxers had attacked American minister Edwin H. Conger and his staff along with the European diplomats. They were under siege in the legation at Peking. The European powers immediately set out to rescue their nationals from the Chinese assault. The port of Taku was bombarded and taken by the naval powers and forces were landed to march the eighty miles to Peking. Admiral Louis Kempf, the United States naval commander, refused to join in the bombardment inasmuch as the United States was not in a state of war with China. The first official reaction to Kempf's caution was indignant. Later, however, his refusal to engage in offensive action was perceived as the most intelligent response the United States could have made. It enabled the Chinese government to differentiate between her American "friends" and the powers that willfully assaulted the installations of a government ostensibly unable to control the Boxer forces.

As the rumors of Chinese barbarism increased, the President took action. He ordered 5,000 Americans to China to participate in the march on Peking. The troops that landed at Tientsin for the rescue mission came from our new base in the Philippines. The imperialist press crowed that annexation had enabled American soldiers to do their duty to their imperiled fellow citizens. One intervention was used to justify another.

Three American infantry regiments (some 2,900 men) participated in the assault on the Imperial City. The Americans, assigned the job of taking the government citadel itself, were enraged when they were ordered back at the last minute. Higher councils had decided to permit the Dowager Empress and her court to escape in order to preserve the myth of the noninvolvement of the Chinese government. The rebellion collapsed at the first vigorous blows struck by European and American force and the United States military was ensconced on the mainland of Asia. McKinley, despite the counsel of some of his principal advisers, including Secretary of State John Hay, wanted to withdraw as quickly as possible. Controversy had already erupted in the wake of his decision to intervene. Some of it was stimulated by members of his own party.

Representative Bromwell, from the President's own state of Ohio, took the position that acquisition of the Philippines was insufficient for American purposes. "The fact that we have the Philippines will not insure us full commercial advantages if China goes into the hands of Europe." The Congressman put it bluntly. "If the Chinese Empire has to be divided, I am most certainly in favor of getting the proportion of territory that belongs to this country." The *Nation*, while lauding the President for the "prompt, efficient and discreet action [for the] rescue of American citizens," warned that the American Republic would be disgraced if our occupation of the Philippines was used to "seize Chinese territory for no other purpose . . . than to promote our commerce and trade." Other organs of opinion disagreed. One newspaper argued that American troops must remain in China "*to protect all our interests.*" Anticipating the constitutional question of congressional authority to declare war, the *Brooklyn Eagle* told its readers that there was no need for an extra session "merely to determine the employment of force. *The President's power in this respect without the Congress is complete.*"

McKinley, however, was listening to other voices. "If there is to be a war it is for the people to declare [through the Congress]," said one newspaper in the Middle Western heartland. Perhaps the New York *Herald* best summarized the views in which McKinley finally acquiesced. The Chinese affair found constitutional warrant only in the assumption that the President and his Cabinet were engaged in the protection of American lives, the *Herald* editorialist wrote. Only from that viewpoint can the *refusal* to call Congress be justified. "If the President has not gone beyond his prerogative he has obviously carried it to an extreme unprecedented in our history."

William McKinley had had enough of domestic dissent. In using his power as Commander in Chief during one legal war to engage illegally in still another, he had gone far beyond the conception he held of his office when he first took the presidential oath. Now, on the eve of an election campaign, he had no desire to initiate further upheaval. Despite the Navy Department's halfhearted attempt to arrange for another coaling station in Fukien Province, McKinley's eyes were at last turned homeward. When Secretary of State Hay attempted to persuade him to maintain an American presence as a bargaining weight, the President wrote peremptorily that "I know of no way to get out but to come out." His note to Hay was drafted in September, 1900. By late October American troops had been withdrawn to the Philippines. Many Americans in the 1970's must bitterly reflect that McKinley's simple assertion was the essence of political wisdom.

William McKinley literally bridged the nineteenth and twentieth centuries. His personality was structured in an era when Presidents were expected to assume, at least publicly, that the executive branch of the government was coordinate with the legislature and the judiciary. But the currents of the age swept him into executive actions that exemplified a presidential supremacy that is nowhere to be found in the written Constitution.

The United States was fortunate that McKinley himself was not a "personal imperialist." He did what he felt he had to do in order to maintain his political grip in a new age. McKinley gave the American people what he thought they wanted. When his political senses told him that further expansion would not be to their liking, he pulled out of China with as much determination as he had marched into the Philippines.

The McKinley Administration also marked another stage in the abandonment of principled constitutionalism. Americans have always been pragmatic in their politics, and the Constitution has often protected them from the results of carrying that pragmatism too far. But the protection of a written document can be effective only when those who read it and interpret it are willing to abide by its explicit direction. Lincoln, too, had discarded the constitutional separation of powers. But we have seen that Lincoln's evasions occurred in the heat of great national peril. McKinley never claimed that such was the case during his term in office. He simply permitted policy requirements to preempt the precepts of fundamental law. Public opinion, McKinley felt, called for a new reading of what the war powers meant and for enlargement of the Commander in Chief role to whatever degree was necessary in the Philippines. Congress too signed away its own constitutional authority with little or no struggle. The popularity of the war with Spain and the exuberance of the urge to power inhibited any tendency to raise the question of constitutional means and ends. Congress was too little aware of what it was giving away; McKinley was hardly aware of the significance of the gift. But his successor would understand its magnitude. He would use it to the fullest. He would ask for more but he would *take* what he thought he needed.

XIII

TR: "I Have Been President Emphatically"

THEODORE ROOSEVELT acted during his administration to deprive Congress of the right to decide on war or peace and successfully undermined the Senate's treaty-making power. The Roosevelt era was marked by across-the-board expansion of executive power. I have written elsewhere that "he made the Presidency the vital center of action." McKinley had opened the door. TR charged through with a series of assertions of presidential prerogative that stunned and outraged his opposition, while at the same time they added an enormous weight of precedent to the claims made for presidential authority later in the twentieth century. He joined the battle for executive supremacy with a combination of self-confidence and self-righteousness that was based on solid domestic achievement.

"I did and caused to be done many things not previously done by the President and the Heads of the Departments. I did not usurp powers, but I did greatly broaden the use of executive power."

"The Constitution did not explicitly give me the power to do what I did—it did not forbid me to do what I did."

"I therefore did my best to get the Senate to ratify *what I had done.*"

"I took Panama."

Each of the above statements bears directly on the Rooseveltian concept of the President as "Steward." He saw himself as the embodiment of the popular will, "bound actively and affirmatively to do all he could for the people . . ."; it was not only his right but his duty to do anything that the needs of the nation demanded unless such action was forbidden by the Constitution or the laws. Such a view of the presidential function expresses the dominant political theme of our time; but when TR enunciated it in action, he was responding to the demands of a new age with a new concept of presidential responsibility. He applied the "stewardship" standard across the full range of executive activity. Its potential for constitutional trespass came to full flower in a clash with Congress and a sector of public opinion over the question of the Panama Canal. If Roosevelt's post-Presidency boast that "I took Panama" was an overstatement, the truth was in itself a worthy example of an increasing executive reach for power and congressional impotence when confronted with a usurpation of its authority on behalf of an enormously popular national objective.

American foreign policy had aimed at a trans-isthmian canal for over fifty years. Roosevelt himself, his biographer Henry Pringle notes, had been an ardent canal advocate from the earliest days of his interest in foreign policy. A waterway between the Atlantic and Pacific Oceans would multiply the effectiveness of the nation's military and naval power, and increase the speed, range and profitability of America's international commerce.

Treaty obligations and the presence of European powers in the area long prevented the United States from fulfilling its desire to build such a canal. In fact, much of the naval maneuvering in Central American coastal waters during the nineteenth century was designed to eliminate those political obstacles. The new President's accession to power almost coincided with the signing of the Hay-Pauncefote Treaty with Great Britain whereby the United States was conceded full rights to proceed with construction of an isthmus passage. The venture's staggering technical complexity was the only problem left to solve, inasmuch as the fact that Panama was a province of the Republic of Colombia appeared to TR to be of little importance. The Colombian authorities were expected to acquiesce in an American-built and an American-controlled canal. Here the human element upset the calculations of statesmen and speculators. Subtle pressure would not suffice to achieve Roosevelt's objectives on exactly his terms.

The President, in a much abused phrase of our own day, was an "activist." His canal venture gave full expression to that element in his nature. TR offered $10 million and an annual payment of $250,000 for an agreement that would give the United States effective sovereignty over the canal as well as a ten-mile strip of surrounding territory. Roosevelt was outraged when the Colombian senate rejected the Hay-Herrán Treaty. He regarded the refusal to ratify the treaty as an act of bad faith and denounced the Colombians as "bandits" and "thieves." At a later date other men were to take a different view but Roosevelt was very much the pragmatist when it came to questions of international power. He once vigorously informed Secretary of State Hay that any nation had the right to abrogate its treaty obligations when it was in its interest to do so. But a South American senate's rejection of a treaty in which he was vitally interested was intolerable. He was determined to override Colombian intransigence by whatever means were necessary.

The Colombian refusal to ratify the Hay-Herrán Treaty was based in large degree on the fact that one of its articles (a blatant interference with Colombian sovereignty) stipulated that Colombia could not negotiate a settlement with reference to the construction rights it had granted to the New Panama Canal Company. The stipulation, in effect, guaranteed that a private French enterprise, represented by a prominent American lawyer named William Cromwell, would receive a payment of $40 million from the United States Government, a sum four times as large as the price to be paid for encroachment on the sovereignty of the Republic of Colombia. Further, the United States stood as guarantor that the company would not be required to share its windfall with the government that had provided it in the first place. Cromwell and Philippe Bunau-Varilla, the chief engineer, were quite as determined as President Roosevelt not to permit Colombia to obstruct American acquisition of canal rights in Panama.

The company's two principal agents were fully aware that their forty million dollars was contingent on American acquisition of the Panama site. Congress, on June 28, 1902, had authorized Roosevelt to conduct negotiations for a canal route with Colombia within "reasonable time" on "reasonable terms." If such an agreement was not forthcoming, Congress directed, *the President was to seek an alternative canal route in negotiations with Nicaragua and Costa Rica.* Because the United States had a number of options available, a trans-isthmian canal would inevitably be built and controlled by the North American Republic. There was, however, nothing inevitable about the payment to the New Panama Canal Company.

Bunau-Varilla and Cromwell moved to protect the forty million dollars that would accrue to Cromwell's clients only if the Panama route was quickly negotiated. Roosevelt's impatience and indignation with those who stood in the path of presidential power were the principal factors in helping the Canal Company achieve its objectives and in assuring a successful Panamanian revolution against a Colombian government that had dared to assert its sovereignty in negotiations with a powerful neighbor. Roosevelt was to assert the "might makes right" principle on a number of later occasions but Panama affords us the most explicit example of how that principle operates in action.

Philippe Bunau-Varilla was a Frenchman who modeled his engineering career after Ferdinand de Lesseps, the builder of the Suez Canal. De Lesseps later foundered on his failure to repeat his canal success in South America. Bunau-Varilla was determined to salvage something from his hero's misadventure. He had all of the dash required to initiate and carry through an essentially opera bouffe revolution, with the assistance of the United States Government. The tragic perspective of the 1970's lends a two-dimensional and somewhat comic flavor to this early venture in CIA-style diplomacy. But it was one of the precursors to the much larger commitments that have brought us to our current pass. If Roosevelt's concern with style and presidential prestige enhanced his domestic accomplishments, its spillover

into the international arena was less well received by other political figures and his later explanations for the Panama incident
were belligerently defensive in tone. Although the President himself played no active role in fomenting the revolution, private
comments that received wide circulation, and the cooperative
atmosphere he established for the activities of Engineer Bunau-
Varilla and Lawyer Cromwell, made their success inevitable.

In the summer of 1903, agents of the Panama Railway Company, a subsidiary of the Canal Company, paid a series of visits
to Bunau-Varilla's suite at the Waldorf Hotel in New York City.
Some newspapermen later dubbed the uprising the "Waldorf Revolution." A physician employed by the railroad named Manuel
Amador was selected as the revolutionary leader and a junta of
Panamanians with company connections made plans to secede
from Colombia if the government refused to go through with the
Hay-Herrán Treaty. During one visit, Bunau-Varilla was kind
enough to provide the Panamanians with a flag that his wife had
designed, as well as a national anthem. He later expressed pique
that the revolutionaries, in a show of independent ardor, had
designed their own flag. Perhaps this slight to their Waldorf ally
was a mark of dismay that Bunau-Varilla had been unable to
produce a written commitment from Secretary of State John Hay
to provide American armed support for the insurrection. The
insurgents also had reason to be somewhat displeased at the
ephemeral quality of Attorney Cromwell's commitment to their
cause. He at first offered them considerable assistance and
visited with both President Roosevelt and Secretary Hay to discuss the course of future events. When the Colombian authorities
warned Cromwell that if he persisted in dealing with potentially
subversive Panamanians the Company's concession would be
revoked immediately, Cromwell conveniently sailed for Europe
in order to avoid further direct involvement. Care was taken,
however, by parties unknown, to fuel the revolutionary movement with generous funding.

As the summer waned, it became increasingly apparent that
the Colombian senate would not be pressured into passing the
treaty. Roosevelt wrote in letters marked "private and confidential" that he would be pleased if the Panamanians took their in-

dependence. Two United States Army officers were sent on a tour of Central America. They stopped off in Panama where the possibilities for an uprising were assessed. On their return to Washington the two men were taken to the White House. They informed the President that revolution was "inevitable."

The Panamanian patriots, however, were having second thoughts. Money from private sources and encouragement from Washington was well and good. But the revolutionaries wanted more. An American warship was required. On October 27, Bunau-Varilla wired Amador that an American warship was on the way and that it would arrive in Panamanian waters on November 2.

With this assurance in hand, Amador's wife stiffened the spines of the patriots. According to an account in the *New York Post* published shortly after Amador had been named president, she told them that they had gone too far to turn back. The revolutionaries "struck." The American warship *Nashville* arrived in Panama on the night of November 2, 1903, timed almost perfectly to Bunau-Varilla's schedule. A day later, other warships arrived on the Pacific side of the isthmus. Colombia at last sent a contingent of the troops that the revolutionaries had feared.

When some five hundred soldiers attempted to take up positions in the provincial capital, Theodore Roosevelt entered the picture in his role as Commander in Chief of United States Armed Forces. Marines were landed to "assure free passage" across the isthmus. In order to avoid conflict that would endanger the lives of those attempting to cross Panamanian territory, the Marines and the Railway Company refused to permit the Colombian Army to use railroad facilities to proceed to the provincial capital at Colón. The generals commanding the Colombian forces were persuaded to continue the journey without the main body of their troops and a crisis was averted. The colonel left in charge of the stranded Colombian troops accepted eight thousand dollars in gold and two cases of champagne before reembarking for Colombia. The two generals who had gone to Colón ahead of their soldiers were arrested by the patriots, and Colombian troops already stationed in the city received fifty dollars a man. A flag (designed by Mrs. Amador) was raised and the revolution was over. Panama was a free and independent republic.

Seventy-two hours after the revolution was proclaimed, Washington recognized the new government. The revolutionaries appointed their old friend, the French engineer, Bunau-Varilla, as Minister Plenipotentiary to the United States. Within two weeks he had succeeded with astonishing ease in negotiating a treaty that embodied the exact principles that Colombia had rejected. The Panamanian patriots had second thoughts about the Bunau-Varilla appointment. The three-man junta sent a commission to assist the French engineer in his discussions in the hope that they would be able to improve on the arrangements rejected by their former masters. But they were to be disappointed. By the time the commission arrived the treaty had been signed by both parties, and it was made clear to the new government that it would be expected to stand by the signature of its "minister."

The American conscience was later aroused by the episode at Panama. But in the immediate aftermath of the revolution, the treaty and the events preceding it were regarded by most public opinion as a signal American triumph. The United States wanted and needed a canal and Roosevelt had not permitted any piece of paper to prevent us from getting it. A treaty of more than half a century's standing was abrogated by the stronger power (a congressional statute directing the President to negotiate with Nicaragua or Costa Rica in case of an impasse with Colombia was also tossed into the waste bin) and the Constitution disregarded by the President of the United States when he made war without congressional writ.

The ineptitude of the revolutionaries and the blatantly manipulative actions of their corporate mentors and of the President of the United States do lend themselves to caricature. But Colombia and Panama were not the only losers. On each occasion that an American President is enabled to interpret his powers in such a way that those of the Congress are diminished, the balance required to preserve democratic institutions is further disturbed. No one in Theodore Roosevelt's time would have dreamed that in late 1972 the largest aerial bombardment in history would be conducted against North Vietnam by a President whose only "legal" justification lay in his duty as Commander in Chief to "protect" the forces under his command. No one would have dreamed that such authority would be exercised without consultation or report either to the people or to their elected representatives in Congress—the only body with the authority to make war. No one would have believed it, but the seeds had been planted long before. The episode in Panama, its consequences and origins, offer an example of presidential encroachment and congressional acquiescence worthy of study.

The controversy over the Panama Canal was an outgrowth of a treaty the United States had concluded with New Granada (later called Colombia) in 1846. The terms of the agreement provided that the United States and its citizens were to enjoy right of access across the Panamanian isthmus by whatever means of transit then available or to be made available in the future. In return for such access the United States obligated itself to guarantee the neutrality of the isthmus and the sovereignty of Colombia over the isthmus itself. On a number of occasions in the years between American accession to the treaty and the revolution of 1903, United States forces had intervened to preserve Colombian authority and to assure access to both oceans. On most of those occasions American intervention had occurred at the request of Colombian authorities. Only once did a United States intervention prevent Colombia from enforcing its own sovereignty. The American Secretary of State apologized for the error. In the half century of the treaty's life Colombian sovereignty was frequently tested by weak government or revolt in Panama. The United States, under the treaty of 1846, always backed Colombian authority. Only when the Colombian senate asserted its prerogative to negotiate more equitable arrangements on the question of canal rights did the United States interpret the treaty of 1846 in such a way as to enable American power to destroy Colombian sovereignty over the isthmus.

On December 7, 1903, President Roosevelt sent Congress a message that incorporated a number of interesting assertions. He told Congress that when they had "directed" him to make a treaty with Colombia for canal rights, "the essence of the condition, of course, referred not to the government which controlled that route, but to the route itself . . . the purpose of the law was to authorize the President to make a treaty with the power in actual control of the Isthmus of Panama. This purpose has been fulfilled."

Roosevelt went on to contend that he had been "more than just" in the negotiations with Colombia and that American generosity had perhaps "gone too far in their interest at the expense of our own . . ." He described a revolution in which the people "rose as one man," and acknowledged that the United States "*gave notice that it would permit the landing of no expeditionary force,* the arrival of which would mean chaos and destruction . . . and an interruption of transit as an inevitable consequence." In justifying the actions of his administration the President said that Colombia "forced us, *for the sake of our own honor . . .* and the people of the civilized countries of the world," to end an "intolerable" condition.

On December 9, Senator George F. Hoar of Massachusetts directed a series of questions to the President. He wished to know whether the Colombian constitution authorized secession and whether the United States had helped to prevent Colombian authorities from "attempting to assert its authority." To a country that had only recently emerged from establishing its own sovereignty after an attempted secession, the question was fundamental. Hoar was further interested in knowing whether any of those involved in negotiating the treaty with Panama had any "private interest" at issue. Mr. Bunau-Varilla had already become a figure of considerable notoriety as a result of the intense coverage given to the revolution by much of the American press. The Massachusetts Senator noted the remarkable synchronization of the actions of the revolutionaries with the movements of the United States Navy and United States Marines. Casting his observations in the form of queries, Hoar asked "whether this mighty policeman," instructed to keep the peace on the isthmus, "seeing a man about to attack another, before he had struck his blow, manacled the arms of the man attacked, so that he could not defend himself, leaving the assailant free, and then instantly proceeded to secure from the assailant the pocketbook of the victim, on the ground that he was the *de facto* owner?"

Speaking scornfully of the "five-minute act of revolution," the Senator observed that Colombia was a friendly nation with whom we had treated on the canal as a matter of her right. He then raised the ultimate question: "Is not this an act of war upon a friendly though weak nation?"

Many observers felt that the Administration had inadvertently answered affirmatively in a speech delivered by Francis B. Loomis, Assistant Secretary of State. Loomis told diners at a New York banquet that President Roosevelt had displayed courage, knowledge and patriotism of a high order when he instructed the Marines to intervene in Panama. He then provided a play-by-play account of the events that took place on the isthmus from the viewpoint of the Roosevelt Administration. Turning to the "bad faith" exhibited by the Colombian congress, Assistant Secretary Loomis commented that the Panama revolution had been "long expected" and that Roosevelt had ordered the Marines to "do what they could to preserve peace, order and unimpeded transit across the isthmus . . . He promptly recognized the *de facto* government as soon as he learned it was in peaceful possession of the country."

This attempt to laud presidential wisdom is reminiscent of events of a later day on at least two counts. Loomis was an early practitioner of a "school" of public opinion manipulation, in which the citizenry is encouraged to "sleep better at night" because the great problems are in the hands of the master solver in the White House. The idea that one presidential head is better than that of five hundred in Congress has become the conventional wisdom of the latter part of the twentieth century. Sometimes the attempt to create a graven executive image produces a backlash of disenchantment. So it was with Loomis' attempt to apotheosize the Roosevelt of Panama.

Senator Arthur Gorman, noting that Loomis had spoken to a banquet audience about the Panama exploit before the President even sent his message to Congress, remarked that according to the State Department official "we virtually seized, by military power, a part of the territory of Colombia." The Maryland Senator accused the President of usurpation and commented that newspaper critics were now comparing TR with Napoleon.

> Has it come to this, Mr. President, that we have a Napoleon . . . taking action amounting to a Declaration of War, which the Constitution says Congress alone has the power to declare . . . and then . . . sifting out information through a Deputy Secretary of State at a banquet in New York?

Senator Joseph Foraker of Ohio, defending the President's use of the Marines, told his colleagues that "we do not have to wait until there is actual war." He contended that the landing was designed "to prevent those conditions that would have followed but for our intervention."

The opposition to Roosevelt's new treaty with Panama crystallized around the possibility of using the Nicaraguan route for a canal. It was contended that the President had violated congressional instructions when he helped to organize a dummy republic in Panama that would negotiate a treaty with him, instead of finding an alternative route when the Colombian negotiations proved unsatisfactory. The President was repeatedly charged with committing an act of war and withholding information from Congress in order to achieve his ends. The demand was made by an Oklahoma Senator that "the Executive have respect for Congress and special consideration for the Senate when it comes to the negotiations of treaties." Roosevelt was warned that he would be unable to get a treaty passed unless he bowed "to the right of the Senate to be informed of all the facts." The threat was later proven empty, but the anguished quality of the protest reflected a general helplessness felt even then in the face of a successfully completed *coup*. Acknowledgment of Roosevelt's success was implicit in the arguments made by men who charged the President with a willful usurpation of congressional authority.

Senator Edmund Pettus remarked that if the United States was displeased with Colombia's response to our treaty overtures,

> . . . you [Congress] have a perfect right to declare war and to make war on Colombia if you want to. But whoever heard

that the President of the United States could make war without the authority of Congress?

War is being made according to the President's own declaration. He is making war for the purpose of securing that ten miles of land through that country. God forbid that Congress or the people of the United States either should ever approve such a war!

But a large number of Americans did approve the results of Roosevelt's action, whether or not it was a war. The *Brooklyn Eagle* said that the President's "defense of our treatment of Colombia and Panama is unanswerable." The Hartford *Times* thought that "the whole world is likely to agree that summary ending of such conditions was justified and necessary." The New York *Mail and Express* argued that "time is certain to vindicate the actions of the American President, and speedily." The *Mail and Express* felt that Roosevelt had intervened "in the interests of peace, not temporary, but permanent." Perhaps the most acute pro-Roosevelt editorial appeared in the Democratic Atlanta *Journal*. "The President has actually accomplished more toward *getting digging operations started* than any of his predecessors." The *Journal's* pragmatism was expressive of an increasingly large segment of American public opinion. Roosevelt's "get the job done" attitude, with its implied disregard for petty legalisms, was in keeping with the ethos of a new century in which much social attention would be riveted on managerial techniques; sometimes at the expense of the issues to which those techniques are applied. In 1904, however, there was still a large body of opinion that reflected a different aspect of the American character.

The New Orleans *Picayune* declared that Roosevelt's explanation of his actions in Panama "is the argument that the strong always uses with the weak," and the Philadelphia *Record* acidly commented that "it is seldom that the brutal doctrine that the might of the strongest makes right against the weak has been asserted with more cold-blooded cynicism than in this message of one of the Doctors of political ethics, with trite maxims of the sacredness of public obligations almost constantly on his lips."

The New York Times called the American action a step on

"the path of scandal, disgrace and dishonor," and the New York *American* suggested that it would be better to do without a canal than to get it "by such means as this." One newspaper contended that Roosevelt was a "very unsafe and uncertain President," and the Charleston *News* accused him of using the canal enterprise, "on which the heart of American people is set, [*as*] *a pretext for engaging in war with Colombia,* without giving the people of this country time to think, for the enlargement once more of our Army and Navy, and *to extend the power of the Executive.*" It is the latter accusation with which we are principally concerned and it was made repeatedly during both Roosevelt Administrations.

But despite the uproar, the Republican majority and a significant portion of the Democratic minority were in favor of the Canal treaty. Constitutional questions had been settled by action. In the words of the President himself,

"The only question now before us is that of the ratification of the treaty [with Panama] . . . a failure to ratify the treaty will not undo what has been done, will not restore Panama to Colombia . . . The question is not that of recognition of Panama as an Independent Republic. *That is already an accomplished fact.* The question, and the only question, is whether or not we shall build an Isthmian canal."

The Senate answered yes to the question by a substantial majority.

Roosevelt's attitude with respect to the canal controversy and his relations with Congress were expressed with remarkable consistency. Perhaps his most succinct assessment of the proper executive posture when faced with congressional opposition was delivered in a speech at Berkeley in 1911:

"I am interested in the Panama Canal because I started it. If I had followed traditional, conservative methods I should have submitted a dignified State paper . . . to Congress, and the debate on it would be going on yet; but I took the Canal Zone and let Congress debate and while the debate goes on the Canal does too."

The failure of congressional opposition to rally support during and following the Panama affair was perhaps a principal factor in encouraging the President to continue his expansion of executive authority in foreign affairs. *The Times* noted that "Congress has abdicated its authority as the sole war-making power," and another publication commented with asperity that Roosevelt should have been pleased with such a "good" Congress, such a "quiet" Congress. Whether Roosevelt needed such encouragement is a moot point. He had already succeeded in using his constitutional authority to "recognize" a government in such a way as to breach a treaty passed by the United States Senate. He had at the same time so construed his powers as Commander in Chief as to violate another government's sovereignty (in international law, an act of war) and he had used his constitutional authority to negotiate a treaty with the new government of Panama that would, if the Senate approved it, validate the unconstitutional acts he had committed in order to achieve his treaty objectives. The President won on all counts. Despite the bitter debate about morality and constitutionality, the American people wanted the canal and a majority of them did not care to examine the means by which they got it. Neither did a majority of the United States Senate. I remarked earlier in these pages that no one has suggested that California be returned to Mexico. The same was true of the Panama Canal Zone.

The Constitution may not always be read in the light of the election returns and, according to the Supreme Court, it need not always follow the flag. But history does tell us that it's usually read in the light of executive action and, with notable exceptions, that it tends to follow executive policy.

One of the principal sources of the inadequacy of congressional response to presidential encroachment on the war powers is related to the Executive's ability to aggregate a group of his constitutional powers in such a way as to impinge, with at least an appearance of constitutional sanction, on powers explicitly delegated to Congress. An attack launched on executive usurpation on one front is countered with a presidential move on another. Congress, on the other hand, has been unwilling or unable to use its constitutional authority to similar effect. One may guess that at least a partial reason for such reluctance is the finality of such powers as Congress is endowed with. The fund cutoff and impeachment are the ultimate sanctions within congressional reach. The fund cutoff had not stood a serious chance of implementation until the Vietnam War, while impeachment has been tried only once in American history. And then, this drastic step failed. The Executive has the advantage of numerous powers lesser in degree, but overwhelming in cumulative effect. The executive will is also a single entity (no matter how embraced by conflicting counsel) while Congress is dependent on a collective will that can respond as "one" only in extreme circumstance. Twentieth-century Presidents have come increasingly closer to requiring us to face this circumstance. Theodore Roosevelt's Panama adventure was but the first in a series of attempts to establish a "stewardship" that would override congressional authority and responsibility when the President thought it necessary to do so. His attempt to substitute executive agreements for treaties requiring the consent of the Senate was still another enlargment of presidential power.

The executive agreement with Santo Domingo that the United States would collect the duties at Santo Domingo's ports was a milestone on a path that has led us to a point where the United States in 1973 is bound by some four thousand substantive agreements with foreign powers, many so crucial that they should not have been arrived at without the constitutionally required "advice and consent" of the United States Senate. That situation first rose out of TR's concern with the stability of the Caribbean area. He was troubled by the possibility that European powers would use force and occupy territory in order to collect debts owed by Santo Domingo to European nationals. The President had good reason to be worried. German and British power had been brought to bear on Venezuela and Roosevelt was anxious that no precedent for similar action arise in the future. He conceived of the United States as the policeman of the Caribbean and he overtly distinguished between the obligation to recognize and respect the rights of the stronger powers and the obligation to impose our own national will on those unable to defend themselves.

Roosevelt's attitude was realistic and understandable in the context of his age. But the implementation of his views brought us far along the path to a different order of international involvement and to a situation in which executive power sometimes seems to be beyond the control of the "coordinate branches" of the Federal Government. The use of the executive agreement before TR's time had been confined to "housekeeping" details with little or no relevance to policy. Such was not the case in Santo Domingo. The agreement was made in the aftermath of a presidential message in which the Chief Executive carefully articulated what has come to be called "The Roosevelt Corollary."

Any country whose people conduct themselves well can count upon our hearty friendship. If a nation shows that it knows how to act with reasonable efficiency and decency in social and political matters, if it keeps order and pays its obligations, it need fear no interference from the United States. Chronic wrongdoing or an impotence which results in a general loosening of the ties of a civilized society may in America, as elsewhere, ultimately require intervention by some civilized nation, and in the Western Hemisphere the adherence of the United States to the Monroe Doctrine may force the United States, however reluctantly, in flagrant cases of such wrongdoing or impotence, to the exercise of an international police power.

Roosevelt's words served as a warning to the European powers that the United States reaffirmed its commitment to the Monroe Doctrine barring intervention in the Western Hemisphere. At the same time he articulated as a principle the view that American power would rightfully be brought to bear on any sister republic whose conduct offended the United States conception of proper international behavior. Many contemporary historians insist, and events lend support to the view, that we have, since 1945, exported the Roosevelt Corollary around the world. TR, in any event, wasted little time in applying it in Santo Domingo.

The Dominican Republic had long been a center for official and unofficial American interventions. It will be remembered that it was there that Ulysses Grant was halted when he attempted to annex the island by treaty with a corrupt president. Roosevelt, perhaps learning from President Grant's experience, at first avoided the perils of treaty submission. The Administration took a novel approach.

On December 30, 1904, Secretary of State Hay, through the American minister to Santo Domingo, suggested to the beleaguered President Morales that he request the United States to collect the customs at each of the island's principal ports. Morales was confronted with a painful decision. The American offer came during a period in which Santo Domingo had been threatened by the Belgian and French governments with forcible collection of debts owed her citizens. Fully aware that the overwhelming majority of his people were opposed to American intervention, Morales knew that the American "suggestion" left him little choice. After a struggle of some weeks, in which he overcame domestic opposition, he made the "request," and on January 20, 1905, the initial version of the Dillingham-Sanchez Protocol was signed. Commander Dillingham, a naval officer with considerable experience in the area, agreed on behalf of the United States to guarantee the Dominican Republic's territory, to collect its customs and to turn over 45 percent of the receipts to the Dominican Republic. The United States would use the other 55 percent to pay off the European creditors. The circumstances in which the agreement was signed indicate that Roosevelt at first had no intention of asking the Senate to treat his "protocol" as a treaty. United States warships appeared in Santo Domingo waters immediately after the signing and the date of its implementation was to be in early February, hardly enough time for senatorial consideration. At this point a dispatch from Santo Domingo appeared on the front pages of American newspapers in which the details of the agreement were described with considerable accuracy.

The Senate suddenly responded to an obvious executive encroachment. Senator Augustus Bacon of Georgia introduced a resolution in which he demanded an explanation of Roosevelt's actions. When Henry Cabot Lodge attempted to sidetrack the resolution, Bacon argued vehemently that the Senate must judge "the powers of the President to make a treaty which shall virtually take over the affairs of another government, without submitting that question to the consideration and judgment of the Senate." He told an attentive chamber that the affair involved "the most serious and fundamental prerogatives of the Senate and questions of the relative divisions of power between the Executive and the Senate."

Senator Bacon was not alone in his concern for the treaty-making power. Foraker of Ohio, an ardent Roosevelt partisan, said that he "could not imagine that the President has undertaken to exercise the treaty-making power without consulting the Senate," but acknowledged that appearances seemed otherwise. All through January, opposition to the "protocol" jelled in the Senate. Senator Henry Teller of Ohio observed that "under the Constitution it is not possible for the President of the United States to change the character of a document by calling it a protocol or calling it an agreement if it is a treaty." Teller, his words directed to the ear of the President, said that there was no way for TR to "avoid consideration by the Senate . . . there is not any kind of a treaty that can be made that can thus escape the supervision of this body."

The Administration reassessed its position in the light of the quickly developing opposition. The Indianapolis *News,* a paper reputed to reflect the views of Vice President-Elect Fairbanks, said that "if this performance is allowed to pass unchallenged, it will be exceedingly difficult to put any limit on the President's power." The *Evening Post* termed the protocol an "amazing document," and the New York *Sun* said that if Roosevelt was permitted to overthrow the constitutional provisions for senatorial "advice and consent" on treaties, "the Republican form of government which has blessed this nation for more than a century would cease to exist." It was apparent to the President that discretion in this case would be the better part of valor. The Administration began to assert in astonished tones that it had always intended to submit the treaty to the Senate for consideration. The delay in such consideration, however, proved costly to the President, the Senate and to posterity.

The Senate struck a number of themes when it rejected the treaty. The Roosevelt Corollary, whereby the Executive would determine standards of international conduct and take action to maintain them, was unpopular with a good number of the anti-imperialist lawmakers. The clause in which the United States guaranteed the *status quo* in Santo Domingo was also offensive to many of the legislators, and the presence of United States warships in Santo Domingo waters prior to Senate approval of the document caused still others to withhold approval. The Senate struck the treaty down once more, following Roosevelt's inauguration for a second term. He faced the alternative of acquiescing in the decision or finding a way around it. Running true to form, TR opted for the latter course.

After private consultation with a number of influential Senators, the President established a *modus vivendi* with Santo Domingo whereby he would, unofficially, "recommend" an American citizen to collect Santo Domingo revenues and an American bank in New York to disburse them according to the formulae previously established under the treaty-protocol. Roosevelt, it should be noted parenthetically, knew how to work with Congress when it served his purposes. He was a politician in the highest and the best sense of that much abused word. In a letter to Secretary of State Hay who was ill, the President described a meeting in which he participated with some of the Senators who had opposed the treaty. According to Roosevelt, Senator Gorman, an avowed foe of the treaty, acknowledged the necessity of a *modus vivendi,* though he would publicly oppose it. Roosevelt recalled that the one awkward moment of the conference came when "rather to my horror Taft [Secretary of War] genially chaffed them about going back on their principles as to the usurpation of the Executive. But they evidently took the view that *it was not a time to be overparticular about trifles."*

For twenty-eight months Roosevelt's *modus vivendi* with Santo Domingo operated without the advice and consent of the Senate. The same obligations and processes rejected through the legislative process were effectively implemented by "unofficial" executive fiat. The President took no pains to disguise the plain fact. He openly described the activity of his agents in the Dominican Republic during an address at Chautauqua in the summer of 1905. Roosevelt pointed with particular pride to the fact that the presence of this unofficial American presence "has completely discouraged all revolutionary movement." Not everyone in the government was so sanguine as TR.

Champ Clark of Missouri noted in the House of Representatives that "Sancho Panza said, 'God bless the man who first invented sleep.' Other persons must say, 'God bless the man who invented that convenient phrase *modus vivendi.*' Like the mantle of charity it covers a multitude of sins."

"Perhaps what has been done has been done for the best," Senator Isadore Raynor remarked, "but I want to avoid the precedent, because *precedents live forever and bad precedents make good law.*" Senator Teller, attacking the same theme, remarked almost prophetically that he was not willing to admit that any President could constitutionally make an agreement with a foreign power and put it in operation. If such an admission were made, asked Teller, "where will be the barricade that protects the people from executive aggression?" He queried the Senate as to what the consequences of these acts would finally be for the American people. "This thing will keep piling up and take almost the form of delegated authority of the Constitution. You can keep on piling up one precedent upon another until it takes at last the place of principle as well as policy." Was it beyond the realm of possibility, he wondered, that the United States might have "a future President who may imagine he is doing the best thing by upsetting the law and substituting his own judgment?"

On February 25, 1907, the United States Senate ratified as treaty a substantially amended Santo Domingo protocol. President Roosevelt asserted in his memoirs that the Senate had made "some utterly unimportant changes" in the treaty he had originally presented. The record does not bear him out. The treaty, as finally passed, eliminated both a guarantee of territorial integrity and an American right to intervene in the internal affairs of the republic when the United States considered such intervention to be desirable. Roosevelt nevertheless had the pragmatic advantage of the argument. For as he observed, "I went ahead and administered the proposed treaty anyhow, considering it as a simple agreement on the part of the Executive . . . which would be converted into a treaty whenever the Senate chose to act." The former President accused his opposition of "having left the country in the position of assuming a responsibility and then failing to fulfill it." Roosevelt thus identified the "country" with the Presidency. The United States Senate was not entitled, in this view, to function as an independent branch of government. Rather the Senators who opposed him had "shirk[ed] their duty . . . somebody had to do that duty and accordingly I did it."

Roosevelt's position on Santo Domingo was the same as the "I took Panama" posture he had adopted in 1903. According to George Milton, writing on presidential power in 1944, Theodore Roosevelt's primary contribution to the evolution of the Presidency was the new conception of that office that he left with the American people. Milton notes that in a quiet era TR had a "positive genius" for creating issues which might be magnified into Armageddons where he could battle for the Lord. I cannot help but think that Theodore Roosevelt would have taken pride in that assessment.

Roosevelt continued to live according to his standards of stewardship until the very end of his term in office. A document found in his private papers after his death reveals that he had reached an informal agreement with Japan to the effect that the United States would act in concert with that country and Britain to assure the stability of the Far East. TR's Secretary of War also informed Japan that the President would regard with favor the establishment of a Japanese protectorate over Korea. Professor Corwin has observed that this agreement, which Roosevelt signed two weeks before Japan took control of Korea, was "the most remarkable secret executive agreement" to be signed prior to those made by the second Roosevelt at Cairo and Yalta. The executive agreement has since been refined into one of the principal instruments of unrestrained executive power. But it was the first President of this century who found the way to prevent the Senate from effectively exercising its responsibility to "advise and consent."

TR's presidential effectiveness is beyond question. He offered the American people a vibrant and progressive image of what they were and stirred their imaginations as to what they could be. If he prepared the way for the executive encroachments of our own day, he did so in response to the rhythms of a new age that required action. "I have been President emphatically," he once said in defense of his Santo Domingo *modus vivendi*. "In showing the strength of, or giving strength to the Executive, I was establishing a precedent of value."

Theodore Roosevelt tilted the scales firmly on the side of presidential power. But the conflagration of two great world wars institutionalized the imbalance.

XIV

Wilson Moves
from "Watchful Waiting"
to Total War

WOODROW WILSON's Administration marks the emergence of the age of total war. We have lived in that age ever since and only now are we becoming aware of it. Most of the men and women who make national policy have been molded by intellectual training to think of war as an aberration; a departure from the normative behavior of nations. Indeed, that norm was codified in the Hague Convention of 1907 in which rules pertaining to declarations of war were solemnly debated and decided. The rules, requiring preambles of justification and notifications of intent, were handsomely adapted to the age of the Congress of Vienna. Like generals who prepare their armies to fight the last war, statesmen all too frequently look to the future not as a continuum but as a repetition of the familiar past. Although declarations of war continued to be made for a few years after the Hague Convention, they were shortly to become the exception to the savage rule of "fight now—talk later." In a world in which our most powerful leaders feel required to announce that "we arm to parley" it should not be surprising that the President means to have the last word in both.

Woodrow Wilson's tragic destiny was to preside over the fortunes of an America about to plunge into a conflagration from which we have yet to emerge. The brief periods of armistice between the great battles of the twentieth century hardly deserve to be called "peace." The issue as to Who Makes War becomes the great question of such an age. We have seen the intentions of the Constitution-makers in that regard continuously undermined by an increasing weight of historic precedent. Almost every Chief Executive to hold office through the first one hundred and twenty-five years of national life contributed to the aggrandizement of presidential war power. Most Congresses acquiesced in the diminution of their own constitutional responsibility. History forced decisions that seemed to leave no alternative to executive supremacy. But it was in the Wilson Administration that the nation first began to live in our own threatening time.

Woodrow Wilson appeared to be a figure who would concentrate the national energies on the reform of our political institutions. Such was not to be the case. He first made presidential war on Mexico and was then forced into an international conflict which future historians will probably perceive as continuing to this very day. Wilson has been psychoanalyzed and psycho-historicized to the point of diminishing return. Suffice it to say that his scholarly training and first-class intellectual powers were used in behalf of the politics of moralism. An approach to internationalism which still shadows much of America's contemporary policies flowered fully in the President's "missionary diplomacy" and during the first great war with Germany.

Although Woodrow Wilson fully believed in democratic processes, he saw no paradox in the imposition of his own views on the peoples of neighboring republics. This was particularly true when he was persuaded that his interventions in their affairs were founded in a genuine concern for their right to free institutions. Wilson's background as educator and his upbringing as the son of a Presbyterian minister endowed him with a pedagogic attitude that influenced the style of his Presidency. He was able to say to the British minister in Washington that he would "teach them [the people of South America] to elect good men," and then to another audience, with the passion of complete conviction running through his voice, exclaim that if "the Mexicans want to raise hell, let them raise hell. We have got nothing to do with it. It is their government, it is their hell."

In reality Wilson's evangelical qualities precluded a willingness to see any man in hell until he had been proselytized on behalf of the secular religion of democracy. This became increasingly evident in the course of the presidential adventures in Mexico.

Prior to Wilson's inauguration, the Mexican dictator, Porfirio Díaz, had been overthrown and a revolutionary upsurge swept the country. A popular struggle rooted in the economic deprivation of the Mexican peasant and worker seemed at first to have won an overwhelming victory when a Social Democrat, Francisco Madero, took power in Mexico City. His triumph was destined to be short-lived in the "barrack uprising" atmosphere of Central American politics. Madero was overthrown by General Victoriano Huerta, who for a time appeared to be Woodrow Wilson's nemesis. Huerta made little pretense at "constitutional legitimacy." He had come to power using power. But he had broken a cardinal rule when he permitted his predecessor's murder. In the process he had also incurred Woodrow Wilson's lasting enmity. Wilson's anger with General Huerta was reflected in the Administration's refusal to recognize the new Mexican government.

For well over a century, the United States had made it a practice to recognize any new government that demonstrated its control over the population and territory it claimed to represent. Such a policy was in accord with dominant international practice and no moral significance was attached to the recognition. James Buchanan, when he served as Secretary of State, commented as follows: "We do not go behind the existing government to involve ourselves in questions of legitimacy. It is sufficient for us to know that a government exists, capable of maintaining itself; and then its recognition on our part inevitably follows." Woodrow Wilson was determined to change that policy. On March 11, 1913, he declared that the United States could have "no sympathy with those who seek to seize the power of government to advance their own personal interests or ambition." Although Wilson did not mention the Mexican chieftain by name, Washington's pressures for new elections in which Huerta would not offer his own candidacy, along with the continued refusal of official American recognition, left little doubt as to whom the President had in mind. The question of the recognition power is another one of those superficially secondary levers which enables a President to create a climate that will determine war or peace. Such was the case in 1913.

The record indicates that Wilson badly misjudged the Mexican situation. He wished to improve the political lot of the Mexicans and he certainly had no desire to go to war with them. Nevertheless, Wilson's diplomatic use of powers on behalf of objectives that were outside the limits of his constitutional responsibilities produced a conflict that he did not anticipate.

Woodrow Wilson was his own Secretary of State. He ignored the advice of State Department counselors who warned him against adopting too restrictive a Mexican policy. When he was angered at Britain's recognition of the Huerta government despite the stiff American posture, the President was reminded that "it had never been considered necessary for foreign powers to ask our consent" to recognize a sister republic. But England was on the eve of a major conflict with Germany and the last thing Lord Grey's government needed was a dispute with the United States. British concern with Mexico was related principally to her need for the Mexican oil that fueled a fleet that had been recently converted from coal. On Wilson's assurance that the oil properties would be protected, the British withdrew recognition from the Huerta government.

The President's pressure on Huerta was relentless. Unofficial emissaries were sent to most of the factions vying for power in Mexico. Messages on Mexico and elections and on the nature of democracy poured from Wilson's portable typewriter. He circulated a note to the European powers in which he decried Huerta's "usurpations" and declared his intention to "discredit and defeat such usurpations whenever they occur." The note went on to assure its recipients that the United States would await the results of Huerta's "isolation" with "patience and without irritation." The press, describing the American attitude as "watchful waiting," noted the President's promise that only if "force of circumstance" was insufficient to remove Huerta would the United States use "less peaceful means" to assure his disappearance from the scene.

Wilson's remarkable assertion of American intentions did much to alienate those Mexicans who had most to gain by

Huerta's elimination. Venustiano Carranza, the "Constitutional-ist" successor to Madero's mantle, rebuffed a Wilson overture with a denial of "the right of any nation on this continent, acting alone or in conjunction with European powers to interfere in the domestic affairs of the Mexican Republic." The Mexican spirit was still marked by the memory of the American invasion of 1846. Carranza rejected the suggestion of armed intervention from the north as "unconceivable and inadmissible on any grounds or any pretext."

The President was seriously embarrassed. When Huerta failed to fall at Wilson's will, when the Mexicans in the capital did not respond to his signal to rise against their master, when the Con-stitutionalists rebuffed his attempt to influence their course, he at first appeared to retreat. "Watchful waiting" seemed to have become a euphemism for bewildered impotence. But Wilson had an iron will. He was able to absorb the lessons of his defeat and find new rationales and new methods for achieving the same ob-jectives. The President's aims, it must be remembered, were in keeping with the imperatives that guided his reform attempts on the domestic front. If foreign policy was a new area for him, he was a master of quick study and incisive analysis.

Coming to grips with the reality that Carranza's forces were the only hope for Huerta's overthrow, Wilson was able to con-vince himself that the Constitutionalist stubbornness could be re-garded as a sign of that very independence he wished for Mexico. The President concluded that support for Carranza was "an in-evitable course of action in the circumstances." He then lifted an arms embargo that had crippled Carranza's forces. But Huerta still hung on.

The Constitutionalists' inability to take full advantage of Wil-son's shift confronted him with the necessity of "recognizing" the Mexico City government or finally taking steps to see that it fell. The President's excessive moralism had placed him in a position in which he would have to accept defeat, or, acting as Com-mander in Chief, force war on Mexico and the United States. His use of presidential authority to withhold recognition had not achieved his objective. His unofficial attempts to influence Mexi-can opinion had rallied support to his enemy and the use of his foreign policy prerogatives to articulate American hostility merely called international attention to Huerta's survival. But Wilson could still choose armed intervention.

Secretary of State William Rogers, during his testimony on the War Powers Act of 1971, noted the factors that encouraged such presidential action in the earlier part of this century. "Presidents were acting in the context of a generally popular consensus in the country that the United States should assume a posture consistent with its emerging power, particularly in the Western Hemisphere." Although Congress and public opinion expressed misgivings about the enlargement of presidential power, dissent on this score was relatively mild. One could account for this in part, the Secretary observed, because a large majority of the actions "occurred in the Caribbean, where this country's power was so predominant that there was little or no chance of forcible response to our actions." Therefore, Rogers contended, "the risks to the nation which Article 1, Section 8, was designed to reduce never arose. In short, there being no risk of major war, *one could argue there was no violation of Congress' power to declare war.*" This readiness to accede to executive violence in the absence of effective response from the victim has been, in my judgment, one of the principal factors in establishing the precedent for executive incursion in the more dangerous world of the 1970's. Wilson's Mexican intervention already offered strong hints that executive authority, no matter how noble its intent, could not be indefinitely extended beyond our borders without a challenge to American power.

On April 9, 1914, members of the crew of a small American naval vessel were arrested by Mexican authorities in a minor incident at the port of Tampico. When General Morelos Zaragoza, commander of Huerta's forces in the area, learned of the episode he was stunned. Zaragoza immediately ordered the release of the prisoners and apologized to Admiral Henry T. Mayo. But the commander of the American squadron in Tampico waters chose to escalate the controversy with a demand that the American flag be greeted with a twenty-one-gun salute. A series of communications passed between Washington and Tampico and Washington and Mexico City dealing with the possibility of compromising the

American ultimatum, but Wilson seized the opportunity to force a clash. The President ordered the entire North Atlantic fleet to Tampico. A day later, on April 15, he ordered all warships in the Pacific to Mexico's western coastal waters. Huerta was looking for a way out but he refused to surrender to Washington's insolent demands that he comply with the letter of Admiral Mayo's injunction.

Wilson now consulted with the Foreign Relations Committees of both houses of Congress. The President orchestrated the crisis theme to a crescendo. He informed them that Mexican insults had forced a stern response and that he intended to blockade both coasts of Mexico and seize Vera Cruz if the salute was not fired.

A sense of the ludicrous must have haunted that White House meeting. The President of the hemisphere's greatest power, in conference with influential members of the body constitutionally empowered to declare war, focused his attention on an artificial "point of honor" at the same time as he moved great naval fleets and announced that he was about to seize foreign territory without asking for a *declaration of war*. Wilson told the committee members that he intended to ask for congressional approval of the actions he was determined to take.

On April 20 the House of Representatives gave overwhelming support to a resolution stating that the President was justified "in the employment of armed forces," to satisfy American demands for a salute from the unrecognized Mexican chief of state. Prolonged Senate debate prevented the resolution from taking effect in time to anticipate the presidential move. Wilson's timetable had been upset.

Word had been received that a German ship, the *Ypiranga,* was about to dock at Vera Cruz with a load of ammunition earmarked for General Huerta's armies. Anxious to cut off Huerta's supplies, Wilson ordered one thousand Marines and sailors to take immediate possession of key areas of the city and to seize the customhouse in order to lay hands on anything the Germans chose to land.

The President did not think it appropriate to seize the shipment directly from the German ship, but he found it quite reasonable to invade Mexican territory in order to prevent its arrival.

Once again an American Chief Executive was ready to use force on a nation he deemed unwilling or unable to defend itself, almost at the same time as he explicitly recognized a different international law with respect to a strong or "great" power. Inasmuch as Wilson's moral aspirations were so much higher than those of most political figures, his failure to match action to precept looms larger on the historical scene. It should also be noted that such failure is infectious. The resolution, passed by the House before the invasion and by the Senate after its successful conclusion, read in part to the effect that "the United States disclaims any hostility to the Mexican people *or any purpose to make war on Mexico.*"

The Mexican army units and naval cadets who opened a steady fire on the American invaders were overwhelmed by superior numbers and weaponry. Three hundred twenty Mexican casualties, including nearly two hundred dead, momentarily solidified the Huerta and Carranza forces in a feverish rage at the Americans. Woodrow Wilson, shaken by the unexpected resistance, had second thoughts about the proper course of action. His military advisers, as is the way with military advisers, recommended more of the same and the President was pressed to move on to Mexico City to "protect American lives." Instead he cast about for a way to end the fighting while at the same time forcing Huerta from office. Refusing to take the capital, Wilson accepted an offer of arbitration from Argentina, Brazil and Chile.

With the Americans holding Vera Cruz, Huerta's career was on the wane. He attempted to bargain through the arbitrating nations but it was no use. Wilson dominated their proceedings and would accept nothing less than the provisional president's resignation. On July 14 Huerta, like Porfirio Díaz before him, gave up his office and sailed for France. Carranza Constitutionalists moved into Mexico City and "the First Chief" became Mexico's second revolutionary president. In mid-November American occupation troops left Mexican soil; Woodrow Wilson had won his recognition battle; a democratic regime was temporarily in power in Mexico. But in the United States, Congress had seen the Executive use a portion of his foreign policy prerogatives in conjunction with his authority as Commander in Chief to further whittle away at congressional war powers.

Wilson's request for a congressional resolution is of particular interest today as it offers an early example of the employment of Congress as an executive auxiliary. The President's words when he spoke to the joint session on April 20, 1914, leave no room for doubt that he was fully aware of the use to which he was putting Congress.

> No doubt I could do what is necessary in the circumstances to enforce respect for our Government without recourse to the Congress and yet not exceed my Constitutional powers as President, but I do not wish to act in a matter possibly of so grave consequence except in close conference and co-operation with both the Senate and House. I therefore come to ask *your approval* that I should use the Armed Forces of the United States in such ways and to such an extent as may be necessary to obtain from General Huerta and his adherents the fullest recognition of the rights and dignity of the United States [applause] even amidst the distressing conditions now unhappily obtaining in Mexico.

After explicitly asserting his independence of Congress and asserting that such independence was in the frame of his constitutional prerogative, the President asked for "*your approval*" of a predetermined course. It was a case of "consent" without "advise." We have since become jaded by the spectacle of Presidents seeking support before the fact in order to prevent the expression of dissatisfaction with the consequences of presidential action. Wilson probably wished to accomplish the same end. But I think there was more involved.

The President had already improved on Theodore Roosevelt's use of his office as a "bully pulpit." His decision to deliver the State of the Union message in person dramatized the declaration that he was more than "a department of government" at "the other end of Pennsylvania Avenue." Rather, he told his listeners, he was a man who wished to work closely with the legislature in achieving their common objectives.

Wilson was, like Jefferson, a party leader as well as a President. He was, like Theodore Roosevelt, a propagandist for the powers of the Presidency. I would judge that his speech to Congress on Vera Cruz was designed to bind his listeners to his policy, but that he was primarily intent on asserting by implication the supremacy of the Executive in areas bordering on war and peace. His attitude and the frankness with which it was expressed is illustrated by an exchange between Senators John Weeks and Benjamin Shively.

Weeks, noting that he had heard a rumor that troops were already in Vera Cruz, commented that it was "a farce for the Senate" to further consider a resolution in which "the State Department asked us to give the President authority to use the armed forces in Mexico." Shively replied incisively and with considerable impatience:

"I thought it was understood by this time that there is no resolution here asking Congress to give the President authority . . . He has only asked the counsel and support and approval of Congress for things that he has the authority to do without coming to Congress."

The debate was sharp. Senator John Williams of Mississippi observed that Mexico's right to self-government included the right to misgovernment and that "we have no right to sit in judgment." He demanded that the resolution be written in a way that would prevent it from being used as an excuse to stay in Mexico. "I want it so narrowed down that if Huerta shall die or be assassinated or shall resign or shall salute the flag, all we shall have to do will be to come on back home." Senator Joseph Bristow of Kansas raised the perennial question.

We are told that a disapproval of [the resolution] will be alleged to be a refusal . . . to sustain our country when engaged in war with an enemy. I do not propose however to be put in that attitude. It has been said here tonight that we are to approve or disapprove what the President has done. I think he has done wrong and I intend to say so by my vote.

The response, too, has become part of the litany of acquiescence. "The things the President has done . . . have now become history. We have got to face it from the viewpoint of the present." The words were spoken by Senator Moses Clapp, but their sense was repeated throughout the acrimonious debate. One Senator thought that "the spectacle of the President asking Congress to pass a resolution which contains no authority whatever will remain as one of the novelties of the present time." He was proven wrong, as the *pro forma* passage of such resolutions became the rule rather than the exception in the case of succeeding presidential wars. The Senate, many of its members expressing reluctance, recorded its *ex post facto* approval of Wilson's small war by a 72 to 13 vote.

The move into Mexico aroused little enthusiasm in the country at large. Unlike previous interventions in which "manifest destiny" was involved, Americans were confused as to the reason for getting caught up in an internal squabble. The New York *World* hoped that "by 2015 at least," there would be a centennial observation of peace on the Rio Grande. The Wall Street *Independent*, a month after the invasion was successfully concluded, thought that "possibly our Congressmen are afraid to go home," and the *Christian World* found hope in what it perceived as "the passing of the war spirit." Twenty years earlier, the *World* said, "the lust for war would have swept the nation . . . but none of this happened when the President took Vera Cruz last month. Congress *reluctantly* upheld him and did so hoping no war would come from it . . . the great body of people throughout the land prayed the President not to enter upon war."

The President obviously sensed the national mood when he accepted the arbitration offer that attained both a cessation of hostilities and Huerta's deposition. But Wilson's experiment in warlike intervention was expensive.

Mexican hostility had been fanned to a pitch that blocked the two countries from a normal relationship for years to come. When the bandit chief, Pancho Villa, attacked an American settlement in New Mexico, the Mexican government was unable to cooperate effectively with United States authorities in apprehending him. Any government in Mexico City that acquiesced in the "hot pursuit" proposed by Washington would have been overturned.

Villa's bloody ploy was intended to provoke war. He almost succeeded. Wilson, however, despite a number of provocative incidents, had learned something from the earlier intervention. His
actions during the campaign against Villa were designed to apply
the least possible pressure to Mexico's sense of sovereignty.
Woodrow Wilson's policy on Pancho Villa was a complete re-
versal of the form he had displayed in the Vera Cruz incident.
But he would never again feel free to withhold executive strength
from war. The rest of his political life would be spent in expanding presidential power so that the United States could win a war
"to make the world safe for democracy."

The Wilson Presidency brought to center stage all of the
forces that had been gathering for years on behalf of overwhelming and undiluted executive power. With world war as the focal
point of the nation's energies and emotions, it was inevitable that
presidential authority would assume the large dimensions that it
has yet to relinquish. Wilson's own intellectual power and his
authoritarian personality were fit instruments for the political
providence that has shaped our contemporary institutions.

The President had been a ranking political scientist in the
days before he plunged into his own public career. His *Congressional Government* offers an interesting insight into the development of his views. In the edition published in 1885 Wilson wrote
that the national power was effectively vested in the Congress.
The Presidency was, in his eyes, an executive adjunct that would
much better serve its purpose if it were reorganized along the
lines of the British cabinet system. Time was to change that position radically. In 1908 when he published a series of essays
entitled *Constitutional Government* Wilson had this to say about
the Presidency.

> Our President must always, henceforth, be one of the great
> powers of the world, whether he act greatly and wisely or
> not . . . we have but begun to see the presidential office in
> this light; but it is the light which will more and more beat
> upon it and more and more determine its character and its
> effect upon the policies of the nation . . . [the President]
> must stand always at the front of our affairs and the office
> will be as big and influential as the man who occupies it.

Wilson himself was determined to act according to his own prescription. He had noted that the presidential role in foreign affairs was of particular significance. His control was "absolute," Wilson felt, and when war came he moved to assert that supremacy. Like Lincoln before him the President was the leader of forces engaged in a struggle that required total mobilization. But he was determined to avoid constitutional questions insofar as he could by using congressional statute to back up his authority.

There was no question about the legitimacy of the congressional declaration of war against Germany on April 6, 1917. Only two members of Congress had voted against the resolution and they did not return the following year. The struggle over the war powers, however, continued undiminished, and it continued to move in the direction of unrestrained presidential prerogative. Wilson's consolidation and expansion of that power was assisted by the enormous popular support for the war. He was aware that the Presidency symbolized the nation to its people and he took advantage of it. "If Congress be overborne," he had written, "it will be no fault of the makers of the Constitution—it will be from no lack of constitutional powers on its part, but only because the President has the nation behind him and Congress has not."

Even before war was declared, the lines of dispute over war powers were drawn when the President asked Congress for permission to arm merchant ships carrying goods to Europe. He asked that "the authority and power of Congress" be placed behind a measure that he considered within his own power to enact "without special warrant of law, by the plain implication of my constitutional duties and powers." A filibuster by a small number of "willful men" prevented the overwhelming majority of the Congress from endorsing the presidential request for their support. Wilson, convinced of his own legal authority, gave notice on March 12 that he intended to proceed to arm the ships. Confrontation never came about because the war itself followed a few weeks later and the national sentiment was overwhelmingly behind Wilson's program. The President, meanwhile, using "the executive power" of Article 2, began to create a series of advisory committees under the Council for National Defense that would blossom into instruments of executive authority when war was officially declared. The War Industries Board under Bernard Baruch and the Food Administration under Herbert Hoover are archetypal examples of instruments designed to make and enforce rules and regulations with the full power of law. In each case these instruments began to work under the Wilsonian concept of the Commander in Chief and executive powers and were greatly expanded in their scope when Congress added statutory authority to the presidential initiative.

Wilson's interpretation of his rights, powers and duties did not go unchallenged. Senator James Reed, during debate on a measure broadening presidential authority, cried out that "more and more we cringe . . . the lash is laid across the legislative back." Reed's outburst came in the context of a move to give the President total powers over the nation's economy. The food supply, the railroads, natural resources and access to cables and communications links were all mobilized into the national service under the authority of the Commander in Chief. When Baruch assumed his power as chairman of the War Industries Board, he did so under the simple mandate of a presidential letter. A national propaganda agency under the direction of George Creel was created by executive authority despite considerable congressional opposition. The nation's first total war had set the stage for a total response that tolerated little or no dissent.

Wilson's ability to override opposition to his assumption of the entire war power was an outgrowth of a national fury at the enemy that knew no bounds. The German language had been banned from many schools and German music had been dropped from the repertory of distinguished American orchestras. Citizens of German extraction had been mobbed in the course of "liberty bond drives." In such an atmosphere constitutional questions are bound to receive short shrift. But some members of Congress doggedly continued to battle on behalf of the separation of powers and for congressional authority to act under the war powers constitutionally delegated to the lawmakers.

In an age when price controls and profit ceilings have come to be regarded as normal weapons in the national arsenal during times of peace as well as war it is difficult to imagine the animosity roused when they were first introduced into American life. The food bill that Wilson asked Congress to pass included authority to control prices and regulate distribution. The chairman of the Senate Agriculture Committee called it "unconstitutional legislation." He reminded the Senate to "cherish the Constitution in times like these." Senators Thomas Gore and Henry Cabot Lodge both feared the one-man rule they saw being created under the pressure of war. The passage of the Lever Act, as the food statute was called, marked a turning point in American political history. The legislation granted unprecedented authority to the President and his agents but it did far more than that. Grants of power under the Lever Act were so huge that Congress passed the responsibility for its implementation to the Executive. The President was authorized to create any agencies, boards and panels that he thought suitable to administer the act. In effect Congress had delegated legislative powers to the other end of Pennsylvania Avenue. It is a pattern that has continued to this very day. But in 1917 it was new on the American scene and there were loud if scattered cries of protest that were drowned in the demand for any measures that would assure victory. One Senator announced that he was unconcerned about the fate of "a paper constitution" that had been "more or less suspended" under the exigencies of war. Others didn't say as much, but they voted as though they were in full agreement that victory justified the most drastic kind of change in constitutional relationships.

By the end of 1917 the President had at his disposal all of the power a Chief Executive could ask in order to prosecute a total war. The last numerical restrictions had been removed from his authority to draft men under the selective service act. Executive agencies had proliferated under blanket congressional authorization; the President stood supreme. He consolidated that supremacy in the aftermath of a congressional attempt to create a new agency that would have limited the powers of the Commander in Chief.

During the debate over the food bill, Weeks of Massachusetts had offered an amendment that would have created a Joint Committee on the Conduct of the War, modeled on the Civil War committee that bore the same name. Wilson objected that such a group would interfere with the efficient conduct of the war. He cited Lincoln's experience as evidence that congressional participation in war-related activity would amount to harassment of the Executive. Although Congress dropped the plan, Henry Cabot Lodge remarked that unrestrained executive authority would lead to "a day of reckoning which we shall all deplore."

The reckoning first appeared to have come when a bill to create a War Cabinet was introduced in the Senate. The proposal was made in January of 1918, following a series of disclosures of inefficiency in the newly created war agencies. Three men, to be chosen by the President and confirmed by the Senate, would exercise in substantial degree a good many of the powers constitutionally delegated to the Commander in Chief. Wilson, furious at the assault on his authority and fearful that the bill would pass in the name of efficiency, had a bill of his own introduced that would improve executive capabilities and validate his power once and for all. The Overman Act, named for the Chairman of the Judiciary Committee, gave the President free rein to reorganize the executive branch. The bill's provisions authorized him to eliminate or consolidate departments at his discretion and to delegate any of the Chief Executive's authority to any department he chose. If Wilson decided to make foreign policy through the Postmaster General and to send the mail through the State Department, the Overman Act gave him all the authority he needed to do so.

The debate on the Overman Act crystallized the division of opinion on the President's constitutional authority during time of war. Congress debated the bill for six weeks. Some of the members warned prophetically that such a delegation of authority under the stress of war could also shape the country's peacetime institutions. But few questioned the need for increased efficiency and it was noted that past Presidents had also wanted to reorganize the executive branch. The constitutional implications of such reorganization and the way in which it came about were left for later Congresses to consider. In 1917, as in most periods of war or domestic conflict, the question was what to do now.

Senator Albert Cummins of Iowa carried much of the burden for those who were concerned with increasing presidential power.

"The bill is unconstitutional because it attempts to delegate legislative power to the President," Cummins said. But his attack was much more far-ranging than that. He expressed bitterness that men and women who had differed with presidential policy were branded "throughout the land" as "traitors." Cummins also contended that the President's war powers were no greater than his powers were in time of peace. The Constitution, said the Iowa Senator, was the bulwark of a Republic that was strong enough to meet the challenges of war and peace under the free institutions that should not be abandoned under stress. He noted that President Wilson already had the specific power to conduct the war without hindrance and he took sharp issue with those "who come before the Senate saying . . . the President wants this power, that because he wants it he ought to have it," and that those who questioned the wisdom of the delegation were guilty of disloyalty. Such an attitude would "ultimately destroy the strength of the American people." But the heart of the Cummins argument rested on the premise that in Congress resided the powers "we must employ in order to carry on the war successfully." He argued that it was "delusion" to think that all of the powers of government rested in the executive branch during time of war. Constitutionally, Senator Cummins thought, the powers of the President that could be "justly exercised" were but "a tithe" of those entrusted to Congress.

Senator Philander C. Knox, a former Attorney General, gave partial support to Cummins. He contended that the President *had no war power as such.* The key factor in the widespread view that presidential power expanded during hostilities, in his opinion, was based on the unquestionable fact that *the Commander in Chief powers operated on an expanded and multiplied range of activities during hostilities.* That activity loomed so large in the public eye that it was often confused with the relatively limited war power conferred on the Commander in Chief.

Senators Cummins and Knox were in the minority. Wartime fervor carried the day. Many Congressmen who had reservations about the increasing powers accorded the President in order to wage total war were carried along by an attitude that found expression in the words of the Senator who said, "Our toast now, Senators, should be 'Our President, more power to him.' "

Passage of the Overman Act was the ultimate extension of presidential authority to make war. By 1919 a noted scholar, Lindsay Rogers, was able to say that "Wilson has exerted an almost absolute authority over Congress." The reaction came of course when the President attempted to ride over senatorial sensibilities during the peace negotiations. His wartime powers had given Wilson a heady sense of executive prerogative and the League of Nations fell victim to the break between President and Congress. The famous Lodge Reservations to the League Treaty were in reality reassertions of the congressional authority to make war. If Wilson had been willing to negotiate with the United States Congress in the same spirit as he negotiated with the Allies it is probable that the United States would have become a member of the League of Nations. Whether that would have changed the disastrous course of events that led to the Second World War is an open question, but it is certainly worth considering. In the context of the American situation in the 1970's, the fact of presidential isolation and insulation from dissenting opinion is one of our most profound problems. When almost absolute power is granted to a single individual, entirely too much comes to depend on the nature of his personality, his staff and advisers, as well as the image he feels compelled to project in his dealings with others. We have generally been fortunate in the character of the men in whom we trusted. On other occasions we have been less so.

Woodrow Wilson was deserving of their gratitude for the unsparing energy and powerful intellect he placed at the service of the highest aspirations of the American people. They called forth much of the best in the national tradition. But his weaknesses must be said to have been the weaknesses of "the Emperor who had no clothes." The sense of his own moral rectitude, of the rightness of his own perceptions and of the evils of his enemies, prevented him from achieving the very objectives for which he strove. The war to end war planted the seeds of still another and greater conflict. The President who had gathered more power to himself than any other before him died broken and alone. The wartime willingness of Congress to surrender its constitutional responsibilities had blinded him to the fact that he would have to deal with very different responses when peace came.

Woodrow Wilson's fate is a tragic example of the frailty of human personality and the wisdom of the constitutional separation of powers that protects against that frailty. Lord Acton was not writing of Woodrow Wilson when he coined the aphorism that "power corrupts, and absolute power corrupts absolutely." But he might have been speaking of any man who has been encouraged by circumstance and permitted by his peers to assume the powers that belong to others. During the perils of war members of Congress should recall Sam Rayburn's response when he was asked how many Presidents he had served under. "I've served *with* eight Presidents," Rayburn replied. "I haven't served *under* any."

XV

FDR: Commander in Chief of Our Generation

THE Roosevelt years were marked by domestic and foreign crises that solidified the hold of the Presidency on the American people. The institution flourished in the personality of the man who held the office; for this President, with a personality uniquely fitted to the task, was afforded the opportunity to express himself across a web of communication available to no previous Chief Executive. The fireside chat, the twice-weekly press conference in the President's office, air travel across the nation and the world, conferences with other world leaders at far places with romantic and exotic names served the public purpose of a man uniquely endowed with the ability to exploit the dramatic circumstance and the new technology of the age in which he wielded executive power.

FDR's Presidency was the natural peroration of the long history of the expansion of White House authority. The great wartime precedents laid down by Lincoln and Wilson combined with the only slightly less significant advances of Theodore Roosevelt and William McKinley to forge an arsenal of executive power for a man with the will to use it! War with Hitler's Germany and the Japanese Empire provided the occasion and Franklin Roosevelt had the ability and determination to gather the partially hidden resources of his office and transmute them into an instrument of such power as to change the nature of our political institutions. The Second World War has been over for nearly thirty years but we live under executive powers that were first shaped to fight World War II's battles and that have never been relinquished by FDR's successors to the Presidency. As Professor Corwin noted at war's end, a "constitution of rights" had become a "constitution of powers."

Although the Roosevelt years are rapidly receding into a historic past, they are still close enough to condition the attitudes of many of the men and women who currently occupy positions of public responsibility. Indeed, World War II and its aftermath were the major factors in the development of the political and social attitudes of the large majority of the American people. The conflicting impulses and the volatile expressiveness of the postwar generation are belated reflections of an age that embraces four years of worldwide violence, the explosion of the first atomic bomb and a quarter century of Cold War that climaxed in the fury of Vietnam.

In such a context, analysis of President Roosevelt's use of the war powers is inevitably affected by the biases of those who participated in the war and in public life since its conclusion. Historic perspective is foreshortened by active involvement and I am no exception to that rule.

I believed at the time that it was vital to American survival that Hitler be defeated: Whatever reservations I had about FDR's Presidency, I believed in 1940 that it was essential that he be reelected for a third term because I felt that a Roosevelt defeat would have been worth two million men to the Axis Powers. It is ironic that thirty years later I write in criticism of the overwhelming imbalance of war powers that evolved so profoundly during the Roosevelt Presidency. Yet, had I served in Congress during World War II, I would have probably acceded in large measure to the broadening scope of presidential war power. The situation was analogous to the crisis faced by Lincoln during the Civil War and quick and bold executive action was necessary to assure survival.

I must nevertheless acknowledge that the United States has paid a high price for FDR's use and extension of the Commander in Chief powers. Emergencies have a way of being codified into standard operating procedure and the liberties of the people are directly affected by the failure of legislative constraints on presidential authority to make war. In the mid-seventies that is the problem we must solve and it is from this angle of vision that we must assess the impact of FDR's wartime administration.

The America of the thirties and early forties was a vastly different place from the United States of the seventies. The abundance that has come to symbolize America to the rest of the world is almost grotesque when juxtaposed against the desperation of the depression years. Hope for a more secure future was a driving impulse behind the popular acceptance of the New Deal. Perhaps the most important difference between those years and now is the quality of belief. Americans, by and large, were ready to trust their elected leaders. The tendency was to believe that the people in Washington were telling the truth. The liars were foreign enemies. American virtues were taken for granted. Rectitude, straight dealing and compassion were seen as ends in themselves. I don't mean to oversimplify a set of national responses. There were bitter divisions among us, but we took for granted the basic premises. We knew that our institutions were, in the final analysis, based on trust. Whether or not that trust was abused became one of the major issues of the postwar years and it was first raised in the context of how we got into war with Japan and Germany. The nature of presidential authority and influence was closely related to the answer to that question.

Franklin D. Roosevelt's understanding of public opinion was matchless. Some of his biographers and several members of his administration seem at times to have been exasperated by the close attention he paid to that opinion and how he appeared to let it guide his actions and influence the national posture. Secretary of War Henry Stimson, who had been an intimate of Theodore Roosevelt, once noted in his diary that the President ought to be a "leader" of public opinion rather than a "representative." He was convinced that although FDR was dedicated to the defeat of the Axis Powers, his concern with public reaction to American involvement might result in a German victory. Stimson's apprehensions were in direct contrast to the fears of those who were convinced that the President was maneuvering us into war. Roosevelt's behavior gave credence to both views. His insight into the popular mood of disenchantment with the European involvements of the past led him to the conviction that American participation in the war would have to be related to purely American interests as perceived by the American people. He did everything he could as President to encourage that perception.

FDR's activities as leader of public opinion seem to me to have made it possible for the country to engage in a four-year world war with overwhelming popular support. Our own recent experience in Vietnam underlines the importance of such support in waging any war. Yet World War II was the last occasion in American military history in which the nation was united from beginning to end. Even the isolationists who bitterly opposed American intervention rallied behind the national effort in the aftermath of Pearl Harbor. Their challenge to America's participation in the conflict had been based in part on the belief that FDR bypassed the Congress and the people to create a situation in which war was the inevitable outcome. He had used presidential power, in this view, so as to preempt the constitutional war-making authority of Congress. The declaration of war on December 8, 1941, was to them a simple recognition of war begun by presidential action. Senator Arthur Vandenberg wrote on December 11, "Perhaps it was ultimately inevitable that we should be involved—no one can successfully deny that thesis. But I contend that this inevitability was certain in the light of the foreign policies which we pursued. We 'asked for it,' and 'we got it.' The interventionist says today—as the President virtually did in his address to the nation—'See! This proves we were right . . . this war was sure to involve us.' The non-interventionist says (and I say)—'See! We have insisted from the beginning that this course would lead to war and it has done exactly that.' "

In the light of subsequent testimony and events it is hard to escape the conclusion that what Vandenberg called our "foreign policies" led to the final plunge into World War II. I believe, however, that the line between "foreign policies" and "war powers" as executed by President Roosevelt was so vague as to be nonexistent. He used all of the Constitution's "executive power" (and a good many extra-constitutional precedents) to enable him to lead the country into a conflict he saw as inevitable if the Republic was to survive. We are concerned here, not with the merits of his assessment, with which I agreed, but with the presidential tools he used to attain his objective and with the question of whether or not those tools were his by right.

In his wartime memoir, *The Grand Alliance,* Winston Churchill testifies to the enormous impact of presidential action on British fortunes *before* America's official entry into the struggle. "In January, 1941," Churchill tells us, "secret staff discussions began in Washington covering the whole scene, and framing a combined world strategy . . . Preparations were started to meet the needs of joint ocean convoy in the Atlantic." This was during a period when the President fenced with press conference interlocutors over the convoy question by insisting that American ships would "patrol" the waters of the Western Hemisphere. When he was pressed on the difference between "convoy" and "patrol" the President remarked that "you can call it standing on your head if you've a mind to. I call it 'patrol.' " As the nation became more deeply involved first in acts that bordered on war, and then as the President erased that border without legislative sanction, FDR carried out his purpose to do everything within his power to assure British survival and to bring public opinion along with him.

Roosevelt, with the depression experience behind him, knew how to shape the crisis atmosphere to the end he had chosen. "Emergency" was the key to an ever-expanding use of presidential authority. A Republican Congressman, Bruce Barton, complained as early as March, 1939, that "a study of President Roosevelt's messages and speeches disclosed that the country was now in its thirty-ninth emergency since 1933." Barton accused the President of "manufacturing continuous crises" and lashed out at the repeated presidential use of phrases like "national emergency," "unprecedented condition" and "serious menace." Barton did not concern himself with the realities to which these phrases were addressed. He understood full well, however, that use of "national emergency" as a tool for the justification of presidential edict was sanctioned by Lincoln's Civil War precedent and the passage of wartime legislation in 1917. Congressional action *taken a quarter of a century earlier* could invoke a wide range of executive powers when the President declared a national emergency. Franklin Roosevelt used that power to its fullest extent and he amplified its effects with a broad *prewar* application of the Commander in Chief power.

Roosevelt expressed his sympathy for the Allies in a series of addresses calling for "quarantine" of the Axis Powers and commitment of American resources to the struggle as "the arsenal of democracy." But he backed and filled, presumably seeking to stay with the tides of public opinion. The first major break with that pattern and the first full-scale assertion of new executive war power came with the Destroyers for Bases deal with England.

In the spring of 1940, Churchill had approached the President with a request for American naval vessels to help Britain resist the German U-boat onslaught. British resources were stretched to their limits and materiel from the United States was essential to survival. Not until September, 1940, was FDR able to find a way out of the constitutional (and public relations) difficulties that threatened to prevent him from making such an arrangement. He was able then to give Britain fifty overage United States destroyers in exchange for the lease of naval bases on eight of Britain's North Atlantic island possessions. For Churchill, the arrangement was a dramatic symbol of the connection between a desperate Britain and a sympathetic if wary United States. For Roosevelt, it was, among other things, the first time he chose to defy congressional authority over military dispositions. A naval appropriations bill that had been enacted earlier in his administration explicitly prohibited the President from giving military hardware to foreign governments unless it had been certified by the military as "useless to the defense of the United States."

The law was intended to prevent FDR from involving United States forces in the European war without congressional authorization. But the President was determined to build a bridge to the Allies and to assert his authority as Commander in Chief. Rather than appeal for congressional support, he chose to link the destroyers to the bases in such a way as to validate the measure as a "strengthening" of American defense. I do not doubt at all that the Destroyers for Bases deal did exactly that. FDR's action was, however, a challenge to congressional war powers. His independent behavior was calculated to assure him of a psychological advantage on the eve of a struggle for complete control of the military forces.

Attorney General Robert Jackson's opinion that the President was entitled to make the trade was based on a commander's duty to "dispose" the forces at his command. Jackson said that meant that the Commander in Chief could dispose *of* those forces and their equipment on his own authority. The construction Jackson put on the Commander in Chief power, and his use of the right to "dispose," was later challenged by Professor Corwin, who observed that the Constitution specifically grants Congress the right to raise, equip and regulate the armed forces. Jackson also cited the President's constitutional responsibility for foreign relations. He rejected the contention that the Senate at least should have been consulted because the arrangement had the weight of treaty, when he observed that the destroyer deal embodied no future American commitments that would require senatorial consent under the Constitution. Because there was no financial obligation on the part of the United States, there was no constitutional requirement for the Senate to ratify *"an opportunity that entails no obligation."* But the Attorney General might just as well have said that "a *fait accompli* entails no ratification."

Although press response to the Destroyers for Bases arrangement reflected the split between interventionist and isolationist sentiment, the constitutional question did not go unnoticed even among those who cheered the policy of closer ties with the Allies. *The New York Times*, brushing aside the question of whether Roosevelt had the authority to make the deal, observed that "the present agreement would be even more desirable if it had the formal stamp of congressional approval on it." The *Times*'s Washington Bureau Chief, Arthur Krock, noted that during a period when democratic processes were "scorned and abandoned throughout the world," the United States "should be sedulous in maintaining them." Krock went on to observe that Mr. Roosevelt *"is already too greatly disposed to sink the legislative function in the executive."* The Boston *Post* contended that the whole thing was accomplished in "a manner far removed from our rightful democratic processes," and the St. Louis *Post-Dispatch* headlined "Dictator Roosevelt Commits an Act of War."

In Congress, the critics focused on the Constitution while FDR's supporters cried "emergency." One Representative said that "there is no longer any need for Congress," and a Senator accused FDR of "an act of war," but the Democratic majority rallied to the President with a series of statements addressed to British need and gallantry and the American obligation to sustain her. The lines were drawn on policy rather than constitutionality. World War II was to be filled with episodes in which major attention was focused on the grave issues at hand. The Constitution was sometimes pressed into the service of policy; where it could not be used, it would be quietly ignored. The Destroyers for Bases deal was only the first of dozens of incidents illustrative of the erosion of congressional authority during the course of hostilities.

President Roosevelt and his aides were convinced that effective British resistance against the expected German onslaught would be impossible without full-scale American support. They were determined to provide that support to the degree necessary to sustain British arms. No one in the Administration represented a contrary view although there was considerable and substantial dissent in Congress. Until December 7, 1941, an essentially adversary relationship existed between the President and a bipartisan congressional minority that was rooted in the traditions of midwestern isolationism and pacifist populism. That minority gave voice to its doubts over Roosevelt's direction during the battle over Lend-Lease.

On January 6, 1941, the President told Congress in his State of the Union message that the United States must provide "billions of dollars' worth of weapons," to the anti-Axis forces. He emphatically contended that such an effort would not be an act of war, "even if a dictator should unilaterally proclaim it so to be." The President sought blanket authority to manufacture or purchase any weapon, ammunition, vessel or airplane and to exchange defense information with any government he selected and to provide whatever weapons and supplies were necessary to the support of the armies of any power he deemed suitable. The Chief Executive was to be authorized to take such actions without any limitation of cost and these new powers were to override the provisions of any other law. No President had ever asked for such wide-ranging authority over American production and supply in time of peace or war. More limited precedents had been established during the Wilson Administration but the need had never before been so great or the pressures for quick action so intense. According to William L. Langer and S. Everett Gleason's study, *The Undeclared War*, Roosevelt wished to supply the Allies without continual reference to Congress and without the risk of time-consuming controversy. But the bill itself was the lightning rod for the controversy Mr. Roosevelt feared. The New York *Daily News* produced this headline, "Defense Bill Gives All War Power to Pres." The story, written by John O'Donnell and Doris Fleeson, had the same flavor.

> The Peace bloc in Congress declared immediate war tonight on President Roosevelt's sweeping bid for one-man dictatorial power to lend or lease this nation's fighting equipment, its military secrets and the future output of its mighty economic machine . . . At an opening of the greatest test of strength between Congress and the White House since Roosevelt entered the White House . . . isolationists charged that Roosevelt was demanding the abdication of Congress and its power to declare war.

The historian Charles Beard sounded the constitutional warning when he testified before the Senate that the Lend-Lease proposal should be preambled with the words, "All provisions of law and the Constitution to the contrary notwithstanding, an Act to place all the wealth and all the men and women of the United States at the free disposal of the President . . . to authorize him to wage undeclared wars for anybody, anywhere in the world, until the affairs of the world are ordered to suit his policies." Beard's hyperbole obscured the considerable truth in his assertion. HR1776, as Lend-Lease was called when it was introduced, provided powers that were stunning in their potential for the aggrandizement of presidential power. Secretary of the Treasury Morgenthau, who had been entrusted with the responsibility for drafting the bill, discussed its intent with considerable frankness. The President wanted a free hand in the manufacture and distribution of war materiel, Morgenthau told key treasury officials. There was to be no subterfuge in achieving the objective. "We want to do this thing right out and out," the President had remarked.

A six-week struggle ensued over the bill's provisions. Although Roosevelt's Cabinet members testified to the importance of the Act in the context of an administration policy tied to British survival, Congress focused on the questions raised by Beard in his assault on the measure's constitutionality. Senator Wheeler charged that the bill violated international law and that "Congress coldly and flatly [has] been asked to abdicate." The Montana isolationist, who had been resisting presidential encroachments on congressional authority since the days of Woodrow Wilson, warned that passage of Lend-Lease "means war, open and complete warfare." He was joined by Representative Clifford Hope of Kansas. "The present bill will put us in the war in the end just as surely as if Congress had voted a declaration of war. We will be in for all purposes and to the finish. We will be in without any vote of Congress on the question and without the great majority of our people having any idea that this momentous step has been taken." An interesting light is cast on these passionate congressional remonstrances by the memoirs of Secretary of War Henry Stimson, written in the third person with McGeorge Bundy:

> Stimson did not publicly preach to the American people the necessity of fighting; any such outright appeal would at once have lost him his hearers; always his statements were framed to preach rather the absolute necessity of preventing a Nazi triumph. *Although constantly pressed for such an admission by isolationist members of Congress, Stimson never allowed himself to say that the final result of President Roosevelt's*

policy would be war . . . As he gradually became convinced that war was inevitable, he was bound to silence by the requirement of loyalty to his chief.

If Stimson, one of Roosevelt's closest advisers and an ardent exponent of active American intervention in the war against Hitler, was aware of the inevitable war to come out of presidential policy, it is hardly likely that the Chief Executive himself was any less cognizant of where the country was heading. It is here that the constitutional obligation of "advise and consent," along with the congressional responsibility in a decision to make war, were aborted by the President's assessment of the necessities of policy. If the President had openly declared his intention to commit specific acts of war if they were necessary to assure Hitler's defeat, he might have precipitated a constitutional crisis that would have prevented effective United States action. Although Harry Hopkins once remarked that Roosevelt was fully prepared to stand the risk of impeachment, it was exactly that kind of dilemma and its consequences that he was determined to avoid. Roosevelt's problem was a classic illustration of the strain placed on executive leadership when it must operate during a time of international crisis within a constitutional system of checks and balances. Anyone who lived through the period sharing Roosevelt's concerns and convictions can take little satisfaction out of convicting him of abusing the Constitution he was pledged to uphold. Almost every act FDR took prior to the declaration of war was hedged with qualifications designed to dilute the credibility of such an accusation. While Stimson, Navy Secretary Knox and other key advisers pressed for an increasingly belligerent public posture, the President himself looked at public opinion polls that reflected the paradox of majority opposition to American involvement at the same time as that majority expressed an awareness that war was simply a matter of time.

Roosevelt himself has been charged with creating a climate of hesitancy; if so, he must also be credited with using the Presidency in such a way as to elicit mass recognition that there was no long-range alternative to active intervention.

The debate over Lend-Lease was an early manifestation of

FDR's full-scale commitment to war. It was, at the same time, marked by the disingenuous quality that earned him the criticism of supporters as well as enemies. Arthur Krock, assessing him at the end of the war, wrote in his notes that FDR was "too ready to persuade himself that the national interest justified glossing over or withholding the facts due the people." That readiness certainly colored his relations with Congress. Administration witnesses on behalf of Lend-Lease persisted in describing it as a last hope for peace. Yet almost every responsible member of the executive branch truly regarded Lend-Lease as an effective instrument of war and some of them were convinced that the isolationists were right in judging it to be the precursor to full-scale participation.

Secretary of State Hull, while acknowledging the bill's dangers, called it "the safest course." Stimson said that Lend-Lease was not a breach of neutrality at the same time as he avowed that "there was no obligation to be neutral in the face of aggression," and Secretary of the Navy Knox told the House committee that he would be opposed to the use of "manpower" to aid England if Lend-Lease failed of its purpose. Roosevelt cannot be said to have presented Congress with an objective and complete administration assessment of the ultimate effect of such broad-scale aid to England especially when combined with unparalleled executive power. But an ambience of increasing danger was created by the hearings themselves, and this he must have calculated as part of his arsenal of psychological preparation. He had set the stage with a radio address that informed the American public of his determination to do everything necessary to help the Allies to defeat the Axis and the warnings of those who opposed the bill did much to heighten the drama.

Charles Lindbergh, the most prominent of the isolationists, and Joseph Kennedy, FDR's former ambassador to Britain, both testified that HR1776 would lead the United States into the war and it is unlikely that the President was unduly upset over the warning. Each step the Administration was to take was an inevitable outgrowth of the one before and each was accompanied by a chorus of warnings that war was on the way.

Analysis after the fact leads inevitably to the conclusion that presidential war had actually begun at the beginning of Roosevelt's third term when he responded to Churchill's appeals for assistance with an increasingly close strategic relationship and the fifty destroyers that were later recognized as the first example of Lend-Lease in action. That presidential war was to mount in intensity and effectiveness until the end of 1941. A congressional majority, still unwilling to enter the conflict, was in the firm grasp of an administration privately committed to full intervention. The last congressional opportunity to alter the course of events disappeared on March 11, 1941, when Lend-Lease passed both houses of Congress. The "constitutionalist" minority asserted itself in the final text with provisions that required congressional authorization of expenditures under the bill and a clause empowering Congress to repeal the act by joint resolution. But the battle over Lend-Lease was a last gasp for active congressional participation in the decision process as it related to the making of war. FDR now had the major power resources at his disposal and he used them fully until the Japanese attack at Pearl Harbor gave Congress the opportunity to validate what Roosevelt himself had finally called a "shooting war."

The road to that shooting war was defined by presidential decisions on the implementation of Lend-Lease. Even before congressional deliberations had been concluded, high-level military staff talks between British and American officers were secretly conducted in Washington under the code name ABC-1. The British participants, dressed as civilians, were ostensibly members of a supply mission. But they and their American counterparts were making plans for the closest possible military cooperation. ABC-1 expressed a relationship between the two countries that Robert Sherwood has described as "a common law alliance." Sherwood, who worked closely with Harry Hopkins, the President's top wartime aide, wrote in *Roosevelt and Hopkins* that "the alliance which existed between the United States and Great Britain following the passage of Lend-Lease . . . was certainly not 'recognized' in such jurisdictions as Congress." He went on to say that if Congress had been aware of its extent, the demands for Roosevelt's impeachment would have been considerably louder.

That alliance, formalized only after the Japanese attack, was a direct outgrowth of the close personal bonds that had developed between the British Prime Minister and the American President. When Churchill described to Roosevelt the increasing U-boat menace to the supplies now beginning to pour from the American production lines, the President began to move toward the next step.

The word "convoy" means little in the context of the seventies. But in 1941 it was synonymous with an act of war. Germany, Italy and Japan were embargoed, restricted from military purchase on the American market, even as the Allies (first Britain and then Soviet Russia) became the recipients of guns, planes, munitions and the other sinews of war on an increasingly staggering scale. The Administration was in no mood to see the bulk of that material sent to the bottom by German submarines and convoy appeared to be the answer. But during the debate on Lend-Lease the warning that the next step would be military escort for materiel destined for Britain, was repeated by the bill's opponents and administration spokesmen had been forced to deny any such plans. Secretary Knox, pressed by his questioners, had conceded that "convoy" would be "an act of war." He angered some of the committee members when he argued that he would be obliged to order such convoys if the President instructed him to do so. Knox, in effect, had contended that Roosevelt as Commander in Chief was constitutionally empowered to commit an act of war even without a congressional declaration. These exchanges and the heated discussion of the issue in the press took place in a situation very unlike the Vietnam conflict. The presidential response, however, made it almost mandatory for later Chief Executives to act on their own in behalf of military objectives they considered vital to the national interest. The giant scale of Roosevelt's maneuvers had reduced the psychological barriers to smaller scale international "police actions." FDR, after all, played for huge stakes and without undue deference to the Constitution. The pre-Pearl Harbor war was worldwide in scope, and the President's determination to act was clear. His insistence that the United States was engaged only in the defense of the "hemisphere," his refusal to acknowledge that

American actions violated international law and offered a legal cause for war to Hitler enraged his political opposition. But his posture provided a cover of constitutionality to actions that otherwise would have caused a domestic confrontation and it enabled public opinion to catch up with the realities of the situation as Roosevelt understood them.

Roosevelt's resistance to the term "convoy" was part of the fabric of guile that he employed to achieve American goals without the loss of the majority support he had obtained for actions that he doggedly insisted were "short of war." American planes and ships tracked the movement of German vessels in the hemisphere waters and reported on their disposition to British supply convoys and naval craft. When FDR was pressed by his Cabinet to shift to outright escort he was unwilling to take the plunge. Secretary of War Stimson wanted the President to go to Congress for the authority to use armed escorts, but his chief feared a congressional rejection. He, therefore, redefined "hemispheric waters" to encompass the entire western Atlantic and intensified the patrol. FDR, in announcing the broadened scope of American naval and air support for the Allies, once again described his move in the context of hemispheric defense. He had first written to Churchill that he might not announce the action at all, but the clamor from the interventionists forced a public statement. The President's essential caution, even as he took the boldest executive action since Lincoln, is highlighted by an exchange with his Secretary of War. Although Stimson would have preferred an even more aggressive stance, he was pleased by the presidential decision to step up the "hemisphere patrol." During a conference with FDR, Stimson noted that the President

kept reverting to the fact that the force in the Atlantic was merely going to be a patrol to watch for any aggressor and to report that to America. I answered there, with a smile on my face, saying, "But you are not going to report the presence of the German fleet to the Americans. You are going to report it to the British fleet." I wanted him to be honest with himself. To me it seems a clearly hostile act to the Germans, and I am prepared to take the responsibility of it. He seems to be trying to hide it into the character of a purely reconnaissance action which it really is not.

Roosevelt's public posture with regard to the convoy question was even more ambiguous. "Obviously when a nation convoys ships . . . there's apt to be some shooting—and shooting is awfully close to war," he remarked to reporters in the early part of 1941. He then observed that such action might "almost *compel* shooting to start." FDR appeared to be moving on a course that would force the Nazi government to respond with an act of force. Henry Morgenthau later recalled that the President had told him that he was "waiting to be pushed into the situation."

Roosevelt's sense of timing was one of his greatest political gifts. Although many of his closest associates sensed an aimless drift during 1941, FDR's historic clock was accurate. As the months went by, he took control of Iceland; American troops were sent to Greenland. The "patrol" system was turned into a pattern of "limited escort" partway across the Atlantic, and the President declared a state of "unlimited national emergency." At every step of the way, the nature and extent of American involvement became increasingly clear. Perhaps the most explicit and dramatic acknowledgment of the realities came in the President's Labor Day address: "I know that I speak the conscience and determination of the American people when I say that we shall do everything in our power to crush Hitler and his Nazi forces." Three days after that speech Roosevelt received the reply he had long anticipated.

The U.S.S. *Greer*, an American destroyer on patrol, sighted a German submarine in Icelandic waters and proceeded to track it for several hours. The U-boat at first attempted to escape the American surveillance. As the destroyer continued its dogged pursuit, broadcasting the submarine's location to the British fleet, the German commander turned on his tormentor and fired two torpedoes at the *Greer*, missing each time. The *Greer* returned the fire. We do not know to this day whether that German submarine was struck by American depth charges. But we do know that the incident was just what FDR had been waiting for. Expressing indignation at the Nazi "violence" and "intimidation," the President went on the air to offer the American people a new definition of "attack" and a prescription for future American response. "If submarines or raiders attack in distant waters, they can attack equally well within sight of our own shores. *Their very presence in any waters which America deems vital to its defense constitutes an attack.*" The President, asserting the principle of freedom of the seas, declared that the United States would in the future protect from Axis attack any and all vessels engaged in commerce with the Allies. That protection meant, in Roosevelt's words, that we would not wait for German ships to "strike their deadly blow—first." At last, it was to be "shoot on sight."

FDR linked his response to the *Greer* incident with Jefferson's strike at the Barbary pirates one hundred fifty years earlier. That early precedent of limited presidential war was cited as constitutional justification for an act that would bring us into world war. Presidential semantics enabled FDR to obscure the reality. "It is not an act of war on our part when we decide to protect the seas . . . ours is solely defense." But from that point until Pearl Harbor, United States forces engaged in an undeclared war in the Atlantic. Hitler failed to respond with a declaration of hostilities only because he had determined to concentrate on victory along the Russian Front before turning on his Atlantic enemy.

Roosevelt's use of the *Greer* incident to rally public opinion behind naval action against Germany established a precedent President Lyndon Johnson used when the Gulf of Tonkin became the focal point for another sea crisis.

Johnson was an admiring young Congressman during the Roosevelt Administration. One can speculate that memories of the *Greer* and its aftermath at least echoed in the presidential mind when he first received reports that the North Vietnamese "navy" had attacked an American warship in the Gulf of Tonkin. He would have had good reason to ponder the lesson, for American public opinion overwhelmingly favored FDR's new policy of "shoot on sight." Congressional opposition to presidential war was reduced to a minimum under the pressure of an "attack" on American forces. When the Germans continued to respond with torpedoes to American pressure at sea, the national temper was further inflamed. If there was a constitutional question about the war power, it had been decided by calculated presidential action, conceived and executed so as to expose the Chief Executive to as little constitutional criticism as possible, while he pursued the policy he considered essential to the military defeat of the Axis Powers. I wrote earlier that I regarded American participation in World War II as essential to the survival of our institutions. But those institutions were weakened by the very processes with which they were defended.

President Roosevelt's extraordinary use of the Executive's constitutional responsibility for foreign affairs created a situation in which our active involvement in hostilities became inevitable. His genius as a master of public opinion enabled him to join the fight at the same time as he built the national consensus essential to the successful prosecution of war. That consensus frayed during the next four years, but it maintained enough strength to stand the strain of continued expansion of executive power as the war became an oppressive yet exciting background to the everyday life of most of the American people.

Total war implies the use of the nation's total resources. The power to marshal those resources must, of necessity, reside in the national government. In 1936 the Supreme Court noted in the Curtiss-Wright decision that "a political society cannot endure without a supreme will somewhere. The powers to declare and wage war, to conclude peace . . . *if they had never been mentioned in the Constitution,* would have vested in the Federal Government as necessary concomitants of nationality." That inherent power of the national government did much to rationalize the use of FDR's Commander in Chief power on the "home front." Citing emergency in the pre-Pearl Harbor war, and the war itself after December 7 had given it constitutional sanction, Roosevelt seized a number of industrial plants in order to "keep the defense efforts of the United States a going concern." Attorney General Jackson justified these actions as resting on the President's "civil and military authority" during wartime. Roosevelt also had a base of legislation that had been enacted at

Wilson's behest during the First World War. Provisions in the National Defense Act of 1916 and the Espionage Act of 1917 had never been repealed. Roosevelt was able to use powers delegated to an earlier President in order to prosecute an even greater war. The "head start" provided by the Wilson legislation enabled FDR to assert executive authority over the full range of American life.

Nothing was untouched by the President's war power. Congress itself again delegated legislative authority to the President when it passed a series of war powers acts designed to control the country's resources and regulate labor and production. A series of alphabetic agencies exploded across the national landscape. WPB, OPA, WMC, ODT, OCD, OES and literally hundreds of other executive offices came into being as expressions of the presidential will to regulate the most minute aspects of American society. One constitutional authority asked rhetorically for the "constitutional and legal status" of the administrations, authorities and offices set up by executive fiat. Professor Corwin points out that the Constitution stipulates that "all civil offices shall be established by law." The Senate must advise and consent to presidential appointments, unless Congress provides otherwise. But during World War II, Congress made no provision for these offices, nor did FDR present his nominees for the Senate's approval. Roosevelt simply cited his authority as Commander in Chief as sufficient ground for the creation of the new wartime agencies. Occasionally he would refer to the "First War Powers Act" as ancillary authority, ignoring with Rooseveltian insouciance the simple fact that the act authorized him only to "redistribute" functions of executive agencies already in being.

Only once during the course of the war did the courts consider presidential authority to reorganize the executive branch, ruling that the agencies were "advisory" and therefore judicially "unreviewable." The reality, of course, was that the war bodies were administrative arms of the executive branch. It must be noted, too, that Congress itself did nothing to challenge their constitutionality. The legislature, just as anxious as the President to conduct the war with "efficiency," either delegated away its own constitutional powers or acquiesced in the executive assumption of powers that hitherto had not been exercised by any branch of government.

As the Presidency grew in wartime power and prestige, congressional authority waned. FDR took the initiative on the battlefields abroad and on the production line at home. The economy itself became increasingly subject to the needs of the war machine as seen by the Commander in Chief. It must be said that he was frequently more responsible in his assessment of the country's requirements than Congress appeared to be. His national constituency was aware of it and when Roosevelt and Congress finally came to loggerheads over a constitutional issue FDR once again had public opinion in his corner.

The Economic Stabilization Act of 1942 provided the occasion for the most explicit constitutional clash between the executive and legislative powers yet to be seen in wartime. Roosevelt had asked Congress to repeal a farm subsidy that threatened to produce a serious wartime inflation. His request for action was ignored despite repeated urgings. The President smoldered. He noted during one of his press conferences that he had been able to get measures through Congress at the rate of two or three a week when the depression threatened the national pocketbook. Now that the country's very existence was at stake, FDR charged, he could get Congress to do nothing at all.

Finally, on September 7, 1942, Roosevelt appeared on Capitol Hill.

I ask the Congress to take this action by the first of October. Inaction on your part by that date will leave me with an inescapable responsibility to the people of this country to see to it that the war effort is no longer imperiled by threat of economic chaos.

In the event that Congress should fail to act, and act adequately, I shall accept the responsibility and I will act . . . The President has the powers, under the Constitution and under congressional acts, to take measures necessary to avert a disaster which would interfere with the winning of the war . . . I will use my powers with a full sense of my

responsibility to the Constitution and to my country . . .
When the war is won, the powers under which I act automatically revert to the people—to whom they belong.

Roosevelt's astonishing ultimatum was cast in a form that
was bound to arouse the support of most of the American people.
During the fireside chat that followed his message to Congress
he spoke of food prices and of the sacrifices of a bomber pilot
who had died in battle over the Coral Sea. It was in the middle
of his address on price stabilization that FDR awarded the war's
first Medal of Honor. The battle was joined and if Roosevelt was
the inevitable victor he did not go unscathed.

Franklin Roosevelt had literally threatened to suspend the
Constitution if Congress failed to give him what he demanded.
The New York Times put the question: "If he can carry out this
threat on this occasion . . . what constitutional barrier would
prevent his using the same plea for whatever other powers he
wished to exercise, for whatever other laws of Congress he wished
to suspend? What effect would this have on our constitutionally
guaranteed liberties of all kinds? It may be replied that the President would assume only the powers necessary to win the war
. . . Should the President be the sole judge of what congressional
laws interfere with the winning of the war . . . would not this
whole doctrine leave Congress, as Senator Taft has said, 'a mere
shell of a legislative body'? The President has taken a grave position that cannot be allowed to pass unchallenged."

In Congress itself other voices were raised in anger. Taft
called the President's message "revolutionary and dangerous to
the American form of government . . . an assertion that the
laws of this country can be made by executive order." Senator
Vandenberg remarked that "there is less need for even greater
executive power. The need is for more efficient use of those
powers already in existence," and the minority leader, Senator
Charles McNary, observed that Roosevelt's "intimations are probably in excess of his constitutional powers." Unqualified approval
was rare even among Democrats. Senator Guffy equated the
President's threat with an attempt to "suspend Congress for the
duration of the war." And Senator Pat McCarran used the word

"dictator" to describe the President's ultimatum. Even the most ardent of Roosevelt's supporters spoke of "uncharted seas" and "unsatisfactory solutions." But in the country at large there was widespread support for a presidential posture of impatience with footdragging while there was a war going on. The New York *Herald Tribune*, a Republican newspaper, reflected that view in an editorial that termed FDR's speech "a necessary and salutary shock!" The "incisiveness of his demand on Congress," according to the *Herald Tribune* was just "what the country had been waiting for."

Congress, in the end, agreed. Within a week of FDR's speech, measures embodying most of his recommendations were reported out of committee in both houses.

FDR had won a tactical legislative victory by a threat to the fundamental law. In the rush of wartime events, the presidential ultimatum was soon seen as just another one of yesterday's headlines. But the vantage point of thirty years offers quite a different perspective. Not even Lincoln had asserted the right to overrule Congress on a matter of law. FDR had literally threatened to repeal a statute enacted by Congress. He asserted that the Constitution itself empowered him to do so. Inasmuch as he cited no particular clause, one must assume that the Commander in Chief power was his point of reference. If the President had carried through his threat there is little question that the balance of powers would have been fatally impaired. Checks and balances imply mutual restraint among the three branches of government. The overwhelming power available to a wartime President looms so large in its potential for abuse that its very presence may ultimately change the nature of the federal system. But FDR was no constitutional lawyer and one must assume that he was not aware of the significance of the closing passage in his speech to Congress: "When the war is won, the powers under which I act automatically revert to the people—to whom they belong."

The entire structure of representative government is destroyed when the Executive considers that his powers emanate not from law but from the body politic itself. Roosevelt's assertion could be easily read as a call for a new set of power relationships that would bypass Congress altogether and establish a government based on the connection between President and people. We would, under such terms, live in an elective monarchy.

The pressures of the twentieth century's total wars and the rapid change in technological forces at the disposal of national governments have combined to accelerate the thrust to increasing executive power in most of the countries of the world. In that sense, at least, we are not alone. Britain's parliamentary democracy turned during World War II into a government in which the Prime Minister became, to the public, the symbol of the State itself, and, in the day-to-day workings of government, practically the equivalent of the President of the United States. Today, the French Republic is led by a man with even greater constitutional powers than our own President. Throughout Europe and the Third World the trend to executive authority has been a response to the exigencies of a complex world order that appears to demand quick decision and instant response. The solution of executive supremacy was a natural outgrowth of the almost unrestricted activities of the Commander in Chief during World War II. While few would question Franklin Roosevelt's success in that role, the dangers in the unrestrained breadth of its scope were not adequately recognized during the period he dominated the world stage. Great battles tend to obscure the forces at work behind the lines but those forces often determine both the quality of the lives we live when the battles are over and the reasons for battles as yet unfought. Nothing better demonstrates the relationship of the wartime authority of the Commander in Chief to the erosion of the constitutional institutions he is sworn to uphold than the treatment accorded to Japanese American citizens during World War II.

Almost immediately after Japan attacked Pearl Harbor, an outcry was raised in the western states against the Nisei minority. As historian Roger Daniels recently noted, the "fifth column" danger dominated much of the press and demands for evacuation of the Japanese Americans from their rich farmlands were repeated with hysterical intensity. The Los Angeles *Times* was relatively restrained in its comment that "treachery and double-dealing are major Jap weapons." *Times* columnist Ed Ainsworth, writing immediately after Pearl Harbor, advised his readers to "be sure of nationality before you are rude to anybody." Ainsworth suggested that one way to differentiate between the yellow races was the fact that "Chinese and Koreans both hate the Japs more than we do."

JAP BOAT FLASHES MESSAGE ASHORE . . . JAPANESE HERE SENT VITAL DATA TO TOKYO . . . NETWORK OF ALIEN FARMS COVERS STRATEGIC DEFENSE AREA OVER SOUTHLAND. Dozens of similar headlines popped up in newspapers all over California.

By early February the *Times* had become infected enough with the virulence of the period to editorialize that "a viper is nonetheless a viper wherever the egg is hatched—so a Jap-American, born of Japanese parents—grows up to be a Japanese, not an American."

But perhaps the headline that best exemplifies the strain of war read, CAPS ON JAPANESE TOMATO PLANTS POINT TO AIR BASE.

President Roosevelt's military advisers were not immune to the pressures of post-Pearl Harbor nerves. Secretary of War Stimson and his aide, John McCloy, both pressed Roosevelt to "relocate" the Nisei inhabitants of the West Coast. With the casual remark, "Be as reasonable as you can," the Commander in Chief set in motion "the most drastic invasion of the rights of citizens of the United States that has thus far occurred in the history of our nation." The words were spoken by a prominent constitutional scholar, although the sentiments have become part of our own conventional wisdom. Yet only thirty years ago the Commander in Chief, acting in order to "effectively prosecute" the war, ordered over 110,000 citizens from their California homes to concentration camps in ten southwestern and northwestern states.

Roosevelt, citing "the authority vested in me as President of the United States, and Commander in Chief of the Army and Navy," directed "all executive departments, independent establishments and other federal agencies, to assist the Secretary of War or the said military commanders in carrying out this executive order." Constitutional due process had taken a legal holiday. Indeed, the Supreme Court almost said as much in one decision denying an appeal by a citizen of Japanese extraction. Chief Justice Harlan Stone, speaking for the Court, defined the war power as "the power to wage war successfully." Such a definition clearly implies the absence of any restraint on such power. Stone's biographer has written that wartime pressures pushed the Chief Justice and the Court to a point where he was ready to sanction "shrinking judicial review of the war powers almost to the vanishing point." It should be observed, if only to underline the change in perspective that change in office sometimes entails, that Justice Robert Jackson dissented. The former Attorney General wrote:

"It is said that if the military commander had reasonable military grounds for promulgating the orders, they are constitutional and become law . . . if we cannot confine military expedients by the Constitution, neither would I destroy the Constitution to approve all that the military may deem expedient."

Jackson went on to observe that a military breach of the Constitution is merely "an incident," but that legal approval of such a breach "becomes the doctrine of the Constitution."

I have tried to confine this history where possible to situations in which the President's actions breached the separation of powers. But the Japanese relocation tragedy was staged by all three branches of Federal Government. Congress did enact, at the request of the Secretary of War, a two-line resolution imposing criminal penalties on anyone who disobeyed the initial executive order. This retroactive validation of presidential initiative was similar to the congressional approval of the war measures Lincoln took in 1861 during the three months before he called Congress into special session. Presidential initiative in the relocation of American citizens was an expression of excessive concern with military danger and a response to the popular anger at the Japanese aggressor. It was never suggested that citizens of Italian or German extraction be interned and it should be noted that not one espionage or sabotage case involving Japanese Americans was ever uncovered. Even more important was the readiness of the Executive to abandon constitutional safeguards in the struggle for victory and the *ex post facto* acquiescence of Congress and courts.

We have been confronted throughout our history with situations in which the Constitution has sometimes been adapted and sometimes distorted to meet the requirements of policy. World War II imposed a strain on the constitutional substance from which it has yet to recover. If the War Relocation Authority was the framework for the large-scale invasion of the personal rights of American citizens, the executive agreements reached with foreign powers as the war reached its climax were the precursor to a postwar situation in which American Presidents have felt free to commit armed forces to action without "advice and consent," or even adequate information. The executive agreement has become synonymous with the secret agreement. Although the trend began with Theodore Roosevelt's arrangements with Japan and Santo Domingo it received its most impressive impetus from the outcome of his cousin's meeting with Churchill and Stalin at Yalta.

The demonology of World War II includes a Roosevelt plot for the assault on Pearl Harbor and a Roosevelt "surrender to the Reds" at Yalta. It is not my purpose to indulge either fantasy. Nevertheless myths arise out of a hardrock of reality. The meeting at Yalta has come to symbolize the planting of the seeds that led to the Cold War. Three men, conducting large-scale military operations all over the globe, and bound by the secrecy attached to such operations, made decisions as to the future shape of the map of Europe without regard to America's constitutional processes. Stalin was responsible to no one but his political clique, Churchill's parliamentary responsibilities were unwritten, but the American Commander in Chief was obliged to seek the advice and consent of the Senate before committing the United States to substantive international agreements. Here again Roosevelt gave no evidence of consciously avoiding his constitutional obligations. Indeed, at Teheran he had discussed with Stalin the congressional role in determining the extent of United States involvement in an international organization. The President, however, was confronted with the necessity of making military decisions in the context of a geopolitical struggle. He attempted to walk a thin line in the negotiations, repeatedly adverting to the attitudes of the American people and their concern with the borders of postwar Poland. At one point Andrei Vishinsky, the

Soviet Deputy Foreign Minister, remarked that the "American people should learn to obey their masters."

In the context of a history of the war powers Yalta is significant. For that is where an American President agreed with other heads of government on the structure of world organization and on substantive changes in the international maps of the future. Roosevelt's principal objective was to win the war with Germany and Japan as quickly as possible. A timetable was set and plans were made for Russian entry into the war against Japan. The compromises reached on the structure of the United Nations and Polish boundary must have seemed to FDR to be of secondary consequence in the glow of the accomplishments relating to military strategy. Our concern is with the fact that portions of the Yalta agreements were secret. FDR and Churchill had agreed to Stalin's demand for three UN General Assembly votes for the Soviet Union and two of its member republics. Roosevelt, who at first had been angry with the demand, later toyed with the idea of asking for forty-eight votes for the United States, one for each state in the Union.

The President's return from Yalta was climaxed with an address to Congress in which he spoke hopefully of the San Francisco Conference to be held to form the United Nations. He made no mention of the vote concession given to the Soviet Union. Its later inadvertent revelation before the Conference began caused an uproar over Yalta secrecy. Reading the Conference minutes one must agree with the conclusion that the deliberations did indeed incorporate "understandings" that were not made public. The Cold War battles of the late 1940's brought those understandings into the public forum as weapons in the ideological conflict. I am concerned with them only as "process." For while one or another arrangement was violated by the former allies, the concept of authority on which they rested was absolutist in tendency. The Commander in Chief function was extended to embrace the authority to commit the national entity to policies without the "advice and consent" of the Senate, and the postwar years have been a calendar of the continuation and extension of that process. The wartime conferences of the three Great Captains foreshadowed a history of meetings between relatively junior officers of the executive branch and their foreign equivalents, in which more substantive business is dealt with than has been accounted for to Congress and the people. Executive agreements today govern much of the military disposition of the United States around the world and are subject to no direct veto by the Congress.

These pages have perhaps not given full weight to the burdens of the Presidency during total war. The responsibility, almost inevitably, is also total in the presidential view. The victory of American arms and the survival of American institutions certainly justifies Roosevelt's extraordinary Presidency. But historically his accomplishments must be examined also in the light of their effect on our political system.

The Second World War consolidated the popular attitude toward presidential leadership. Emergencies became the rule rather than the exception, and the heroic qualities of the leaders on both sides of the contest have left us with an intellectual and emotional hangover that persists to this day in conditioning the attitudes we bring to the settlement of international disputes. Without denigrating the great differences that separate our own institutions from those that dominate most of the Communist world, it must be said that we have attempted in part to apply the solutions of World War II to the problems that have faced us since.

Franklin Delano Roosevelt's superb political leadership accounts in large degree for our current attitudes to world events. Although the conditions in which his leadership flourished are no longer applicable to our needs, we have responded until very recently in almost Pavlovian style to executive domination during a period, now hopefully coming to a close, when the overwhelming national sense was that we faced a war, cold or hot, on many fronts. Only now are we beginning to be able to use once again a good many of the words that World War II had stricken from the international dictionary. In the aftermath of an age when "unconditional surrender" was a national goal, it took the tragedy of Vietnam to restore "negotiations" to the lexicon of acceptable usage.

The Roosevelt era molded habits of thought that were not

easily broken when the crisis of total war came to an end. Perhaps the most significant development of the time was the increasing dependence of both Congress and the people on presidential leadership. For over twelve years FDR had been the American symbol abroad and in his own land. He stamped the Presidency with a regal presence that every one of his successors has sought, each in his own way, to emulate and perhaps to surpass. I think that the magnitude of Franklin Roosevelt's accomplishment and the burden of his legacy were best expressed in a tribute offered at his death by *Yank,* the wartime soldiers' magazine. "He was the Commander in Chief, not only of our Armed Forces, but of our generation."

XVI

The Cold War:
"Curious Delusions"
and "Great Debates"

WHEN Sam Rayburn died, the presence of four American Presidents at his funeral service was recorded in one of those brooding
photographs that etch themselves into the national memory.
There is irony in the poignant recollection of Truman, Eisenhower, Kennedy and Johnson, sitting side by side, as they paid
tribute to a Congressman who never doubted that he was their
peer. Although he supported presidential authority in foreign
affairs, he was the apotheosis of "the hill." Little more than a
decade later, there is no single legislator with power and influence equivalent to that held by Sam Rayburn. Whatever that
tells us about the Speaker, it says a good deal more about what
has happened since.

The vacuum of legislative authority with which Congress is
grappling in the 1970's springs in large part from the demonstrated supremacy of the presidential will in deciding on war
or peace, as well as congressional impotence in the face of a determined Chief Executive. But if Vietnam was the occasion that
brought the country to constitutional crisis, the roots were
planted at the close of World War II when the world once again
divided into two armed camps.

The struggles of the Cold War and their implications for
the future of America's international relationships have been
analyzed and reanalyzed by succeeding historians. These pages

are not intended to add to the literature. However, the growing power of the President to make undeclared war and the tendency of Congress to surrender its prerogatives was history made in the framework of stark reality. A complex of ideological and geopolitical rivalries with the Soviet Union and The People's Republic of China positioned the United States so that we perceived our survival and the survival of our allies to be seriously threatened by the forward thrust of the Communist-bloc powers. While the validity of those assumptions is not at issue here, the mechanisms of response elicited by the very danger are at the heart of this history.

The amazing effect of total war on the United States was discussed in the last chapter. The American people had been conditioned by four years of war to respond to new alerts with the reflexes of disciplined soldiers. It was that very discipline under fire, a virtue in crisis, that resulted in a fundamental shift in our institutions. Inasmuch as I was a participant in many of the events of the fifties and sixties, I should state simply that I was in full accord with most of the foreign policy decisions of the era and would vigorously defend a majority of them to this very day. Events, however, have convinced me that in our desire to put up effective barriers against external peril, we were not sufficiently aware of the dangers to freedom inherent in every appeal for emergency powers. There must come a time when a nation insists on the integrity of its institutions, regardless of the risk. During the past twenty-eight years, we have not been nearly insistent enough.

The line should have been drawn as far back as Harry Truman's Presidency, a period when presidential war power steadily increased, although the country was ostensibly at peace. Roosevelt's successor could hardly have been more different from the Hudson Valley patrician, but he had every bit of FDR's determination to "fill" the presidential office. Harry Truman was not loath to exercise authority and his readiness to accept responsibility was one of his most attractive qualities. President Truman exercised the foreign policy prerogative with a force that might have been kept under better control in the early stages of his administration. Although the transition between alliance and Cold

War with the Soviet Union had already begun before he assumed office, his determination to appear "in charge" had a major effect on the course of the Russo-American relationship. In his first interview with foreign minister Molotov Truman laid down the law, telling the Russian that he should live up to his agreements. The salty Missouri manner may have reassured the new President of his own authority, but it offended the Russians and convinced them that the possibility of maintaining even the façade of the old wartime relationship was highly dubious.

As the Cold War with the U.S.S.R. intensified, the President and his chief advisers found it easy to fall back on the precedents of the wartime emergency. The bipartisan foreign policy, invoked during the crisis of world war, was reaffirmed as a new threat appeared to rise in the East. Inasmuch as there was no love lost among Republicans for the Communist giant, a relatively stable approach was maintained with respect to European affairs. But when the President and his advisers entered deeper constitutional waters, they ran into trouble. Although the Republican opposition was quite willing to stand guard against the possibility of Soviet aggression, there was considerable reluctance to add to presidential power along the way.

In Brussels during the spring of 1948, the countries of Western Europe, with United States encouragement and support, banded together in a Western European Union treaty to ensure collective security against the Soviet Union. The treaty was designed as the forerunner of a larger alliance that would include the United States. Almost as soon as the initial meetings of the seven Western European governments had been completed, the defense ministers flew to Washington, D.C., to open discussions on military aid. A series of conferences was climaxed with the assertion by the first United States Secretary of Defense, James Forrestal, that a generous supply of American arms was required to give meaning to the Brussels Pact. By autumn the Europeans had followed the Forrestal lead with a request that the United States join an Atlantic pact. NATO negotiations began at year's end; after considerable debate, the NATO treaty took effect in 1949.

I have outlined the chronology because it illustrates the

power of the executive branch to order foreign affairs in such a way as to implement and broaden presidential war powers whenever it suits the Executive's purpose. The Western European Union conferences were all deliberately planned way stations along the road to NATO. The treaty was, in the words of Iowa's Senator Guy Gillette, "a vehicle for the transfer of arms and military equipment from the United States to Western Europe." The Western Europeans, in the early stages of recovery from the wounds of World War II, would, after all, have hardly attempted to band together without some assurance from the United States that the industrial heart of the Atlantic community would be at the center of whatever arrangement ultimately took shape. The fear of Soviet invasion of Western Europe was of such magnitude as to require immediate material support of their governments by the United States; NATO, an organization that has since achieved considerable significance as an extra-military entity, was the chosen structure built to receive the necessary assistance.

United States debate on the NATO treaty centered on Article 5, which stated that each signatory would consider an attack on one "an attack against them all." Considerable attention was paid to the possibility that such an agreement would further diminish congressional war power. If an attack on Copenhagen was to be considered an attack on New York, Congress would be completely cut off from the power to determine whether the country should go to war. The treaty's caveat that each country was bound according to its constitutional processes was less than reassuring because of a number of past presidential actions that might appear to offer precedent for executive hostilities. The Administration's arguments on NATO's behalf were sometimes disingenuous in the extreme. Witness after witness before the Senate Foreign Relations Committee brushed off questions about the effect of passage on the congressional right to declare war. Dean Acheson, a man endowed with the ability to formulate his thought with occasionally acid precision, was notably vague.

SENATOR DONNELL: Would you care to indicate in the suppositious case which I have given you [a large-scale Russian invasion of Norway], whether or not the President would have the constitutional right to put this country into a state of war without the actual formal declaration of war by Congress?

SECRETARY ACHESON: I would prefer not to go into cases of that sort . . . I am not the Attorney General and I do not express legal views on this matter. . . .

SENATOR DONNELL: If the United States were to be attacked at the Port of New York by 500,000 troops or by atom bombs or whatever it might be, you would have no doubt about the right of the President, before the Congress took any action at all, to defend this country against that attack?

SECRETARY ACHESON: I would have no doubt.

SENATOR DONNELL: In this Article 5, each of the parties agree that an armed attack against any one or more of them shall be considered an attack against them all. That is correct; is it not?

SECRETARY ACHESON: That is true.

SENATOR DONNELL: So that if the President would have the right to defend this country against an attack on New York, without action by Congress, this would obligate him, would it not, and our country, immediately to take action even though Congress did not go through with the formal declaration of war?

SECRETARY ACHESON: Article 5, Senator, does not enlarge, nor does it decrease, nor does it change in any way, the relative constitutional position of the President and the Congress.

SENATOR DONNELL: In other words, the President would have the entire right to send troops to safeguard this country against an attack on New York without any action by Congress; that is correct, is it not?

SECRETARY ACHESON: He would have whatever right the Constitution gives him.

SENATOR DONNELL: He does have that right, does he not, in your opinion as a lawyer?

SECRETARY ACHESON: I do not want to go into a discussion as to the relative position of the Commander in Chief.

The Acheson-Donnell colloquy is worth examining on a number of counts. In the first place the Secretary requested that he not be pressed to hypothesize American action in specific "attack" situations. Yet the treaty was presented as a tool to deal with just such exigencies. Acheson's refusal to equate an attack on Norway with an attack on New York appears on its face to be a deliberate avoidance of the treaty's principal purpose. Forced to admit the President's constitutional responsibility to respond immediately to an attack on American soil, he refused to take the step of acknowledging that the soil of an ally became the equivalent of American soil under the treaty's Article 5. His assertion that the Article "does not enlarge, nor does it increase" the President's constitutional authority implies at the least an anxiety to interpret the Constitution after the fact, not before. That would ordinarily be sensible enough. But in this case the "fact" was the treaty ratification and the hearings were ostensibly intended to enlighten rather than obscure.

Perhaps the key to the Secretary of State's overall attitude on the question of war power is to be found in his reply to Senator Donnell's question as to whether the President had the right to protect New York from attack without congressional authorization. Although he refused to give an explicit answer, Acheson referred to the relative position of "the Commander in Chief." Nowhere in the exchange had Senator Donnell called the President the Commander in Chief. Acheson's use of the phrase, even as he avoided defining presidential powers under the NATO treaty, offers at least a clue as to his position. Thinking back on this episode and a number of similar events during later administrations, it must be admitted that a number of those of us who were in sympathy with United States foreign policy objectives but solicitous of the separation of powers did not take a hard enough look at the procedures whereby foreign policy was being implemented. We did not ask the hard questions until some of the objectives themselves began to appear less than provident.

Acheson's reluctance to come to grips with the issue of Who Makes War is typical of the attitudes of most Secretaries when they are confronted with situations in which presidential policy and constitutionality come into conflict. Whenever possible, the historic rule has been to push the constitutional question into the background. The objective is to "get the job done," and to let someone else at a later time worry about the Constitution. There is a good deal to be said for this viewpoint; through much of American history, the Supreme Court itself made a practice of deciding constitutional cases on as narrow a ground as possible. Avoidance of repeated crises is an essential ingredient of social stability. Unfortunately, the war powers issue is one of those in which the desire to avoid confrontation has resulted in surrender of an essential component of the legislative power and the unbalancing of our government.

During the course of the NATO debate, John Foster Dulles, then New York's junior Senator, commented somewhat querulously that "there seems to prevail in some quarters a *curious delusion* that the whole world is bound by the Constitution of the United States, and that there cannot be war until Congress declares it. I wish that were the case. Unfortunately there can be war, and there have been wars, without the Congress declaring war . . . that can happen again." Dulles, a man who spent most of his distinguished public career in the executive branch, was impatient with legislators who displayed an excessive concern with "the constitutional twilight zone in this area between the President and the Congress." He was, himself, fully prepared to equate President Roosevelt's response to Japan's attack on Pearl Harbor with "the right to consider, if we wish, that *an attack anywhere which we think is against us* can be treated as an act of war." That, in the late twentieth century, might also be considered a "curious delusion," but when Dulles spoke he was dealing with a situation in which the United States seemed only a step from another global struggle. The sharp language of the period reflected a continued readiness to eliminate excessive constitutional baggage if it became necessary to survival.

This tendency to cast every such issue in terms of life or death accounts for a considerable part of the erosion of congressional authority in the war powers area. The Senate passed the NATO treaty by an overwhelming majority of 82 to 13 despite a strong number of expressed constitutional reservations as to the implicit increase in presidential hegemony. But many Senators were able to approve the NATO treaty because of the reaffirmation of legislative authority contained in the report of the Committee on Foreign Relations.

The treaty in no way affects the basic division of authority between the President and the Congress as defined in the Constitution. . . . In particular, it does not increase, decrease or change the power of the President as Commander in Chief of the armed forces or impair the full authority of Congress to declare war.

Nevertheless, Iowa's Guy Gillette spoke for many who sensed a growth in presidential authority, when he said that his vote for the treaty was cast with full knowledge that Congress was "nodding its head to already accomplished deeds," because a failure to ratify NATO would have made the country "the butt of ridicule and scorn around the world." But he warned that "one day soon" it would become necessary to redefine the precise powers of President and Congress in what Dulles had referred to as the "twilight zone" of constitutional powers.

Senator Gillette's observation that "this is not the time to raise that thorny problem" exemplifies the pattern of postwar acquiescence in executive supremacy. A willingness to place the decision as to war and peace in presidential hands was expressed with astonishing openness in a cross section of the nation's press. *The New York Times* relished the change in national attitude since the days when Woodrow Wilson went down to defeat in the fight for the League of Nations. "Mr. Wilson in time of peace would not have dared to ask the Senate to commit itself, as Mr. Truman and his advisers are now doing, to go to war if any one of eleven or more nations is attacked. *We should not quibble on this point.* The defense pact means that or it means nothing." One thing is almost certain. *The Times,* twenty-three years later, would regard such a commitment as a good deal more than a quibble.

In the Midwest, the heartland of prewar isolationism, the St. Louis *Globe-Democrat,* endorsing the treaty, spoke a few home truths. "The most repugnant fact of the treaty," according to the *Globe-Democrat,* was the inescapable fact that under its provisions, "Congress would have no more freedom to avoid war than a citizen has to defy the conventions without ostracism. Technically, the right of Congress to maintain an indifferent isolationism would exist; as a practical, moral matter in a world emergency it would not." The *Globe-Democrat* regarded the Communist threat as sufficient to justify acceptance of the treaty's limitations on congressional authority. "The pact should be sold to the American people on that basis. *Half truths are not enough.* If they will not accept it in its true meaning, now is the time for them to say so."

The natural inclination was to shape and endorse policies that would bring American power to bear quickly and efficiently when the need arose. The inevitable consequence of such eagerness has been an almost unconscious reluctance to weigh the "marginal" questions associated with the decision-making process. In the early 1950's, constitutional problems were either buried in the jump pages of "issue-oriented" newspaper articles or given short shrift in the debate over the best way to contain Communist expansionism. Few administration spokesmen were ready to face the war power issue head-on, and too few congressional leaders were prepared in those days to take a stand on the constitutional prerogatives of Congress. Senator Robert Taft was one of those who were. Although he endorsed a policy of firm resistance to Soviet expansion, he was determined to preserve congressional authority.

Taft's conservatism was structured on a bedrock of great intellectual power and integrity. His mastery of the political process had quickly raised him to the top rank of Republican leadership. His observations during the "Great Debate" over commitment of American divisions to the defense of Western Europe were landmarks of insight into the process whereby presidential encroachment on congressional war powers became the rule of the postwar era.

In 1951 the United States was locked in undeclared war with North Korea. The Cold War had intensified to a point where its strategy was increasingly military, and President Truman signaled that American troops were going back to Europe as part of the NATO organization; that was the context in which Taft traced the gradual escalation of American involvement around the world and the increasing role of executive fiat in determining the level of American commitment. He noted that when Congress ratified the UN Charter, provision was made that American troops would be committed to UN action only after a Special Military Agreement had been negotiated with the Security Council and approved by Congress. Constitutional processes had ostensibly been protected in order to assure United States accession to the UN; but that military agreement was never negotiated because of the Cold War between the council's two most powerful members. When President Truman was confronted with the fact of the North Korean invasion, he cited another article of the Charter as justification for American intervention.

Taft contended that the President's action was illegal "under the very terms and provisions of the act which was passed by Congress to implement the charter." Noting the bitter struggle in which the country was engaged in Korea, Taft turned his attention to the call for a renewed troop commitment in Europe. He explored the origins of the North Atlantic Treaty and recalled the testimony of administration witnesses that the "strength and authority" of the pact lay in its general notification that an attack on one member would be an attack on all. Tom Connally, the Chairman of the Senate Foreign Relations Committee, had specifically promised, Taft recalled, that "we are not sending a single soldier to any of these countries for combat purposes. . . ." Secretary of State Dean Acheson, too, gave "a clear and absolute no" when he was asked if the United States would be obliged to send troops. Less than two years later, the President, in a press conference, was warning of exactly that development. Taft charged that "without authority he involved us in the Korean War. Without authority he apparently is now attempting to adopt a similar policy in Europe. This matter must be debated and determined by Congress and by the people of this country if we are to maintain any of our constitutional freedoms."

Taft's desire for a debate on the issues had little effect on the inevitable outcome. But the controversy produced an interesting juxtaposition of statements supporting presidential power. Senator Connally asserted that the President's right to send the armed forces "to any place required by the security interests of the United States has often been questioned, but never denied by authoritative opinion." Secretary Acheson carried the Senator's point even further. "It is equally clear," he said, "that this authority may not be interfered with by the Congress in the exercise of powers which it has under the Constitution." Mr. Acheson had really spelled it out.

The debate was held in Congress, but the decision to send troops to Europe was made at the White House. For Harry Truman had no intention of diluting the powers of the Commander in Chief. Less than a week after the President had ordered American troops into Korea, the State Department was ready with an official memorandum "directed to the authority of the President to order the armed forces of the United States to repel the aggressive attack on the Republic of Korea." According to the State Department, *the President's power as Commander in chief was unlimited.* The document asserted that he was authorized to send troops into combat "without congressional authorization" in pursuit of his constitutional obligation to conduct foreign affairs. Many of the episodes we have discussed in these pages were cited as precedent for the Korean intervention. None of them, of course, were remotely equivalent to the scale of the Korean combat or the size of the American commitment. But the claims for presidential authority were in keeping with the magnitude of the new war, and the determination to resist aggression called forth bipartisan support. In the House of Representatives, the author, then a New York Congressman, spoke to the issue: "The American people . . . took, through the President, this fateful decision of determining to stop [aggression] in Korea with the use of armed force . . . the decision was, I believe, the right one by the President, and I have consistently supported it since."

In the Senate men like Morse, Humphrey and Douglas rushed to defend the President's action as an expression of devotion to the UN and as a proper use of the Commander in Chief authority. The Illinois Senator, while insisting that Truman's intervention was constitutional, did note the dangers inherent in giving the President "discretionary powers to use our armed forces in advance of a declaration of war by Congress." He remarked that "a reckless and militaristic President" could commit the country to a course of aggression. But Senator Douglas thought he had a solution: "If such an act were to be grossly at variance with the national interest and against the public will, the President would render himself liable to impeachment at the hands of Congress. This is certainly something of a deterring influence." Considerable experience since Korea has done nothing to substantiate the view that impeachment is a viable congressional tool in a dispute with the Executive over the use or misuse of war powers. Even then, the imbalance between presidential and congressional authority was illustrated in an exchange between Senator Arthur Watkins of Utah and Scott Lucas, the Democratic Floor Leader. When Watkins remarked that it "had never been determined whether [armed intervention] can be done without the consent of Congress," Lucas retorted in five words, "Well, it has been done."

Some of the congressional leaders who bolstered the case for Harry Truman would express strong reservations when later Presidents accepted the Korean War as an important precedent for independent executive action. But their endorsement of President Truman's firm response to the North Korean invasion reflected the general tone of public opinion. Despite the reservations voiced by Senators Taft and Watkins, there was little disposition to invoke the Constitution against a President who had already gained a considerable reputation as a man of the people. HST simply didn't have the look of a "usurper" about him. Whether or not one agreed with him on a specific issue, his actions were always consistent with the image of a man determined to do his best at a painfully difficult job. Nevertheless, the Korean War was to prove his political undoing, just as the Vietnam War tolled the political bell for Lyndon Baines Johnson.

American Presidents can expect considerable tolerance from their constituents so long as their policies seem to be working well on behalf of sound national objectives. But when the pain of failure induces reflection as to the initial wisdom of presidential commitments, virtue is no longer rewarded with applause. Battlefield agony turned a "police action" into "Truman's war" and belated attention began to be paid to the renewed accusations that the President's intervention had been unconstitutional in the first place. One national newspaper chain took to running the daily casualty count trimmed in black. The principal casualty, however, was beyond statistics. National unity had been shattered.

The Korean War divided Americans over its cause, its strategy and its ultimate outcome. One would have thought that the need for unanimity in war would have been established once and for all. Perhaps the fact that the North Koreans were driven back of the thirty-eighth parallel obscured the enormous costs of the "victory" and it may be that the necessity to justify an unpopular action as a symbol of rectitude imposed unrecognized penalties. For Harry Truman's posture as a man who could stick it out in the face of opposition and obloquy was another accretion to the presidential myth that has had to be borne by his successors. That myth grew in direct proportion to the giant increase in American power. The Presidency, in the age of the Media Revolution, had become more than ever the most viable symbol of the nation itself. When the nation was the richest in the world, when it held for a time a monopoly of the atomic weapon, the symbolism of the Presidency became almost imperial in its dimensions.

Inasmuch as the United States was the principal Western nation, the President became, in the eyes of people concerned with the configurations of power, "the leader of the free world." This partial truth lent credence to the idea that the President of the United States is by definition larger than life. The myth, as it was cut to the specifications of President Truman, was different from the Eisenhower, Kennedy, Johnson and Nixon variations. Allowances were made for the idiosyncrasies different individuals brought with them into the White House; but whatever the changes of style, the myth was insistent on the presence of virtually unlimited power as a component of the American Presidency. Professor Corwin's "constitution of rights" was too mundane a document to serve as more than a historic background against which the President was to play his imperial role.

None of the postwar Presidents created this new ambience.

Each was victimized by its unreality and each of them, in differing degree, assumed prima facie the primacy of the executive branch of the government, along with their own relative infallibility. Ironically, they were supported until recently by a substantial majority of their congressional colleagues. Executive power had expanded to a point where Presidents of the United States were frequently able to substitute executive agreements for treaties which would have had to be ratified with the advice and consent of the Senate. Congressional resolutions now began to be used to stamp "valid" on wars threatened or begun by executive initiative. The events that accelerated the process have been compressed into the last twenty years of American history.

XVII

From Formosa to Vietnam: "According to His Best Judgment"

THE Presidency imposes an enormous burden of precedent on the Chief Executive. No one who enters the office wishes to leave it a lesser instrument on his departure. Dwight Eisenhower, John Kennedy, Lyndon Johnson and Richard Nixon were each borne on a stream of prior executive action from the moment they entered the White House.

Eisenhower's modest bearing was one of his most notable characteristics and the deferential manner he brought to his relations with Congress was extremely flattering considering the enormous role he had played in the national life before he even entered politics. But there was no doubt in his mind that the President had the exclusive right to deploy American forces "according to his best judgment and without the specific approval of Congress." Although Ike's convictions were firm, there was a degree of ambiguity in the way he applied them. In the spring of 1954, during the early days of American involvement in the Indochina crisis, President Eisenhower told a press conference: "There is going to be no involvement of America in war unless it is a result of the constitutional process that is placed upon Congress to declare it."

There was a somewhat disingenuous quality even to that assurance. Congress was occasionally informed of the gravity with which the Administration regarded the impending French defeat and indeed provided funds to support military assistance programs, but the executive branch was itself responsible for any military actions that were taken to fill the vacuum in the south after Ho Chi-minh and the French government signed a truce, and, incidentally, a truce that was implicitly disavowed by Secretary of State Dulles.

The ambivalent attitude of the Eisenhower Administration toward the congressional role reflected a determination to avoid the kind of clash that had marred President Truman's relations with Congress after the Korean intervention. President Eisenhower's request for a resolution to defend Formosa best illustrates both that determination and the inexorable growth of executive war power.

The American commitment to Chiang Kai-shek's forces on Formosa was an outgrowth of the obligations imposed by the wartime alliance against Japan. The Chinese Communist victory on the mainland had been a stunning defeat for American policy and while few responsible statesmen expected the decision to be reversed, the Eisenhower Administration felt obliged to encourage the maintenance of Chiang's authority on Formosa. The Korean War had already frayed Chinese-American relations far past the point of civilized discourse; the only point in question was the nature and extent of the hostilities between the two powers. That was the context in which the President approached Congress for authorization to "employ the armed forces of the United States as he deems necessary" in order to protect Formosa and adjacent islands from Chinese Communist invasions.

Eisenhower himself noted that his message to Congress was designed simply to warn the Chinese that the United States would intervene to save Chiang. The President, in other words, used Congress as a sounding board for a diplomatic message to a hostile power. "I did not imply that I lacked constitutional authority to act," he later observed. A suitable congressional resolution was requested simply to underscore "the unified and serious intentions" of each of the branches of the government. Although the Senate passed the Formosa resolution, 83 to 3, a few men raised their voices in opposition. Wayne Morse, warning that Congress was reducing itself to the role of "Amen sayer," insisted that the Senate had no right to hand over congressional authority to declare war. But the weight of congressional opinion was still with Speaker Sam Rayburn, who was troubled at the possibility that the Eisenhower request might have created a precedent that would limit executive power.

Rayburn was convinced that the President needed no congressional authorization and would have been better off without asking for it. The Administration was certain, however, that the road of prior congressional commitment was the safest road to travel and it continued to use the technique as long as it appeared to be productive.

Unexpected resistance developed when President Eisenhower and Secretary of State Dulles proposed an anticipatory counter move against a possible Communist takeover of the oil-rich Middle East. In a 1957 attempt to further expand executive authority, the Administration sponsored a measure authorizing the President to use armed force in defense of countries "under the threat of international Communism." Sharp questions were raised on both sides of the aisle.

The attack focused on the broad and unspecified nature of the grant. Senator Sam Ervin, an outstanding activist, then as now, on the issue of Congress's constitutional authority, said that he couldn't reconcile an affirmative vote with his reading of the separation of powers. Senator Ervin observed that no specific country was identified as "under attack." There was no definition of "the threat of international Communism," and the Secretary of State was unable to tell the Foreign Relations Committee how a "two hundred million [dollar] military assistance" appropriation would be spent. He also declined to say whether the President was constitutionally empowered to use armed force in the Middle East without a congressional resolution.

For the first time since the end of World War II, Congress attempted at least to put some kind of limit on executive action that might lead to armed conflict. Itemized periodic accountings of the money spent on military assistance were written into the law's requirements and language was drafted whereby the President assumed responsibility for any hostilities in which the country engaged under the Eisenhower Doctrine. In 1958, when the

President sent Marines to support the Lebanese government, he made no reference to the congressional Middle East resolution. Unlike some later Presidents, Ike appeared content to avoid confrontation on constitutional grounds.

Although I voted for the Middle East resolution because I believed in its purposes, the constitutional questions had become sufficiently compelling to require an assertion of my own attitude on the question of Who Makes War. In my mind there is not now and there never was the slightest possibility that Congress could give away its constitutional authority. The following exchange with Senator John Kennedy illustrates the point.

SENATOR KENNEDY: It does not seem to me that passage of the resolution will affect the constitutional powers of the President or the constitutional powers of Congress to declare war.

SENATOR JAVITS: Mr. President, will the Senator yield on the question of law?

SENATOR KENNEDY: I yield.

SENATOR JAVITS: The argument as to constitutionality tends to defeat itself. If a constitutional power is involved, no resolution passed by Congress can relinquish it, because the Constitution can be amended only as provided in the Constitution itself, by amendment ratified by the states. On the other hand, if the resolution is saying that we are going to back the President in our foreign policy . . . then we are only dealing with a policy; we are not giving up any constitutional power. If it is a constitutional power to declare war that we are allegedly trying to give up, we could not do it if we tried. That is the end of the matter.

Although I believe that my position was correct, Senator Morse's comment that it would be difficult to get Congress to reassert a power it had once relinquished has been substantiated by later events. The failure to exercise constitutional rights tends to raise questions about their legitimacy. Constitutional scholars often refer to the "twilight zone" between presidential and congressional war powers. That twilight zone has become in recent years a kind of constitutional DMZ infiltrated by expansionist-minded Presidents. Congress, on the other hand, has retreated to appropriating the funds that fuel the President's foreign power and military programs. The war in Indochina was never specifically authorized by Congress, but successive Chief Executives can point to the Gulf of Tonkin Resolution, congressional appropriations for military assistance and AID programs and later to funds supporting American troops placed in combat by presidential fiat. The process has been cumulative in effect and staggering in its dimensions. Each Chief Executive has seemed to feel under an obligation to amplify commitments of American power made by his predecessor.

The responsibility for our involvement in Vietnam has certainly been bipartisan. If its beginnings could be found in some events in the Eisenhower Administration, it took a quantum leap when President Kennedy made the decision to send 17,500 "advisers" to South Vietnam. American participation climaxed in 1965 when President Johnson decided to deploy large numbers of troops in South Vietnam in order to shore up a government that was then in danger of imminent collapse. The painful events of the Johnson years were the natural culmination of an executive hubris that was cultivated by members of every branch of the government and by the shapers of public opinion as well. The soil was enriched by the support resolutions of the 1950's and transformed by the bold assertiveness of President Kennedy's tragic venture at the Bay of Pigs and later by his successful facedown of Soviet power during the Cuban missile crisis.

The Cuban affair was a prime illustration of the passive congressional role. Although there was substantial opinion in favor of toppling the Castro regime, the President considered the "cover" of the invasion's independent origins to be adequate excuse to go ahead with an armed attack against a neighboring state without congressional authorization. During the missile crisis period, President Kennedy asked Congress to resolve that he already possessed all necessary authority to use "whatever means may be necessary" to prevent Cuba from subverting its neighbors and to prevent the establishment of a Soviet naval base on Cuban soil. When Senator Richard Russell looked at the resolution, he remarked that "I do not believe that the Armed Services Committee is going to make a constitutional assertion that the President of the United States has the right to declare war, and that is what this does." The resolution was redrafted to state that the United States Government, rather than its President, would take the actions suggested by the Kennedy Administration. The difference may have been subtle but it was the first small sign that a reawakening of congressional assertiveness was on the horizon. While the awakening was indefinitely postponed by increasing domestic turmoil and by the tragedy of John F. Kennedy's stunning and senseless assassination, Lyndon Johnson's Presidency brought it to full flower.

Perhaps no event of Johnson's administration did as much to awaken Congress to its constitutional responsibility as the passage of the Gulf of Tonkin resolution. It was the ultimate outgrowth of all the resolutions that had gone before, the extreme point in the process of constitutional erosion that had begun to accelerate at the opening of this century.

On August 4, 1964, the American Destroyer *Maddox* became the focal point for one of the great crises of American constitutional history. Although the facts of what happened in the Gulf of Tonkin are unclear even now, we do know that the President of the United States reported that the *Maddox* had been attacked by North Vietnamese torpedo boats and that the President had warned the North Vietnamese that American patience was not unlimited. When still another attack on the *Maddox* was reported twenty-four hours later, Johnson sent Congress a request for a resolution empowering him to "take all necessary measures to repel any armed attack against the forces of the United States and *to prevent further aggression*." The resolution empowered the President to use armed force to assist any Southeast Asian country requesting assistance in defending its right to self-determination. *The New York Times*, in applauding the President's determination, noted almost marginally that "congressional authority for future military action will, in effect, be delegated to the President by the joint resolution scheduled to be voted today." That delegation of authority triggered a belated congressional reaction that has yet to abate. For in a matter of weeks, the incident in the Gulf of Tonkin was obscured in uncertainty as to whether the *Maddox* had been attacked twice, or even once. One thing is incontrovertible. Lyndon Johnson felt he had a congressional authorization to use American armed force in any way he saw fit. Congress had once again given a President blanket authority to go to war, and President Johnson did exactly that.

Congress was stunned when it began to appear that the Tonkin Gulf resolution actually was being used to justify the involvement of 500,000 American troops in Asian combat, bombing raids conducted on a larger scale than the attacks mounted in four years of the Second World War and the expenditure of 50,000 American lives. Did we have a right to be surprised? On the recond—yes. None of the more recent congressional resolutions authorizing the use of presidential force had actually resulted in military action. The Formosa resolution, the Cuban missile resolution and the Middle East resolution had all achieved their objectives short of war. But luck had run out and Congress had paid too little attention to the possibilities inherent in blanket authorizations.

The language of the Gulf of Tonkin resolution was far more sweeping than the congressional intent. In voting unlimited presidential power most members of Congress thought they were providing for retaliation for an attack on our forces; and preventing a large-scale war in Asia, rather than authorizing its inception. Congressional expectations were shaped by the national election campaign then in progress in which President Johnson repeatedly asserted his determination to keep American boys from "going ten thousand miles from home to do what Asian boys ought to be doing for themselves."

Whatever President Johnson's position, however, Congress had the obligation to make an institutional judgment as to the wisdom and the propriety of giving such a large grant of its own power to the Chief Executive. Indeed, questions were raised in the Senate exactly to that effect when the resolution was debated. Finally, however, all but Wayne Morse of Oregon and Ernest Gruening of Alaska "went along"—including the author. I am convinced that congressional embarrassment at the failure to weigh all the factors involved in the Tonkin resolution has been responsible for the burgeoning assertiveness of the movement in the Senate at long last to curb the war-making power of the President. In any case, Tonkin Gulf was a natural outgrowth of twenty years of congressional acquiescence in the executive preemption of the power to make war and President Nixon's 1970 decision to invade Cambodia without congressional authorization was an inevitable consequence of the almost uniform success attained by his predecessors in their steady assumption of total war power.

The Nixon decision to enlarge the war, along with the bitter convulsions of public opinion across the country, the campus rebellions and the massacre at Kent State, were grotesque warnings of what can happen when substantial segments of society are disarmed of political weapons in a struggle against the overweening power of one of the branches of a representative government of checks and balances. Louis Henkin, a noted authority on the Constitution's separation of powers, has commented recently on the President's ability to frustrate congressional will during the first Cambodian affair: ". . . members of Congress, unhappy with that extension of the war and fearful of further extensions, some of them indeed desiring to terminate the war entirely, sought to repeal the original resolution authorizing the war in Indochina and to limit the continuation of war by forbidding expenditures for certain purposes and beyond prescribed dates."

Noting the President's claim that Congress had no right to challenge his authority as Commander in Chief by trying to control or limit the conduct of the war, Henkin asserts that "constitutionally, in my view, the President was wrong. The power of Congress to declare war is the power to decide for war or peace, and should imply the power to unmake war as well as to make it. In the political context of Vietnam–Cambodia, repeal of the Tonkin resolution did not in fact constitute a congressional decision to end the war. But a clear resolution to that effect would have bound the President and he could not have properly insisted on prosecuting the war thereafter."

During the last five years of the Vietnam conflict, twelve judicial challenges were brought against presidential authority to make war. One of them was a case in which the Massachusetts legislature joined as an expression of its view that the Constitution was being violated. But none of them reached the Supreme Court. The courts in each case, in accord with historic precedent, wished to leave political questions to political action. But the power of decision that President Nixon exercised in Cambodia and through the very end of the Vietnam War had not been stolen. It had been surrendered. The Presidents who exercised the war power in the late sixties and early seventies were convinced that it was inherent in their constitutional obligation. Congressional acquiescence was the result of a surge in American power that had charged the Presidency with an aura of international splendor.

XVIII

The
Imperial Presidency

As the powers of the Presidency have grown, the office has come
to be described in increasingly imperial terms. Whether it be a
"glorious burden" or the "loneliest job in the world," its occupant
is accompanied by a steady fanfare of attention that tends to
obscure the fact that the human being elected President on the
first Tuesday in the November of every fourth calendar year is
still a human being on the following Wednesday morning.

Although there are no gods in Washington, one of the marks
of the age is the almost worshipful atmosphere that has come to
surround the person elected to *serve* as Chief Magistrate. The
tendency is readily understandable when one considers in the
atomic era the fearful implications of presidential war power; and
the sanction of history behind the office. Each of the great
ancient empires apotheosized its leaders. They were literally
worshiped as gods, and the monarchies of the West, in the subtler
style of a later and more sophisticated age, linked the power of
their kings to divine right. But perhaps no human institution has
gathered so much of that mythic aura to itself as has the American
Presidency. The history of the office is a history of the accretion
of both power and pomp. President Nixon, after beginning the
aerial bombardment of Hanoi and Haiphong in the spring of
1972, offered "maintenance of respect for the President of the
United States" as one reason to engage in armed warfare. Al-

though many were displeased at the air war's expansion, his reference to the prestige of his office as a factor in making the decision elicited little comment. Thus the Presidency has itself attained a status that the incumbent is obliged to maintain without reference to other considerations. Winston Churchill's grandiloquent and uncharacteristically imprecise remark that he would not preside over the liquidation of the British Empire is matched by the reverential determination of American Presidents to maintain the powers of the office.

Perhaps the hallmark of democratic institutions and a republican form of government is that reverence is salted with skepticism about the hallowed nature of any human institution. I find the almost idolatrous attitude held toward the Presidency particularly inappropriate for a political office founded to exemplify the spartan virtues of the early Republic. We have moved from a day in which Thomas Jefferson returned from his first inauguration to find every seat filled at his boardinghouse table. No one rose to make a place for the new President except a single woman and he, refusing her offer, wedged himself into a place near the foot of the table. That's a far cry from an age of panoply in which the martial strains of "Hail to the Chief" have come to be synonymous with the dignity of the Presidency. Those citizens of the early Republic may not have been very polite, but they weren't aware that they were seated next to the predecessor of a new "Imperial" breed.

It is fortunate that Jefferson and his nineteenth-century successors had no intimations of the luster that would eventually adhere to the Presidency. If they did, the constitutional crisis through which we have been passing might well have come much sooner. The simple, matter-of-fact attitude that early Americans held toward the Presidency was much closer to the spirit of the Republic as the framers of the Constitution envisioned it. If we have traveled a great distance down the road from constitutional fidelity, it is a reflection of our own passivity in the face of a growing institutional imbalance.

It is too much to ask, at this stage in history, that the President himself remove some of the mystique of the office. A man who has pursued the Presidency has done so not to diminish it but to enlarge its scope and to make it a grander place than it was before he entered it. Such a man is locked into the precedents of those who came before, in a way that holds true for no other office-holder in this country.

A United States Senator or Congressman or Governor feels obliged to do his best in coping with the responsibilities of his position. But he bears no burdensome crown. His constituents have elected him to respond to today's needs. The policy and practice of his predecessors may or may not be relevant to his own conception of his office. He is on his own, with only the Constitution, the laws, the wishes of his constituents and his individual conscience and talents to guide him. The holder of the presidency confronts quite another situation.

The postwar period has seen five Presidents differing widely from each other in personality and in attitudes toward domestic issues. Each of them, although their perceptions of international relations might have been altered over the years, have felt obliged by the actions of their predecessors, in the name of bipartisan foreign policy, to maintain policies that reflected presidential "continuity." That continuity has sometimes been purchased at the expense of responsiveness to the popular will and to emerging realities that were not apparent during prior administrations. Each President has thus been at least partially a prisoner of the past.

The new dimensions of foreign policy breakthrough negotiated by President Nixon were carefully attuned to an awareness of the psychological trauma attached to adopting postures dramatically different from the attitudes that were so long dominant. I am convinced that a vital element in these initiatives was the fact that our inability to extricate ourselves from the Vietnam quagmire forced Congress into the position of making the first break with the Cold War's conventional wisdom. Because successive Presidents were locked into battle lines drawn in an earlier time, Congress had to respond to the urgencies of the "here and now." Although the Executive eventually negotiated us out of the Vietnam War, it did so only after the agony of a divided nation and insistent congressional pressure made it clear that there was no other way. President Richard Nixon was able to move boldly across a wide-ranging series of foreign policy initiatives because Congress was able to break with the dogmas of the past that holders of the Presidency have long felt obliged to defend. One must wonder whether Lyndon Johnson would not have ended the war before leaving office, if he had not been intimidated by a militant image of the President as "leader of the free world" and the echo of phrases from the past like "iron curtain" and "domino theory."

Reading the papers of the past twenty years with an eye to the compilation of this history has afforded me a startlingly different perspective on the debates about foreign policy in which the country has engaged since the Second World War. The advent of television and the general intensification of media involvement in public affairs has had a remarkable and not always predictable effect on public discourse.

For twenty-five years, statesmen, politicians and journalists have been coining phrases like "free world" and "Communist slavery" in order to justify some actions that ought to have been taken simply because they were in the best interests of the United States and others that shouldn't have been taken at all.

An American move to defend Western Europe from a rival social system and to counter an armed takeover in Southeast Asia does not necessarily have to be cast in terms of good and evil. The same media intensity that has brought public affairs sharply into the lives of millions of Americans has made possible a sophisticated response to the realities of world politics. We have failed to perceive that people will probably respond to arguments made on the basis of enlightened self-interest. An explicit affirmation of American interest in keeping the lines of commerce free in Southeast Asia, a twentieth-century version of "the open door," might have made it possible for Presidents to discuss international responsibilities and their related risks in less apocalyptic terms. Adjustments in policy and the decision on making war could have been made within a more rational framework. Once a conflict is dressed in ideological clothes, it becomes almost impossible to retreat from an awkward position. The apocalyptic language of the past has tended to deceive those who used it as well as those who got the message. If Presidents had not been hemmed in behind the barrier of cumulative rhetoric, the tendency to avoid honest confrontation of the issues would have been diminished. Such honesty is a requisite for the preservation of constitutional balance, provident policy and peace.

One does not have to assume that the major Communist powers have become American allies to recognize that some of the assumptions that have guided our foreign policy since the end of World War II are no longer applicable. But the American Presidency, because of the monolithic qualities with which we have endowed it, has continued for too long to pay tribute to myth.

The five hundred thirty-five men and women who serve in Congress have their individual prejudices. They are not all statesmen and they often vote with their eyes on the political main chance. But they are reasonably attuned to the will of their constituents and their very diversity of view assures the clash of ideas that is supposedly the essence of our institutions. We may have come to a point in our history where the Presidency is handicapped by the very dimensions of its powers and where Congress, instead of buckling under to presidential will, must be the institutional factor that insists on the opportunity to deal with the world as it is and as it is likely to be. Enactment of war powers legislation to defend the Constitution as it was conceived by the founders can be a first step on the road back to fully representative government.

XIX

A Matter
of Survival

WHEN President Harry S. Truman attempted to seize the steel mills during the Korean War, the Supreme Court intervened with a decision that reaffirmed the balance of powers of the United States Government. While acknowledging the importance of the President's role as Commander in Chief during periods of emergency, the Court emphasized that the basic law-giving power belongs to Congress. Justice Robert Jackson, ordering the President to return the mills to their owners, observed that the right to seize private property was too important to leave to the decision of one man. He wrote that under the Constitution the great questions must be settled, "*in good times and bad,*" by the American people through their representatives in Congress. It is time to reaffirm that decision.

Over the past ten years we have been forced to confront the fact that constitutional process has eroded, that congressional responsibility has been abdicated, that unfettered presidential power has been asserted and that it's time to call a halt. When the great question of war or peace is at stake, we must be sure that "the collective judgment of both the Congress and the President will apply to the initiation of hostilities involving the

Armed Forces of the United States, and to the continuation of such hostilities."

That language is part of a war powers bill I introduced with Senators John Stennis and Thomas Eagleton in the Senate in 1972 and again in 1973. Senators Lloyd Bentsen and Robert Taft, Jr., along with fifty-seven other senators, served as co-sponsors. The bill is designed to make sure that the democratic process protects us from one-man decision-making. The War Powers Act requires that the President report to the Congress on the circumstances and scope of any hostilities in which American troops are engaged, or in imminent danger of engaging, and that no such hostilities shall continue for longer than thirty days without specific congressional enactment to that end. If Congress wishes to conclude the action prior to the thirty-day period, it may shorten the period by law. The bill also provides that the President may undertake such hostilities only to repel an attack on the United States, its armed forces overseas, to protect the lives of Americans abroad, or to fulfill a national commitment expressed in statute *specifically authorizing* such military action.

A national commitment does not automatically flow from the mutual security treaties to which the United States is signatory. These international agreements specify that they will be carried out in accordance with the "constitutional processes" of the nations involved. The War Powers Act, for the first time, specifically defines congressional concurrence as an element in those "constitutional processes." It further states that the passage of appropriations acts or extensions of selective service do not imply congressional authorization for presidential war.

In Vietnam, we were caught in a conflict waged under the authority of the asserted "inherent powers" of the President as Commander in Chief of the armed forces. The executive branch of the government, using its enormous power to mobilize, deploy and to commit our forces, was able to pursue its own concept of the national interest without paying more than *pro forma* attention to the contrary views of a large body of congressional "colleagues." It is impossible for a representative body to function as a vital branch of government if it allows one of its principal responsibilities to go by default. War powers legislation must reassert those responsibilities, nearly two hundred years after they were first delegated.

Although this legislation is the first attempt to restore constitutional balance, it has drawn criticism from some surprising quarters. The noted historian Arthur Schlesinger has been sharply critical of constitutional lapses in the conduct of the Vietnam War by Presidents Nixon and Johnson, but he has commented that the War Powers Act is an ineffective method of redressing the constitutional balance. Schlesinger has observed that the Act's provisions would have prevented FDR from engaging in the undeclared war in the Atlantic prior to the attack on Pearl Harbor. I agree. If we are to apply constitutional restrictions on the presidential authority to invade Cambodia, we will also inevitably limit executive initiative in conflicts for which many of us might have great sympathy.

New York Times columnist Tom Wicker has complained on the other hand that the War Powers Act, because of its requirement that the President receive congressional authorization to continue a conflict within thirty days after its beginning, "wraps him in the flag . . . and puts the onus on Congress to declare that he was wrong." Wicker contends that Congress would be unwilling to halt executive war after it had begun. Perhaps one of the most important elements in the War Powers Act is the provision that Congress must take specific action to *continue* hostilities before the end of the thirty-day period or else the law would require them to end. In this situation, legislative *inaction* is the key to the prevention of executive encroachment on congressional prerogative.

We must, in any case, recognize that the objective is to restore constitutional balance. Congress has no intention of destroying the President's ability to defend the United States against attack. Unlike Schlesinger, Wicker appears to believe that the President's Commander in Chief function should be given almost no weight at all. The bitterness of the Vietnam conflict must not blind us to the necessity that Congress and President must respect each other's constitutional authority. Where that authority enters the "twilight zone," self-restraint within the context of constitutional responsibility is perhaps the only solution available to either branch. The fact that Congress has not been accorded that consideration in recent years is no reason for it to abandon its own obligations to the Presidency.

I think these criticisms of the war powers bill are important, because although they issue from differing political perspectives, they share one point in common. These distinguished commentators on American life appear unwilling to separate questions of policy from the issue of constitutionality. That problem has complicated the question of Who Makes War since the earliest days of the Republic. We have drawn repeated attention in these pages to situations in which the Constitution was reverentially invoked to make a policy point or relegated to intentional obscurity when it couldn't be stretched to accommodate one or another presidentially perceived "emergency." I don't think we can afford any longer to use the Constitution as an excuse. It alone must determine the division of powers.

One would think that war powers legislation after ten years of Vietnam would come as a relief to the Executive. It can afford little pleasure to a President of the United States to stand responsible alone for any commitment so grave and so costly as the festering involvement in Indochina. At the very least, a division of the burden would have afforded the relief of sharing that awesome responsibility. But Presidents in modern times tend to rise above such home truths. We have observed that executive power has become so imposing in its magnitude that an almost religious significance attaches to both the office and the man who holds it. Such an attachment tends to preclude the rational judgment that any President is *one* elected national official with the normal propensity to human error.

The bombardment of Cambodia in the winter and spring of 1973 may illustrate the point. In 1970, during the initial Cambodian venture, Americans were repeatedly assured that bombardment over this new theater of Indo-China war was solely to protect U.S. troops then in South Vietnam. However, following the signing of the Vietnam cease-fire agreement and the withdrawal of American troops from South Vietnam, the bombing continued, with the actual effect of upholding a military government that was beleaguered in its capital and in the throes of civil war. The executive branch then claimed that its constitutional sanction for the bombing was based on an obligation to force on North Vietnam the Administration's interpretation of a cease-fire agreement it had never asked the Senate to ratify or the Congress to approve. That sorry spectacle was one more demonstration of the weaknesses inherent in one-man decision-making.

But, whatever the case for the wisdom of one in relation to the wisdom of many, the nature of our national policy requires that the Congress speak for its constituency and exercise its judgment, too, on the most important question that can face a powerful people—war. The United States Constitution, a document cited only less frequently than Holy Writ whenever human behavior appears to need justification beyond mere convenience, seems clear enough on the subject. The Constitution specifically endows Congress with the power to declare war and to raise and regulate the forces necessary to wage it. Congressional authority is enhanced by the Constitution's "necessary and proper" clause, which empowers Congress

> To make all laws which shall be necessary and proper for carrying into execution the foregoing powers, and all other powers vested by this Constitution in the government of the United States, or in any department or office thereof.

There were no prophets of the twentieth century at the Constitutional Convention. There was no way to project an age in which wars would not be declared. The absence of a seer at Philadelphia in 1787 has brought us to a pass in which shared responsibility has come to be an historic memory and in which the vital powers of the national legislature have almost atrophied from lack of use. Indeed, the "declaration of war" as understood in the eighteenth century, when it was written into the Constitution, is no longer relevant to the exercise of the congressional authority to decide on hostilities. International conflict may rise out of a "war of liberation," as in Vietnam, or out of a sudden confrontation between the super powers, as in the Cuban missile crisis of 1962. In uncertain situations we must avoid the automatic invocation of treaties and the train of unalterable consequences that may result from a declaration of war. Our responses must have the flexibility required by the circumstances. In an age when an ICBM can travel from the Soviet Union to the United States in approximately forty minutes, declarations of intent to strike would be almost as grotesque as the weaponry at our disposal. Declaring war, however, is only one part of the Congress's constitutionally assigned war power. Article 1, Section 8 also instructs Congress to provide for the common defense, to raise and support armies and navies, make rules for the government and regulation of the armed forces and organize and govern militia. When combined with the "necessary and proper" clause, Article 1, Section 8 offers overwhelming evidence that Congress is required by the Constitution to determine whether the United States makes war or remains at peace.

The fact of the matter is that the expectations of the founders didn't work out in practice. Vietnam was the culmination of a long but slowly burgeoning process in which the "balance of power" between the branches of government became grossly tilted as to armed hostilities in the direction of the President. Congress has underexercised its powers as to war, while President after President has so steadily expanded the Commander in Chief's function that we have reached the point where any effort simply to check the further enlargement of the presidential war-making power is regarded by defenders of a strong Presidency as an encroachment of the office itself. Many advocates of presidential prerogative in the field of war and foreign policy seem to be arguing that the President's powers as Commander in Chief are what the President alone defines them to be. The implication that the Presidency is beyond the range of congressional authority to check in the exercise of the war powers raises a serious constitutional danger. If we accept such a view we accept a situation in which the American people are dependent solely on the benign intent and good judgment of the incumbent President. We may not always be fortunate enough to see a man with such qualities in the White House. Even if we are, our own stature as free and equal citizens is diminished when we hand an individual leader our lives to do with as he will.

Although history has eroded congressional involvement in the war-making power, continuation of the process is not inevitable. History responds to the temper of the age. During most of the nineteenth century, American Presidents paid at least lip service to congressional authority as to war. Jefferson himself once said that "Congress alone is constitutionally invested with the power of changing our position from peace to war." Only gradually did congressional slippage manifest itself in response to the quickening rhythms of an age that demands quick action to influence fast-moving events; and to the post-World War II temptation to pass the headaches on to the White House.

Twentieth-century Presidents from Theodore Roosevelt to Richard Nixon have given the movement away from "advice and consent" its greatest impetus. If this increasing executive assertiveness reflects the burdensome nature of the Presidency, it is, nevertheless, one of the terrible ironies of American history that as war has become more destructive, less humane and less controllable, the power of decision over war has become increasingly concentrated in the hands of one American. This trend of history carries with it a portent of death for millions of human beings in the nuclear age. The American people can reverse this trend by insisting on the reinstatement of representative deliberations over the fearful decision as to war and peace.

President Richard Nixon suggested in his second inaugural address that it is time for Americans to rely on themselves to achieve the goals to which they aspire. Nowhere should the people insist on that self-reliance with greater determination than on the question that ultimately can determine whether the nation survives. No issue is of more importance than the great question with which we have dealt in these pages. If America is to continue as a great republic, only the people, through President *and* Congress, can decide *Who Makes War.*

BIBLIOGRAPHY

SINCE this book is an effort to survey and analyze the evolution of an historical trend, I have decided to provide the text's documentation at its conclusion in the form of a comprehensive bibliography designed to serve as source notes for each chapter, and to assist those who may wish to pursue the subject further.

CHAPTER ONE

Primary Sources

BORDEN, MORTON, ed. *The Anti-Federalist Papers* (East Lansing, Mich., 1965).

BURNETT, E. C., ed. *Letters of the Members of the Continental Congress* (8 vols., Washington, 1921–1936).

COOKE, JACOB E., ed. *The Federalist* (Middletown, Conn., 1961).

CREVECOUR, J. HECTOR ST. JOHN DE. *Letters from an American Farmer* (London and New York, 1912).

ELLIOT, JONATHAN, ed. *The Debates in the Several State Conventions on the Adoption of the Federal Constitution* (2d ed., 5 vols., Philadelphia, 1876).

FARRAND, MAX, ed. *The Records of the Federal Convention of 1787* (rev. ed., 4 vols., New Haven, 1966).

FITZPATRICK, J. C., ed. *The Writings of George Washington* (39 vols., Washington, 1931–1944).

FORD, PAUL L., ed. *Essays on the Constitution of the United States* (Brooklyn, 1892).

———. *Pamphlets on the Constitution of the United States* (Brooklyn, 1888).

HUNT, GAILLARD, ed. *The Writings of James Madison* (9 vols., New York, 1900–1910).

Journals of the Continental Congress, 1774–1789 (34 vols., Washington, 1904–1937).

LODGE, H. C., ed. *The Works of Alexander Hamilton* (12 vols., New York, 1904).

SYRETT, HAROLD C., and COOKE, JACOB E., eds. *The Papers of Alexander Hamilton* (New York, 1961–).

Secondary Works

BERDAHL, CLARENCE A. *War Powers of the Executive in the United States* (Urbana, Ill., 1921).

BOWEN, CATHERINE D. *Miracle at Philadelphia* (Boston, 1966).

BOWERS, CLAUDE. *Jefferson and Hamilton* (Boston and New York, 1925).

BRANT, IRVING. *James Madison: Father of the Constitution, 1787–1800* (Indianapolis, 1950).

CORWIN, EDWARD S. *The President: Office and Powers, 1787–1957* (4th rev. ed., New York, 1957).

JENSEN, MERRILL. *The New Nation* (New York, 1950).

KOCH, ADRIENNE. *Jefferson and Madison, the Great Collaboration* (New York, 1950).

KOENIG, LOUIS W. *The Chief Executive* (rev. ed., New York, 1968).

KOHN, R. "Inside History of the Newburgh Conspiracy," *The William and Mary Quarterly*, XXVI (April, 1970), 187–220.

LYON, HASTINGS. *The Constitution and the Men Who Made It* (Boston, 1936).

MALONE, DUMAS. *Jefferson and the Rights of Man* (Boston, 1951).

MILLER, JOHN C. *Alexander Hamilton: Portrait in Paradox* (New York, 1959).

———. *Alexander Hamilton and the Constitution* (New York, 1964).

ROSSITER, CLINTON. *The Grand Convention* (New York, 1966).

SCHACHNER, NATHAN. *Alexander Hamilton* (New York, 1946).

———. *The Founding Fathers* (New York, 1954).

———. *Thomas Jefferson, A Biography* (New York, 1951, 1957).

THACH, C. C. *The Creation of the Presidency, 1775–1789* (Baltimore, 1922).

VAN DOREN, CARL. *The Great Rehearsal* (New York, 1948).

CHAPTER TWO

Primary Sources

American State Papers, Foreign Relations, 1789–1828 (6 vols., Washington, 1832–1861), I.

BOYD, JULIAN P. *The Papers of Thomas Jefferson* (Princeton, 1950–).

Debates and Proceedings in the Congress of the United States, 1789–1824 (Annals of Congress) (Washington, 1834–1856).

FITZPATRICK, J. C., ed. *The Writings of George Washington* (39 vols., Washington, 1931–1944).

FORD, PAUL L., ed. *The Writings of Thomas Jefferson* (10 vols., New York, 1892–1899).

HAMILTON, ALEXANDER and MADISON, JAMES. *Letters of Pacificus and Helvidius on the Proclamation of Neutrality of 1793* (Washington, 1845).

HUNT, GAILLARD, ed. *The Writings of James Madison* (9 vols., New York, 1900–1910).

LODGE, H. C., ed. *The Works of Alexander Hamilton* (12 vols., New York, 1904).

RICHARDSON, JAMES D. *A Compilation of the Messages and Papers of the Presidents, 1789–1902* (New York, 1907), I.

SYRETT, HAROLD C., and COOKE, JACOB E., eds. *The Papers of Alexander Hamilton* (New York, 1961–).

Secondary Works

BERDAHL, CLARENCE A. *War Powers of the Executive in the United States* (Urbana, Ill., 1921).

BOWERS, CLAUDE. *Jefferson and Hamilton* (Boston and New York, 1925).

CHAMBERS, WILLIAM N. *Political Parties in a New Nation* (New York, 1963).

CORWIN, EDWARD S. *The President: Office and Powers* (New York, 1957).

DE CONDE, ALEXANDER. *Entangling Alliance: Politics and Diplomacy Under George Washington* (Durham, N. C., 1958).

MALONE, DUMAS. *Jefferson and the Rights of Man* (Boston, 1951).

———. *Jefferson and the Ordeal of Liberty* (Boston, 1962).

MILLER, JOHN C. *Alexander Hamilton: Portrait in Paradox* (New York, 1959).

———. *The Federalist Era, 1789–1801* (New York, 1960).

SCHACHNER, NATHAN. *Alexander Hamilton* (New York and London, 1946).

———. *The Founding Fathers* (New York, 1954).

———. *Thomas Jefferson, A Biography* (New York, 1951, 1957).

THOMAS, C. M. *American Neutrality in 1793* (New York, 1931).

CHAPTER THREE

Primary Sources

American State Papers, Foreign Relations, 1789–1828 (Washington, 1832–1861).

Bas v. Tingy, 4 Dall. 37 (1800).

BUTTERFIELD, L. H., ed. *Diary and Autobiography of John Adams* (Cambridge, Mass., 1961).

Debates and Proceedings in the Congress of the United States, 1797–1799.

FORD, PAUL L., ed. *The Writings of Thomas Jefferson* (10 vols., New York, 1892–1899).

HUNT, GAILLARD, ed. *The Writings of James Madison* (9 vols., New York, 1900–1910).

LODGE, H. C., ed. *The Works of Alexander Hamilton* (12 vols., New York, 1904).

Naval Documents Related to the Quasi-War Between the United States and France (Washington, 1935), I.

RICHARDSON, JAMES D. *Messages and Papers of the Presidents* (New York, 1907), I.

Talbot v. Seeman, 1 Cranch 28, 32 (1801).

Secondary Works

ALLEN, GARDINER W. *Our Naval War with France* (Boston, 1909).

BERDAHL, CLARENCE A. *War Powers of the Executive in the United States* (Urbana, Ill., 1921).

BOWERS, CLAUDE. *Jefferson and Hamilton* (Boston and New York, 1925).

CHAMBERS, WILLIAM N. *Political Parties in a New Nation* (New York, 1963).

CORWIN, EDWARD S. *The President: Office and Powers* (New York, 1957).

DAUER, MANNING J. *The Adams Federalists* (Baltimore, 1953).

DE CONDE, ALEXANDER. *The Quasi-War: The Politics and Diplomacy of the Undeclared War with France, 1797–1801* (New York, 1966).

KURTZ, STEPHEN G. *The Presidency of John Adams* (Philadelphia, 1957).

MALONE, DUMAS. *Jefferson and the Ordeal of Liberty* (Boston, 1962).

MILLER, JOHN C. *Alexander Hamilton: Portrait in Paradox* (New York, 1959).

———. *The Federalist Era, 1789–1801* (New York, 1960).

SCHACHNER, NATHAN. *Alexander Hamilton* (New York, 1946).

———. *The Founding Fathers* (New York, 1954).

———. *Thomas Jefferson, A Biography* (New York, 1951, 1957).

SMITH, PAGE. *John Adams* (Garden City, 1962).

CHAPTER FOUR

Primary Sources

ADAMS, CHARLES F., ed. *The Works of John Adams* (10 vols., Boston, 1850–56).

American State Papers, Foreign Relations (Washington, 1832–1861), II.

BOYD, JULIAN P. *The Papers of Thomas Jefferson* (Princeton, 1950–), VII.

CAPPON, LESTER J. *The Adams-Jefferson Letters* (2 vols., Chapel Hill, 1959).

Debates and Proceedings in the Congress of the United States, 1801–1804.

EATON, WILLIAM. *Interesting Detail of the Operations of the American Fleet in the Mediterranean* (Springfield, Mass., 1805).

BIBLIOGRAPHY

LINCOLN, CHARLES H., ed. "The Hull-Eaton Correspondence During the Expedition Against Tripoli, 1804–1805," *American Antiquarian Society, Proceedings,* New Series, XXI (1911).

LODGE, H. C., ed. *The Works of Alexander Hamilton* (12 vols., New York, 1904), VIII.

Naval Documents Relating to the United States Wars with the Barbary Powers, 1785–1807 (Washington, 1939–1945), I, II.

RICHARDSON, JAMES D. *Messages and Papers of the Presidents* (New York, 1907), I.

Newspapers and Periodicals

Boston: *Columbian Centinel, New England Palladium.*
Brookfield, Mass.: *The Political Repository of Farmers' Journal.*
New York: *Commercial Advertiser, Evening Post.*
Philadelphia: *Aurora for the Country, Gazette of the United States, General Advertiser (Aurora).*
Richmond Enquirer
Washington National Intelligencer

Secondary Works

ADAMS, HENRY. *History of the United States of America During the Administration of Thomas Jefferson* (New York, 1930).

ALLEN, GARDINER W. *Our Navy and the Barbary Corsairs* (Boston, 1905).

BERDAHL, CLARENCE A. *War Powers of the Executive in the United States* (Urbana, Ill., 1921).

BLYTH, STEPHEN C. *History of the War Between the United States and Tripoli and other Barbary Powers* (Salem, 1806).

CORWIN, EDWARD S. *The President: Office and Powers* (New York, 1957).

FOIK, PAUL J. "In the Clutches of the Barbary Corsairs," *Illinois Catholic History Review,* IX (1926), 162–176.

GLEESON, PAUL F. "Attacks by Algerian Pirates Create a Demand for the American Navy," *Rhode Island History,* II (April, 1943).

IRWIN, RAY W. *The Diplomatic Relations of the United States with the Barbary Powers, 1776–1816* (Chapel Hill, 1931).

LEVY, LEONARD. *Jefferson and Civil Liberties: The Darker Side* (Cambridge, Mass., 1963).

MALONE, DUMAS. *Jefferson the President: First Term* (Boston, 1970).

MC CALEB, WALTER. *New Light on Aaron Burr* (Austin, 1963).

MILLER, JOHN C. *Alexander Hamilton: Portrait in Paradox* (New York, 1959).

MUNGER, MARTHA. "A Little Known Debt," *Americana Magazine,* XXIII (1929), 11–19.

NASH, HOWARD P. *The Forgotten Wars, 1798–1805* (South Brunswick, N.J., 1961).

PARTON, JAMES. *Life of Thomas Jefferson, Third President of the United States* (Boston, 1874).

[279]

PETERSON, MERRILL D. *Thomas Jefferson and the New Nation* (New York, 1970).

RANDALL, HENRY S. *The Life of Thomas Jefferson* (2 vols., New York, 1858).

SCHACHNER, NATHAN. *Thomas Jefferson, A Biography* (New York, 1951, 1957).

TUCKER, GLENN. *Dawn Like Thunder: The Barbary Wars and the Birth of the United States Navy* (Indianapolis, 1963).

WRIGHT, L. B., and MAC LEOD, J. H. *The First Americans in North Africa: William Eaton's Struggle for a Vigorous Policy Against the Barbary Pirates, 1799–1805* (Princeton, 1945; New York, 1969).

CHAPTER FIVE

Primary Sources

ADAMS, C. F., ed. *The Works of John Adams* (10 vols., Boston, 1850–1856).

American State Papers, Foreign Relations (Washington, 1832–1861), IV, V.

DALLAS, ALEXANDER J. *An Exposition of the Causes and Character of the Late War with Great Britain* (Washington, 1815).

Debates and Proceedings in the Congress of the United States, 1812–1814.

HUNT, GAILLARD, ed. *The Writings of James Madison* (9 vols., New York, 1900–10).

RICHARDSON, JAMES. *Messages and Papers of the Presidents* (New York, 1907), I.

Secondary Works

BRANT, IRVING. *James Madison: The President, 1809–1812* (Indianapolis, 1956).

———. *James Madison: Commander in Chief, 1812–1836* (Indianapolis, 1961).

BROWN, ROGER H. *The Republic in Peril: 1812* (New York, 1964).

DANGERFIELD, GEORGE. *The Era of Good Feelings* (New York, 1952).

HORSEMAN, REGINALD. *The Causes of the War of 1812* (Philadelphia, 1962).

LECKIE, ROBERT. *The Wars of America* (New York, 1968).

PERKINS, BRADFORD. *Prologue to War: England and the United States, 1805–1812* (Berkeley, 1961).

SMITH, ABBOT E. "Mr. Madison's War: An Unsuccessful Experiment in the Conduct of National Policy," *Political Science Quarterly*, LVII (June, 1942), 229–246.

CHAPTER SIX

Primary Sources

ADAMS, C. F., ed. *Memoirs of John Quincy Adams, 1795–1848* (12 vols., Philadelphia, 1874–1877), IV.

American State Papers, Foreign Relations (Washington, 1832–1861), IV, V.

American State Papers, Military Affairs (Washington, 1832–1861), I, II.

BASSETT, J. S., ed. *Correspondence of Andrew Jackson* (7 vols., Washington, 1926–1935).

BENTON, THOMAS HART. *Thirty Years' View* (2 vols., New York, 1854–1856), I.

Debates and Proceedings in the Congress of the United States, 1818–1820.

HAMILTON, S. M., ed. *The Writings of James Monroe* (7 vols., New York, 1898–1903).

HEMPHILL, W. EDWIN, ed. *John C. Calhoun, Papers* (Columbia, S.C., 1959–), VI.

MADIGAN, THOMAS L. *Papers,* New York Public Library.

MERIWETHER, ROBERT L., ed. *John C. Calhoun, Papers* (Columbia, S.C., 1959–), II, III.

MONROE, JAMES. *Papers,* New York Public Library.

RICHARDSON, JAMES. *Messages and Papers of the Presidents* (New York, 1907), II.

U.S. *House Ex. Docs.* No. 14, 15th Cong., 2d Sess., 1818–19.

U.S. *Senate Docs.* No. 73, 16th Cong., 1st Sess., 1820.

Newspapers and Periodicals

Baltimore: *Niles' Weekly Register.*
Washington National Intelligencer.
Richmond Enquirer.

Secondary Works

AMMON, HARRY. *James Monroe: The Quest for National Identity* (New York, 1971).

BERDAHL, CLARENCE A. *War Powers of the Executive in the United States* (Urbana, Ill., 1921).

CORWIN, EDWARD S. *The President: Office and Powers* (New York, 1957).

CRESSON, WILLIAM P. *James Monroe* (Chapel Hill, 1946).

DANGERFIELD, GEORGE. *The Era of Good Feelings* (New York, 1952).

JAMES, MARQUIS. *Andrew Jackson: The Border Captain* (Indianapolis, 1933).

JOHNSON, GERALD W. *America's Silver Age: The Statecraft of Clay-Webster-Calhoun* (New York, 1939).

PARTON, JAMES. *The Life of Andrew Jackson* (New York, 1860).

REMINI, A. *The Election of Andrew Jackson* (Philadelphia and New York, 1963).

STENBERG, RICHARD R. "Jackson's Rhea Letter Hoax," *Journal of Southern History,* II (1936), 480–496.

SYRETT, HAROLD C. *Andrew Jackson* (Indianapolis, 1953).

WARD, JOHN W. *Andrew Jackson, Symbol of an Age* (Fairlawn, N.J., 1962).

WILTSE, CHARLES M. *John C. Calhoun, Nationalist* (Indianapolis, 1944).

———. *John C. Calhoun, Nullifier* (Indianapolis, 1951).

CHAPTER SEVEN

Primary Sources

BENTON, THOMAS HART. *Thirty Years' View* (2 vols., New York, 1854–1856), II.

Congressional Globe (Washington, 1834–1873), 1846–1848.

GALLATIN, ALBERT. *Peace with Mexico* (New York, 1847).

LOWELL, JAMES RUSSELL. *The Biglow Papers* (Boston, 1848).

QUAIFE, MILTON M., ed. *The Diary of James K. Polk During His Presidency, 1845–1849* (4 vols., Chicago, 1910).

RICHARDSON, JAMES. *Messages and Papers of the Presidents* (New York, 1907), IV.

SUMNER, CHARLES. "Report on the War with Mexico," *Old South Leaflets* (9 vols., Boston, 1896–1922), VI, No. 132.

THOREAU, HENRY DAVID. *Resistance to Civil Government* (Boston, 1849).

U.S. *House Ex. Docs.* No. 60, 30th Cong., 1st Sess., 1848.

WEAVER, HERBERT. *Correspondence of James K. Polk* (Nashville, 1969).

Newspapers and Periodicals

Baltimore American, Boston Whig, Hartford Times.

New York: *American Review, Morning News, Times* and *Tribune.*

Washington: *National Intelligencer, Washington Advertiser, Union.*

Secondary Works

BAKER, CHARLES A. "Another American Dilemma," *The Virginia Quarterly Review,* XLV (Spring, 1969).

BARTLETT, RUHL. *Policy and Power* (New York, 1963).

BEMIS, SAMUEL FLAGG. *A Diplomatic History of the United States* (New York, 1955).

BERDAHL, CLARENCE A. *War Powers of the Executive in the United States* (Urbana, Ill., 1921).

BILLINGTON, RAY A. *Westward Expansion* (3d ed., New York, 1967).

CORWIN, EDWARD S. *The President: Office and Powers* (New York, 1957).

DE VOTO, BERNARD. *The Year of Decision, 1846* (Boston, 1943).

DYER, BRAINERD. *Zachary Taylor* (Baton Rouge, 1946).

GOETZMANN, WILLIAM H. *When the Eagle Screamed* (New York, 1966).

GRAEBNER, N. A. *Empire on the Pacific* (New York, 1955).

JAY, WILLIAM. *A Review of the Causes and Consequences of the Mexican War* (Boston, 1849; New York, 1969).

LECKIE, ROBERT. *The Wars of America* (New York, 1968).

LENS, SIDNEY. *The Forging of the American Empire* (New York, 1971).

LEWIS, LLOYD. *Captain Sam Grant* (Boston, 1950).

MC CORMAC, EUGENE I. *James K. Polk: A Political Biography* (Berkeley, 1922).

MC COY, CHARLES. *Polk and the Presidency* (Austin, 1960).

MERK, FREDERICK. *Manifest Destiny and Mission in American History* (New York, 1963).

MORISON, S. E., MERK, F., and FREIDEL, F. *Dissent in Three American Wars* (Cambridge, Mass., 1970).

MORRIS, RICHARD. *Great Presidential Decisions* (Philadelphia, 1965).

PRICE, GLENN. *Origins of the War with Mexico: The Polk-Stockton Intrigue* (Austin, 1967).

REEVES, J. S. *American Diplomacy Under Tyler and Polk* (Baltimore, 1907).

SELLERS, CHARLES. *James K. Polk, Continentalist: 1843–1846* (Princeton, 1966).

SMITH, G. W., and JUDAH, C. *Chronicles of the Gringos* (Albuquerque, 1968).

SMITH, JUSTIN H. *The War with Mexico* (2 vols., New York, 1919).

STENBERG, RICHARD. "The Failure of Polk's Mexican War Intrigue of 1845," *Pacific Historical Review*, IV (Mar., 1935), 39–68.

STEPHENSON, N. W. *Texas and the Mexican War* (New York, 1921).

VAN ALSTYNE, R. W. *The Rising American Empire* (New York, 1960).

WEINBERG, ALBERT. *Manifest Destiny, A Study of Nationalist Expansionism in American History* (Baltimore, 1935).

CHAPTER EIGHT

Primary Sources

Congressional Globe, 1854–1856.

Durand v. Hollins, 4 Blatch 451, 454 (1860).

MANNING, WILLIAM R. *Diplomatic Correspondence of the United States: Inter-American Affairs, 1831–1860* (12 vols., Washington, 1932–1939), IV, *Central America, 1851–1860*, V, *Great Britain*.

RICHARDSON, JAMES. *Messages and Papers of the Presidents* (New York, 1907), V.

U.S. *House Ex. Docs.* No. 126, 33d Cong., 1st Sess., 1854.

U.S. *Senate Ex. Docs.* No. 85, 33d Cong., 1st Sess., 1854.

Newspapers and Periodicals

Boston: *Atlas, Post* and *Transcript*.
New York: *Evening Post, Herald, Times* and *Tribune*.
Washington: *Star* and *Union*.

Secondary Works

BERDAHL, CLARENCE A. *War Powers of the Executive in the United States* (Urbana, Ill., 1921).
GOETZMANN, WILLIAM H. *When the Eagle Screamed* (New York, 1966).
LANE, WHEATON J. *Commodore Vanderbilt, An Epic of the Steam Age* (New York, 1942).
MUNRO, DANA G. *The Five Republics of Central America* (New York, 1918, 1967).
NICHOLS, ROY F. *Franklin Pierce* (2d ed., Philadelphia, 1958).
SCROGGS, WILLIAM O. *Filibusters and Financiers: The Story of William Walker and his Associates* (New York, 1916, 1969).
SPENSER, IVOR D. *The Victor and the Spoils: A Life of William L. Marcy* (Providence, 1959).
VAN ALSTYNE, R. W. "Anglo-American Relations, 1853–1857," *American Historical Review*, XLII (1937), 497.
WALLACE, EDWARD. *Destiny and Glory* (New York, 1957).
WILLIAMS, MARY W. *Anglo-American Isthmian Diplomacy, 1815–1915* (Washington, 1916).

CHAPTER NINE

Primary Sources

Congressional Globe, 1861–65.
Ex parte Merryman, 17 Fed. Cas. 144.
Ex parte Milligan, 71 U.S. 2.
Ex parte Vallandigham, 68 U.S. 243.
Prize Cases, The, 67 U.S. 635.
RICHARDSON, JAMES. *Messages and Papers of the Presidents* (New York, 1907), VI.

Secondary Works

BERDAHL, CLARENCE A. *War Powers of the Executive in the United States* (Urbana, Ill., 1921).
BINKLEY, WILFRED E. *President and Congress* (3d rev. ed., New York, 1962).
CORWIN, EDWARD S. *The President: Office and Powers* (New York, 1957).
KOENIG, LOUIS W. *The Chief Executive* (New York, 1968).

MILTON, GEORGE F. *The Use of Presidential Power, 1789–1943* (New York, 1944).

RANDALL, JAMES G. *Constitutional Problems Under Lincoln* (rev. ed., Urbana, Ill., 1951).

———, and DONALD, DAVID. *The Civil War and Reconstruction* (2d ed., rev., Lexington, Mass., 1969).

ROSSITER, CLINTON. *The Supreme Court and the Commander in Chief* (Ithaca, 1951).

SPRAGUE, DEAN. *Freedom Under Lincoln* (Boston, 1965).

SWISHER, CARL B. *American Constitutional Development* (2d ed., Boston, 1954).

TOURTELLOT, ARTHUR B. *The Presidents on the Presidency* (New York, 1970).

WHITING, WILLIAM. *War Powers Under the Constitution of the United States* (Boston, 1871).

CHAPTER TEN

Primary Sources

BLAINE, JAMES G. *Twenty Years of Congress* (2 vols., Norwich, Conn., 1884–1886), II.

Congressional Globe

HOGUE, A. R., ed. *Charles Sumner, An Essay by Carl Schurz* (Urbana, 1951).

PIERCE, E. L., ed. *Memoirs and Letters of Charles Sumner* (4 vols., Boston, 1877–1893), IV.

RICHARDSON, JAMES. *Messages and Papers of the Presidents* (New York, 1907), VII.

SHERMAN, JOHN. *Recollections of Forty Years* (Chicago, 1895), I.

SUMNER, CHARLES. *Complete Works* (statesman ed., 20 vols., New York, 1900, 1969), XIX.

U.S. *Senate Report* No. 234 (Hatch Report), 41st Cong., 2d Sess., 1869–1870.

——— *Ex. Docs.* No. 17, 41st Cong., 3d Sess., 1870–1871.

Newspapers and Periodicals

New York: *Evening Post, The Nation, Times.*

Secondary Works

BINKLEY, WILFRED E. *President and Congress* (3d rev. ed., New York, 1962).

BERDAHL, CLARENCE A. *War Powers of the Executive in the United States* (Urbana, Ill., 1921).

CORWIN, EDWARD S. *The President: Office and Powers* (New York, 1957).

DONALD, DAVID. *Charles Sumner and the Rights of Man* (New York, 1970).

NEVINS, ALLAN. *Hamilton Fish: The Inner History of the Grant Administration* (rev. ed., New York, 1957).

TANSILL, CHARLES C. *The United States and Santo Domingo, 1798–1873* (Baltimore, 1938).

WELLES, SUMNER. *Naboth's Vineyard: The Dominican Republic, 1844–1924* (2 vols., New York, 1928), I.

WHITE, HORACE. *The Life of Lyman Trumbull* (New York, 1913).

CHAPTER ELEVEN

Primary Sources

Congressional Record, 1898–1901 (Washington, 1874–).

GRAFF, H. F., ed. *American Imperialism and the Philippine Insurrection: Testimony of the Times, Selections from Congressional Hearings* (Boston, 1969).

RICHARDSON, JAMES. *Messages and Papers of the Presidents* (New York, 1907), X.

U.S. Department of State. *Foreign Relations of the United States, 1898–1901*.

Newspapers and Periodicals

New York: *The Literary Digest, The Nation, Times, Public Opinion*.

Secondary Works

BAILEY, THOMAS A. *A Diplomatic History of the American People* (8th ed., New York, 1969).

BEISNER, ROBERT L. *Twelve Against Empire* (New York, 1968).

BERDAHL, CLARENCE A. *War Powers of the Executive in the United States* (Urbana, Ill., 1921).

CORWIN, EDWARD S. *The President: Office and Powers* (New York, 1957).

DENNETT, TYLER. *John Hay: From Poetry to Politics* (New York, 1933).

DENNIS, ALFRED L. *Adventures in American Diplomacy, 1896–1906* (New York, 1928).

DULLES, FOSTER RHEA. *China and America* (Princeton, 1946).

———. *The Imperial Years* (New York, 1956).

———. *Prelude to World Power, American Diplomatic History, 1860–1900* (New York, 1965).

DUPUY, R. F., and BAUMER, W. H. *The Little Wars of the United States* (New York, 1968).

GOETZMANN, WILLIAM H. *When the Eagle Screamed* (New York, 1966).

GRISWOLD, A. W. *The Far Eastern Policy of the United States* (New York, 1938; New Haven, 1962).

LEECH, MARGARET. *In the Days of McKinley* (New York, 1959).

LENS, SIDNEY. *The Forging of the American Empire* (New York, 1971).
LEOPOLD, RICHARD. *The Growth of American Foreign Policy* (New York, 1962).
MAY, ERNEST R. *Imperial Democracy: The Emergence of America as a Great Power* (New York, 1961).
MILLIS, WALTER. *The Martial Spirit: A Study of Our War with Spain* (New York, 1931, 1965).
O'CONNOR, RICHARD. *Pacific Destiny* (New York, 1969).
PLESUR, MILTON F. *America's Outward Thrust: Approaches to Foreign Affairs, 1865–1890* (DeKalb, Ill., 1971).
WOLFF, LEON. *Little Brown Brother* (London, 1961; New York, 1970).
YOUNG, MARILYN B. "American Expansion, 1870–1900," in Barton Bernstein, ed. *Towards a New Past* (New York, 1968).

CHAPTER TWELVE

Primary Sources

Congressional Record, 1903–1907.
HARBAUGH, WILLIAM H. *Theodore Roosevelt: Writings* (Indianapolis, 1967).
MORISON, ELTING E., and BLUM, JOHN M., eds. *The Letters of Theodore Roosevelt* (8 vols., Cambridge, Mass., 1951–1954), III–VI.
ROOSEVELT, THEODORE. *An Autobiography* (New York, 1913).
———. *The New Nationalism* (New York, 1910).
U.S. *House Docs.* No. 8, 58th Cong., 2d Sess., 1903–1904.
U.S. *Senate Docs.* No. 95, 58th Cong., 2d Sess., 1903–1904.

Newspapers and Periodicals

New York: *The Literary Digest, The Nation, Times, Outlook, Public Opinion.*

Secondary Works

BEALE, HOWARD K. *Theodore Roosevelt and the Rise of America to World Power* (Baltimore, 1956).
BEEMIS, SAMUEL F. *The Latin American Policy of the United States* (New York, 1943).
BINKLEY, WILFRED E. *President and Congress* (3d rev. ed., New York, 1962).
BLUM, JOHN M. *The Republican Roosevelt* (Cambridge, 1954, 1961).
CORWIN, EDWARD S. *The President: Office and Powers* (New York, 1957).
DENNIS, ARTHUR. *Adventures in American Diplomacy, 1896–1906* (New York, 1928).
HARBAUGH, WILLIAM H. *Power and Responsibility: The Life and Times of Theodore Roosevelt* (New York, 1961).

HILL, HOWARD C. *Roosevelt and the Caribbean* (Chicago, 1927).

KNIGHT, MELVIN. *Americans in Santo Domingo* (New York, 1928).

KOENIG, LOUIS W. *The Chief Executive* (New York, 1968).

LEOPOLD, RICHARD. *The Growth of American Foreign Policy* (New York, 1962).

MC CLURE, WALLACE. *International Executive Agreements* (New York, 1941).

MILTON, GEORGE F. *The Use of Presidential Power, 1789–1943* (New York, 1944).

MOWRY, GEORGE E. *The Era of Theodore Roosevelt, 1900–1912* (New York, 1958).

MUNRO, DANA G. *Intervention and Dollar Diplomacy in the Caribbean, 1900–1921* (Princeton, 1964).

———. *The United States and the Caribbean* (Boston, 1934).

PRINGLE, HENRY F. *Theodore Roosevelt: A Biography* (rev. ed., New York, 1956).

RIPPY, FRED J. *The Caribbean Danger Zone* (New York, 1940).

STOREY, MOORFIELD, and LICHAUCO, M. P. *The Conquest of the Philippines, 1898–1925* (New York, 1926).

SWISHER, CARL B. *American Constitutional Development* (2d ed., Boston, 1954).

WEINBERG, ALBERT. *Manifest Destiny* (Baltimore, 1935).

WELLES, SUMNER. *Naboth's Vineyard: The Dominican Republic, 1844–1924* (2 vols., New York, 1928), II.

CHAPTER THIRTEEN

Primary Sources

BAKER, RAY S., and DODD, W. E., eds. *The Public Papers of Woodrow Wilson* (6 vols., New York, 1925–1927).

Congressional Record, 1914, 1916–1918.

FORD, H. J. "The Growth of Dictatorship," *Atlantic Monthly,* CXXI (May, 1918).

WILSON, WOODROW. *Congressional Government* (1st ed., Boston and New York, 1885; 15th ed., 1900).

———. *Constitutional Government* (New York, 1908).

———. *The State* (Boston, 1889).

Newspapers and Periodicals

New York: *The Literary Digest, Times, Public Opinion.*

Secondary Works

BEMIS, SAMUEL F. *American Foreign Policy and the Blessings of Liberty* (New Haven, 1962).

——. *The Latin American Policy of the United States* (New York, 1943).

BERDAHL, CLARENCE A. *War Powers of the Executive in the United States* (Urbana, Ill., 1921).

BINKLEY, WILFRED E. *President and Congress* (3d rev. ed., New York, 1962).

BLUM, JOHN M. *Woodrow Wilson and the Politics of Morality* (Boston, 1956).

CLINE, H. F. *The United States and Mexico* (rev. ed., Cambridge, Mass., 1963).

CORWIN, EDWARD S. *The President: Office and Powers* (New York, 1957).

DUDDEN, ARTHUR P., ed. *Woodrow Wilson and the World of Today* (Philadelphia, 1957).

GRIEB, KENNETH J. *The United States and Huerta* (Lincoln, Neb., 1969).

LINK, ARTHUR S. *Wilson the Diplomatist* (Baltimore, 1957).

——. *Wilson: The New Freedom* (Princeton, 1956).

——. *Wilson: Confusions and Crises, 1915–1916* (Princeton, 1964).

——. *Woodrow Wilson and the Progressive Era, 1910–1917* (New York, 1954).

KOENIG, LOUIS W. *The Chief Executive* (New York, 1968).

MILTON, GEORGE F. *The Use of Presidential Power, 1789–1943* (New York, 1944).

MUNRO, DANA G. *Intervention and Dollar Diplomacy in the Caribbean, 1900–1921* (Princeton, 1964).

SWISHER, CARL B. *American Constitutional Development* (2d ed., Boston, 1954).

WEINBERG, ALBERT. *Manifest Destiny* (Baltimore, 1935).

WILLOUGHBY, WILLIAM. *Government Organization in War Time and After* (New York, 1919).

CHAPTER FOURTEEN

Primary Sources

CHURCHILL, WINSTON S. *The Grand Alliance* (Boston, 1950).

Congressional Record, 1940–1943.

Hirabayashi v. United States, 320 U.S. 81 (1943).

Korematsu v. United States, 323 U.S. 214 (1944).

KROCK, ARTHUR. *Memoirs* (New York, 1968).

ROSENMAN, SAMUEL T., comp. *The Public Papers and Addresses of Franklin Delano Roosevelt* (13 vols., New York, 1938–1950), IX–XII.

STIMSON, HENRY L., and BUNDY, MC GEORGE. *On Active Service in Peace and War* (New York, 1948).

United States v. Curtiss-Wright Corp., 299 U.S. 320.

U.S. *Senate*, Committee on Foreign Relations, 77th Cong., 1st Sess. *Lend-Lease Bill, 1941; Hearings* . . . (Washington, 1941).

U.S. State Department. *Peace and War: United States Foreign Policy, 1931–1941* (Washington, 1943).

VANDENBERG, ARTHUR H., JR., ed. *The Private Papers of Senator Vandenberg* (Boston, 1952).

Newspapers and Periodicals

Boston Post, Chicago Tribune, Cleveland Plain Dealer, Los Angeles Times. New York: *Daily News, Herald Tribune, The Nation, Times, Post. St. Louis Post-Dispatch.*

Secondary Works

BEARD, CHARLES A. *President Roosevelt and the Coming of the War, 1941* (New Haven, 1948).

BURNS, JAMES MAC GREGOR. *Roosevelt: The Lion and the Fox* (New York, 1956).

————. *Roosevelt: The Soldier of Freedom* (New York, 1970).

CORWIN, EDWARD S. *The President: Office and Powers* (New York, 1957).

————. *Total War and the Constitution* (New York, 1947).

DANIELS, ROGER. *Concentration Camps USA: Japanese Americans and World War II* (New York, 1971).

DIVINE, ROBERT A. *The Illusion of Neutrality* (Chicago, 1962).

GRODZINS, MORTON. *Americans Betrayed: Politics and the Japanese Evacuation* (Chicago, 1949).

KOENIG, LOUIS W. *The Chief Executive* (New York, 1968).

————. *The Presidency and the Crisis: Powers of the Office from the Invasion of Poland to Pearl Harbor* (New York, 1944).

LANGER, WILLIAM L., and GLEASON, S. E. *The Undeclared War, 1940–1941* (New York, 1953).

SCHLESINGER, ARTHUR M., JR. *The Age of Roosevelt* (3 vols., Boston, 1957–1960).

SHERWOOD, ROBERT E. *Roosevelt and Hopkins: An Intimate History* (New York, 1948).

CHAPTER FIFTEEN

Primary Sources

ACHESON, DEAN. *Present at the Creation* (New York, 1969).

Congressional Record, 1949–1951.

KROCK, ARTHUR. *Memoirs* (New York, 1968).

TAFT, ROBERT A. *A Foreign Policy for Americans* (New York, 1951).

TRUMAN, HARRY S. *Memoirs* (2 vols., Garden City, 1955–1956), II.

U.S. Department of State Bulletin (Washington, July 31, 1950).

U.S. *Senate,* Committee on Foreign Relations, 81st Cong., 1st Sess. *North Atlantic Treaty: Hearings* . . . (Washington, 1949).

————. 82d Cong., 1st Sess. *Assignment of Ground Forces in European Area: Hearings* . . . (Washington, 1951).

VANDENBERG, ARTHUR H., JR., ed. *The Private Papers of Senator Vandenberg* (Boston, 1952).

Newspapers and Periodicals

Chicago Tribune, The New York Times.

Secondary Works

CORWIN, EDWARD S. *The President: Office and Powers* (New York, 1957).

GADDIS, JOHN L. *The United States and the Origins of the Cold War, 1941–1947* (New York, 1972).

GOLDMAN, ERIC F. *The Crucial Decade—and After* (New York, 1960).

KOLKO, JOYCE, and KOLKO, GABRIEL. *The Limits of Power: The World and United States Foreign Policy, 1945–1952* (New York, 1972).

LAFEBER, WALTER. *America, Russia and the Cold War, 1945–1966* (New York, 1967).

NEUSTADT, RICHARD E. *Presidential Power* (New York, 1964).

CHAPTERS SIXTEEN–EIGHTEEN

Primary Sources

Congressional Record, 1954, 1955, 1957, 1961–62, 1964–65, 1970.

EISENHOWER, DWIGHT D. *The White House Years: Mandate for Change, 1953–1956* (Garden City, 1963).

———. *The White House Years: Waging Peace, 1956–1961* (Garden City, 1965).

Public Papers of the Presidents of the United States (Washington, 1960–).

U.S. House, Committee on Armed Services, 92d Cong., 1st Sess. *Vietnam Relations, 1945–1967* (12 vols., Washington, 1971).

U.S. House, Committee on Foreign Affairs, 83d Cong., 2d Sess. *Mutual Security Act of 1954: Hearings . . .* (Washington, 1954).

U.S. House, Subcommittee on National Security Policy and Scientific Developments of the Committee on Foreign Affairs, 92d Cong., 1st Sess. *War Powers Legislation: Hearings . . .* (Washington, 1972).

U.S. Senate, Committee on Armed Services and Committee on Foreign Relations, 85th Cong., 1st Sess. *The President's Proposal on the Middle East: Hearings . . .* (Washington, 1957).

———. 87th Cong., 2d Sess. *Situation in Cuba: Hearings . . . and Report . . .* (Washington, 1962).

———. 88th Cong., 2d Sess. *Southeast Asia Resolution: Hearings . . .* (August 6, 1964), (Washington, 1966).

U.S. Senate, Committee on Foreign Relations, 91st Cong., 2d Sess. *Documents Relating to the War Powers of Congress . . .* (Washington, 1970).

———. 92d Cong., 1st Sess. *Legislative Proposals to End the War in Southeast Asia: Hearings . . .* (Washington, 1971).

———. 92d Cong., 1st Sess. *Transmittal of Executive Agreements to Congress: Hearings . . .* (Washington, 1971).

———. 90th Cong., 1st Sess. *United States Commitments to Foreign Powers: Hearings . . .* (Washington, 1967).

————. 92d Cong., 1st Sess. *War Powers Legislation: Hearings* . . . (Washington, 1972).

U.S. Senate, Subcommittee on U.S. Security Agreements and Commitments Abroad of the Committee on Foreign Relations, 92d Cong., 1st Sess. *Laos: April, 1971* (Staff Report) (Washington, 1971).

————. 92d Cong., 2d Sess. *Thailand, Laos and Cambodia: January, 1972* (Staff Report) (Washington, 1972).

————. 91st Cong., 1st Sess. *U.S. Security Agreements and Commitments Abroad: Hearings* . . . *Part 2: Kingdom of Laos, Part 3: Thailand* (8 pts., Washington, 1969, 1970).

Secondary Works

ADAMS, NINA, and MC COY, ALFRED, eds. *Laos: War and Revolution* (New York, 1970).

AUSTIN, ANTHONY. *The President's War* (Philadelphia and New York, 1971).

BARNET, RICHARD J. *Intervention and Revolution* (New York, 1968).

BICKEL, ALEXANDER M. "The Constitution and the War," *Commentary*, LIV (July, 1972).

CORWIN, EDWARD S. *The President: Office and Powers* (New York, 1957).

FRIEDMAN, L., and NEUBORNE, B. *Unquestioning Obedience to the President* (New York, 1972).

GOLDMAN, ERIC F. *The Crucial Decade—and After* (New York, 1960).

————. *The Tragedy of Lyndon Johnson* (New York, 1969).

HENKIN, LOUIS. *Foreign Affairs and the Constitution* (Mineola, N.Y., 1972).

HILSMAN, ROGER. *To Move a Nation* (Garden City, N.Y., 1967).

KOENIG, LOUIS W. *The Chief Executive* (New York, 1968).

LAFEBER, WALTER. *America, Russia and the Cold War* (New York, 1967).

LITTAUER, R., and OPHOFF, N. *The Air War in Indochina* (Boston, 1971).

RASKIN, M. G., and FALL, BERNARD. *The Viet-Nam Reader* (rev. ed., New York, 1967).

REEDY, GEORGE. *The Twilight of the Presidency* (New York and Cleveland, 1970).

ROSSITER, CLINTON. *The Supreme Court and the Commander in Chief* (Ithaca, 1951).

SCHLESINGER, ARTHUR, JR. *The Bitter Heritage: Vietnam and American Democracy, 1941–1966* (Boston, 1967).

————. "Presidential War," *The New York Times Magazine*, January 7, 1973.

————. *A Thousand Days* (Boston, 1965).

SHEEHAN, NEIL, et al. *The Pentagon Papers* (Chicago, 1971).

SORENSON, THEODORE. *Kennedy* (New York, 1965).

WEAVER, WARREN, JR. *Both Your Houses* (New York and Washington, 1972).

WICKER, TOM. "Making War, Not Love," *The New York Times*, January 16, 1973.

INDEX

INDEX

DATE DUE

GAYLORD			PRINTED IN U.S.A.